Taxation and National Destiny

Taxation and National Destiny

A Tax Systems Analysis and Proposal

Timothy J. Gillis

— MP —
Maximus Profectus

Taxation and National Destiny: A Tax Systems Analysis and Proposal

Grateful acknowledgement is made to the following publishers, authors, and/or individuals for permission to reprint the material indicated: Page 11, portion of 1787 *New York Journal* article from *The Documentary History of the Ratification of the Constitution, Vol. XV.* Copyright © 1984 by The State Historical Society of Wisconsin. / Pages 18, 23, 25 and 29, historical comments from Carolyn Webber and Aaron Wildavsky, *A History of Taxation and Expenditure in the Western World.* New York: Simon and Schuster, 1986. Copyright © 1986 by Carolyn Webber and Aaron Wildavsky, reprinted by permission of Ms. Webber and Mrs. Aaron Wildavsky. / Page 26, excerpt on agricultural subsidies from Gary M. Walton and Ross M. Robertson, *History of the American Economy, Fifth Edition.* Copyright © 1983 by Harcourt Brace & Company, reprinted by permission of the publisher. / Page 39, quote on economic systems from Ayn Rand, *Capitalism: The Unknown Ideal.* Copyright © 1962, 1963, 1964, 1965, 1966 by Ayn Rand. Used by permission of Dutton Signet, a division of Penguin Putnam Inc. / Page 90, comments on tobacco taxes from Henry C. Simons, *Personal Income Taxation.* Published by the University of Chicago, Copyright © 1938 by University of Chicago Press, reprinted by permission of the publisher. / Page 121, quote from Professor Milton Friedman in a 1978 speech on property tax reform in Pasadena, California, before the American Education League.

First Edition. Published by Maximus Profectus, 3811 Colina Dorada Drive, Unit #A-208, San Diego, California, 92124-3806 USA. Printed in the United States of America.

Publisher's Cataloging-in-Publication

Gillis, Timothy J.
Taxation and national destiny : a tax systems analysis and proposal / by Timothy J. Gillis -- 1st ed.
p. cm.
Includes bibliographical references and index.
LCCN: 98-88275
ISBN: 0-9667434-1-5

1. Taxation--United States. 2. Revenue--United States. I. Title.

HJ2362.G55 1999 336.2'00973

— Cover Plate —

"From the Wisdom of the Past to the Prosperity of the Future"

Concept and Design by the Author.

Illustration by GREG HIGH, Escondido, California.

Order information for this Book and for prints of the Cover Illustration is available on page 290.
Colophon is on page 289.

CTRL: 10 9 8 7 6 5 4 3 2 1 PY: 99 00 01 02 03 04 PROY: 1 2 3 4 5 6 7 8 9 10

Table of Contents

Preface

This book involves a mission—a mission to broaden public perspective and induce major policy changes in national government. But few successful missions are launched without effective ground support.

Special thanks to Mr. Joseph Bast of the Heartland Institute in Chicago, businessman and commentator Fred Schnaubelt in San Diego, Mr. Stephen Moore of the Cato Institute in Washington, D.C., and all other organizations and individuals that participated in the review of early drafts of this work prior to publication. I appreciate both the excellent critique and valuable feedback I received, irrespective of the reviewers' philosophical and political leanings.

A great thanks to all who helped in big and small ways including Mr. Gerald R. Lowell, University Librarian, and his kind library staff at the University of California, San Diego, and likewise Ms. Anna Tatar, Library Director, and her good staff in the San Diego Public Library system. I also received research assistance from Ms. Ingrid Vollnhofer in the New Mexico State Library system, and it is to people such as this that I am grateful.

Also, another special thanks to the mission work crew (see their names in the Colophon on page 289) for helping with the construction and public presentation of this book.

As to the significance of those scholars, thinkers, and leaders, past and present, from whom I have drawn information and perspective, I leave the beginning epigraph.

—Timothy J. Gillis, Author

Antiqui aurum effodentes nobis reliquerunt. Ut divites fiamus, modo in luce nobis intuendum est.

Part A: Examination and Comment

I. Introduction

This power, exercised without limitation, will introduce itself into every corner of the city, and country—It will wait upon the ladies at their toilett, and will not leave them in any of their domestic concerns; it will accompany them to the ball, the play, and the assembly; it will go with them when they visit, and will, on occasions, sit beside them in their carriages, nor will it desert them even at church; it will enter the house of every gentleman, watch over his cellar, wait upon his cook in the kitchen, follow the servants into the parlour, preside over the table, and note down all he eats or drinks; it will attend him to his bed-chamber, and watch him while he sleeps; it will take cognizance of the professional man in his office, or his study; it will watch the merchant in the counting-house, or in his store; it will follow the mechanic to his shop, and in his work, and will haunt him in his family, and in his bed; it will be a constant companion of the industrious farmer in all his labour, it will be with him in the house and in the field, observe the toil of his hands, and the sweat of his brow; it will penetrate into the most obscure cottage; and finally it will light upon the head of every person in the United States. . . .

"Brutus" VI, "The Dangers of Unlimited Taxation: 'Give! Give!'" *New York Journal*, December 27, 1787; from the period of debate on and struggle over ratification of the United States Constitution.[1]

The purpose of this book is to review the federal income tax system in the United States and related tax systems and their net impact on the American economy, and to offer an alternative federal tax system to the American people. Absent from virtually all recent public discussions of existing tax systems in this country and proposed changes to them has been the real philosophical basis under which tax systems have been and continue to be advanced and the real practical effect patchwork tax policy has had on individual liberty and prosperity.

Current federal tax policy has been like that of an architect adding to an ever more gaudy, complicated edifice without any previous site plan, soil analysis, or sound structural foundation and putting an irrational and offensive form before even basic function. The community inhabitants of such a building at the least would endure constrained and unpleasant living conditions, and at the most would face a direct threat to their long-term security.

The history, philosophy, and practical effects of taxation in America are examined in the first part of the book. Different taxes are discussed generally, with particular attention given to the federal tax system. The principles discussed, though, could be applied to state and local tax systems as well. The conclusions reached in the first section of the book provide a basis from which new tax theory is built, and that theory is then fully explained in the last section.

This book does not explicitly promote or discourage any particular political or economic policy of government, other than through analysis and critique of various tax systems. The *spending* of money by the government is not the focus; the *assessment and collection of resources* by the government to finance government spending is. Democrats, Republicans, socialists, and libertarians should all agree that it makes no sense to subject an inefficient, wasteful system on citizens when energies and resources that would be lost through that system could be applied to the production of real goods and services.

That being said, this book is not a dry, abstract prescription developed by an accountant or engineer who has been given proscribed conditions under which to develop a governmental billing system. The basic mechanics of tax systems are reviewed, but more important than that are the underlying principles on which the tax systems are based. Those principles are closely examined, and many ideas currently rooted in the fabric of everyday institutions and activities and accepted as untouchable precepts will be open to challenge. Nothing in this book is "tax exempt" from analysis!

For the reader who is comfortable with the philosophy behind current tax policy, and who believes that exploring a totally different perspective in taxation today would be like fifteenth-century Atlantic explorers of yesteryear sailing west into oceanic waterfalls, then he or she may refrain from coming on board. But if a few waves, brisk winds, and a little time on the water could bring a prosperous New World, it might be one's good fortune to look over the charts, test the rigging, and consider investing in the enterprise.

—The Author, 1999

II. American History—From Liberty to Servitude

That government can scarcely be deemed to be free, where the rights of property are left solely dependent upon the will of a legislative body, with no restraint. The fundamental maxims of free government seem to require, that the rights of personal liberty and private property should be held sacred.

Justice Joseph Story, speaking for the Supreme Court in 1829 on the limitation of legislative powers, on the case of *Wilkinson v. Leland.*[2]

The conditions that exist today in the United States under the current system of federal taxation, more than two hundred and twenty years after the birth of the country, are directly related to political and economic concepts developed, implemented or abandoned during the country's history. Taxation does not exist in isolation. The mechanism of governmental revenue acquisition is an important part of how a nation-state does or does not approach various societal problems.

Social and economic problems and their link to fiscal activities of the state, of course, have been analyzed at a functional level in our current century, and various fiscal policies have been implemented in the name of social and economic management or tax reform. For many academic, business, and political leaders today as well as much of the electorate, taxation and governmental spending in America has come to mean a process and imposition on an organization—the country—to effectively manage the resources therein by some combination of regulation, expropriation, and redistribution.

This is not new or original. This philosophy has been the emblem of directorial and managerial activity in nations since antiquity and virtually every country in the world today embraces this philosophy to a greater or lesser degree. A nation is viewed as a unit whose inner workings must be managed by a governmental entity for social stability and for an appropriate award of wealth to individuals in that society based on a need, desire and performance ratio constructed by the state.

Obviously in such a system, varied interests, almost all of whom may have valid desires and goals when viewed independently, will vie for distribution of benefits by the state. Resolution by competing interests is reached through an appeal to legislative arbiters. Politicians, economists, political scientists, and sociologists, as well as particular interest groups, of course, advance theories and policies they think should be adopted by the government to manage the country's resources. Fiscal law is finally passed when enough legislators concur on a particular program, and governmental economic policy is then implemented affecting directly, and indirectly, people's social and economic lives.

Does this not mean then that we in American society should pay increasing attention to the economic management plans offered by legislators, academics, and business experts? Is there not ultimately a good, stable plan that can be found by government and citizens that facilitates directed development and use of resources in the country?

The answer given by most eminent politicians, academics and pundits today is yes. And almost every single plan that has been put forth incorporates taxation not only as a means of acquiring government revenue but as awarding or withholding, directly or indirectly, benefits and resources.

A reasonable person with the facts he has at hand may agree—that specialists inside and outside government must work toward such a universal mechanism, incorporating taxation to some degree or another for resource management and distribution.

But if one has at this reading a vague thought in the back of his mind or maybe a feeling in the pit of his stomach that something is not quite correct or complete, it is not a cause for self-remonstration. Whether by conscious previous acquisition of a different perspective or an intuitive sense of history, action, and process, the reader may possess what has been formally noted in past American history as common sense.[3]

———— ♦ ————

A unique event occurred in the latter part of eighteenth century that turned the course of civilization. It didn't have to happen and accidents or redirection by participants in history could have produced a totally different outcome. Britain had ascended in the century after the European Renaissance as a center of military and naval power, law, science, and political philosophy, and there was no surety during the tumultuous events leading up to that success that England couldn't have been subdued by France or conquered by Spain.

Colonies were being established by European powers around the world and some on the east coast of North America. The settlements in northeastern America under Britain could have been overtaken by other political cultures less favorable to trade and the objective rule of law. The land could have been peopled by opportunists and speculators intent on immediate personal gain with a perpetuation of either Old World despotism under foreign flags or creation of New World predatory dynasties. But what occurred on the edge of a raw wilderness in America, in a climate of self-reliance and innovation, was a further development of law, science, philosophy, and government and a growth in civilization. The eventual outcome was the birth of a new nation.

The real story of American freedom, however, did not start on a sunny summer day in Philadelphia in 1776 with the signing of the Declaration of Independence. It began a hundred or more years earlier with disenchanted emigrants from Europe desiring religious autonomy or escape from economic penury. Dramatic changes in political thought and action would occur with these people on the western side of the Atlantic.

The new immigrants to America had left a physical environment in Europe of confined dwellings and controlled living conditions, and a social environment of rigid class structure and closed or limited economic opportunities and relocated to the polar opposite—vast areas of open land and an effective vacation of almost all government and social services, but also an unlimited potential for trade and development between the colonies and with Indian, French, Spanish, Caribbean, and African, as well as British connections.

The colonists were farmers, craftsmen, merchants, religious reformers or separatists, adventurers, speculators, and indentured servants living in a land that was not always easy. Economic transactions were unsophisticated or basic for the colonists, especially before the middle 1700s.[4] They didn't even have a regular currency or coinage. Whatever was brought into the country was used for money—Dutch, English, and Spanish coins.[5] Barter items were declared legal currency with staple commodities like rice and tobacco traded in the Southern colonies, and cattle, corn, and furs used in New England.[6] Dutch settlers used Indian shell beads called wampum.[7]

There were no commercial banks in colonial America. Credit was extended by merchants who created their own silver coins or issued letters of credit for Americans traveling abroad.[8] Treasury bills were issued by colonial governments in anticipation of tax receipts and then used in trade.[9] Paper money was also produced,[10] but in the absence of printing controls it could be subject to rapid depreciation, and in those circumstances colonists may have wished they had traded in wampum.

Public sector expenditure in the colonies was, not surprisingly, very limited. Colonial legislators met for short periods and if paid at all received nominal salaries. The only large salaried government officials were the royal governors.[11] Care of the poor and sick was a local responsibility, public works were few, and civil service was small. Government often operated on a fee-for-service basis.[12] No colonial navy existed and the army was usually limited to the local militia, except during war with the Indians or French.[13]

Taxes were likewise constrained. Property taxes were assessed on such things as cattle, slaves, houses and land in New England, and taxes on imports and exports were used in the South. Lotteries were run in all the colonies to finance education. Poll taxes were also used, sometimes cost-tiered by economic occupation, and in the South could be paid with tobacco.[14]

Early American religious principles influenced economic transactions and fiscal policy, with the Puritans of New England believing holding of debt immoral and Pennsylvania's Quakers steadfastly refusing to issue paper money to pay for war.[15] The critical need for credit to facilitate economic exchange was not helped when Parliament passed the English Bubble Act of 1719 in England that prohibited bills of credit there and then later extended it to the colonies. Considerable opposition to the act developed in America by 1751.[16]

England was the titular, supervising governmental entity in colonial America, but that could mean little to the practical, everyday lives of colonists when they looked to their immediate communities for local law, social organization and immediate commerce—and perhaps to a visiting neighbor with an extra rifle for protection in a hostile Indian attack. The lack of development and inherent economic limitations in colonial society encouraged personal responsibility and provided a sense of individual and regional autonomy.

Political and economic philosophies were formed or solidified under the hardships and challenges of the time. There was a definite focus on *private production and trade* of resources in the economy—as opposed to modern, centralized *state manipulation* of resources. The early American experience bred an adaptive and resourceful populace that came to prize highly their physical, economic, and to a great extent political, independence.

———— ♦ ————

Migration and re-establishment of communities and separation from sponsoring countries, however, was not new in history. Political evolution of the American colonies could have progressed from the independent settlement stage to the construction of new nation-states, with a rising directorial elite consolidating their power base and enforcing traditional mechanisms of government control and social management. This, to one degree or another, had been the traditional evolution of new societies and governments throughout the world.

There were certainly formidable political and social obstacles to the formation of the new American state to its final, post Revolutionary form. The early American colonial countryside consisted of thirteen different British colonies with people of religious, ethnic, social and regional differences—individuals of English, Scotch, Welsh, German, Dutch, American Indian, and African heritage and other origins who had major social and philosophical differences and political and economic standings; in some cases holding privileged positions and in others totally excluded from regular economic and electoral processes. Modern science and medicine were still in their early youth; roads were poor; land transportation and communication were no faster than a good horse; and sea and river travel were under the vagaries of wind, current and weather. There could be taxes or tariffs between the colonies. And Great Britain was then, and would remain for the next one hundred and twenty-five years, the greatest military power on earth. What could induce a portion of the American populace to become increasingly unsettled and rebellious and unite under such conditions? What would be the catalyst?

The catalyst was taxation. The rebel colonists remembered why they and their forefathers had come to the New World. The colonists were people, or offspring of people, who fled environments where royal favor and grants were common and success could depend much less on what a person did than on whom he knew. They remembered that government taxation and fiscal policy was a primary means of subjugating liberty and imposing tyranny, petty and great. This influenced colonists to construct limited and frugal government. Thus, the parsimony in financial support to early colonial governments by colonists was not just because people of that time had very limited means, it was because they were very interested in preventing government and government officials from obtaining too much power.[17] Government that could not invade their purses could probably not invade their houses.

Fiscal administration in colonial governments in the decades immediately before the Revolution could be difficult, and colonial legislatures, responsible for tax law, wanted it that way. The royal governors in the colonies, appointed by the English Crown, wanted independent appointments and perquisites that had been typical of those positions.[18] The British believed that if the colonists were English subjects they owed their support to governors appointed by the Crown. The colonists, however, thought royal governors—who were not appointed by the colonists and might oppose the local will—should be assigned substantial fiscal restraints, and colonial legislatures went to great lengths to restrict and control governors' budgets and thus limit executive power.[19] The colonial legislatures put period time limits on indirect taxes, excises, and import duties where the tax laws would have to be reenacted in the legislature each year to continue. They made royal salaries temporary, distributed them semi-annually, or reduced them; elected treasurers independent of the governor; precluded direct disbursement of funds without legislative approval, even after allocation, and created extremely long appropriation clauses that prescribed exactly how money was to be spent.[20]

The subsequent British response was to create its own direct tax system on the colonists to finance royal government, and the result was the final contest for America, as described by Webber and Wildavsky:

> The Stamp Acts, duties on tea, and other impositions on the colonists [by the British] were a royal effort to provide independent sources of income for English officials in America. Power, not money, was the issue. . . . : who should rule America.[21]

Colonial legislatures had been adept in their mechanizations to limit appropriations, and the players in the drama understood very well what was at stake when fiscal policy was implemented. The conflict, the American Revolution, ended with success for the new nation after more than eight long years of struggle.

This unexpected, radical emergence of the United States into the world political sphere helped change the view of acceptable government from the traditional model that directed social and economic activity to one where government was expected to protect citizens in their right to freely engage in such activity. The role of government—the state apparatus existing at the consent of the governed and for the benefit of the governed—had moved beyond philosophical concept into political reality.

◆

Why did the early American states effectively unite, or at least unite to the degree that Revolutionary success was achieved, and grow in a different political direction than other countries in history? What conditions existed that provided for a successful Revolution and stable government and society afterward, especially in light of so many political revolts in past history and in modern times that have not produced lasting, improved conditions for their citizens?

Four conditions could be stated for the success of the American Revolution. First was the existing culture. There was a cohesive moral, religious or metaphysical base, or reference, for individual action and reaction that reflected personal responsibility and what we embrace today as civilized behavior. The base of culture and morality was inherited from Western Europe, and although not always attended to by an individual, it provided a sound basis for a peaceful and productive society and for organized action to perceived injustice. A unique American cultural ethos further emphasized personal liberty and its corollary, personal responsibility, and provided a disposition toward industry, trade and accomplishment.

The second condition was stable law and government. Established American colonial government already existed prior to the Revolution, and American society had the Continental Congress and Articles of Confederation as a relatively ordered transition before the Constitution was implemented after the Revolutionary War. Americans did not—unlike citizens in other political revolutions—have to endure reigning juntas or unstable, experimental governments in a society without democratic experience. American colonial law was also based on British law, the most advanced of the time, which provided for an objective review of disputes, protection of basic property rights, and the maintenance of social order.

The third condition that allowed success was the right political leadership at the right time. Leaders in the American Revolution had the depth of thought, prescience, and courage to lead a revolution and then guide the nation into a stable and democratic aftermath.

Last was the will to implement the new state. Dedicated leaders and individual citizens made the commitment, investment, and sacrifice required for success. And linked to all these conditions was a philosophy of individual rights—*and a demand for proper governmental accountability in taxation and spending.*

It is ironic that politicians in the modern American state are no less resourceful than their forefathers, only in the opposite direction—in the *expansion* of centralized power and the associated *increase* in taxation and spending.

♦

Increased stability and prosperity arrived in the new American nation when new government organization was implemented with the adoption of the American Constitution in 1789. The new Constitution allowed certain forms of federal taxation, and in George Washington's tenure as the nation's first President customs duties and collection systems were implemented.[22] Until the Civil War, the nation relied almost completely on customs duties for federal revenue, with miscellaneous excise taxes sometimes placed on such products as sugar, salt, snuff, proceeds of auction sales, legal instruments and bonds.[23]

A federal excise tax on whiskey was also implemented in 1794 that brought problems for the new nation and a situation that could have ended in much worse circumstances than it did. The event, now known as the Whiskey Rebellion, was a revolt in a frontier district in western Pennsylvania against an imposition of the whiskey tax there. President Washington eventually sent in troops to quell the uprising and enforce collection.[24]

The Whiskey Rebellion demonstrated a problem that would occur and reoccur later in American history in the development and application of taxes, but would be minimized or ignored repeatedly by policymakers and legislators: the underlying validity of an assessment and rate to the assessed. Frontiersmen in western Pennsylvania probably did not understand why one of their limited interests or pleasures in life—in this case the libation of whiskey—should be the focus of a strong excise tax.[25]

Tax policy principles, questions and problems, including assignation of user cost and propriety of "sin taxes," were not resolved, if ever addressed, at a philosophical or policy level at the time of the Whiskey Rebellion. This may have had relatively little consequence for a small country with tariffs and a few excise taxes. But the consequences would later be enormous when twentieth-century politicians ignored the same issues in their extension of increasingly broad, complicated and bizarre tax schemes, everything from income tax oilfield depletion-credits to punitive tax actions on subsidized tobacco.

The Whiskey Rebellion itself was successfully quashed and twenty of the alleged participants marched to Philadelphia for trial. Some of the accused rebels were acquitted. The other defendants, including two men sentenced to hang, were later pardoned (in what was probably a politically judicious move) by President Washington.[26] The government had made its enforcement point, but only limited revenue ended up being collected under the whiskey tax[27] and it was finally repealed in 1802.[28]

Taxation, though, was but one element of fiscal management in the new federal government. The nation under the new Constitution had a stronger central government than under the previous Articles of Confederation, and with this change came the legal authorization to administer a strong, centralized fiscal policy for the government. Basic federal taxation had stabilized under a system of tariffs and excise taxes, but the proper policy in handling the national debt was still not clear. Two competing philosophies arose at this time in a now famous conflict between Thomas Jefferson's Republicans[29] and Treasury Secretary Alexander Hamilton's Federalists.[30]

Substantial Revolutionary War debt remained in the form of unpaid bonds that had been issued by the Continental Congress during the war, and this represented a legal debt by the new nation to the bondholders. Hamilton believed this debt should be paid in full and that purchasers of the government securities were entitled to every penny of profit for risking their capital and financially supporting the nation in its darkest hour. But previous experience with treasury bills and paper money issued in the colonies had influenced many of the original purchasers to sell their securities at a discount. Republicans feared that government payment of the bonds in their original, legally obligated amounts would be a massive payoff to speculators who now held the bonds and that the cost of the payoff would be borne by farmers, soldiers, and others who had earlier sold off their securities at below face value.[31]

The Federalists, though, eventually won the debate with an appeal to legislators to establish the "full faith and credit" of the United States government in its financial dealings with citizens.[32] The legislative appropriation and subsequent full payoff of the bonds has since been hailed in history as a foundation for American governmental financial stability and private sector prosperity.[33]

Unrecognized by most, however, has been the significant aspect of this decision with respect to the principle of individual liberty. The "ability to pay" concept that was later to wend its way into American intellectual advocacy, popular belief, constitutional amendment, and finally extensive income tax legislation was effectively repudiated here by early American government. The federal government had an obligation to maintain objective standards in the construction and application of fiscal policy: It was not the government's prerogative to intervene in private sector transactions (the private resale of the original bonds) and reconstruct benefits by relieving current bondholders of their payment and the government (or non-bondholding citizen taxpayers) of liability.

Thomas Jefferson's and the eighteenth-century Republican Party's affinity for agrarian egalitarianism, however, could hardly constitute an extended advocacy for government interference in the private sector.

Jefferson, who became President in 1801, pushed governmental frugality and repayment of the general debt. He believed one generation should not be saddled with another's debt and that all debt should be paid off within twenty years. He also preferred cutting spending to raising taxes and suggested a Constitutional amendment to require a balanced budget.[34]

Jefferson's eventual retirement of the national debt, projected surpluses from tariffs, and a growing nation in need of expanded infrastructure led to an advocacy in the country for federal expenditures for rivers and harbors, canals, lighthouses, beacons, piers, and roads. Traditional Republicans like John Randolph and John Taylor opposed federal expenditures in those areas, and Jefferson was caught between the practical demands of a growing nation and uncertain Constitutional authority to provide for those needs through federal expenditures.[35] Building of the Cumberland Road and National Pike had already been initiated by 1805 by Jefferson's Treasury secretary, Albert Gallatin, and Jefferson recommended a Constitutional amendment to dispel any uncertainty about the propriety of federal government expenditures for infrastructure, arts, manufacturing, education and "the other great objects within each State."[36]

Modern day politicians and financiers may look back at this period of time and view the debate on federal spending on infrastructure as provincial, quaint, or academic, but it was actually just the opposite. The debate of the period demonstrates the seriousness to which early Americans took government, law, economic liberty and the limitations on federal power. Individual states, being viewed as closer to the people and less likely to engage in abuse of power, did not have the same moral and legal sanctions against public spending.[37] The states also, of course, did not control the national money supply.

Expanded federal spending occurred in administrations following Jefferson's, and the reasons for concern in federal fiscal policy started to become evident in real-life fiscal management. Federal expenditures of a sometimes questionable nature were soon labeled "pork-barrel" legislation, a metaphor for legislators awarding federal project appropriations for their districts (like dipping their hands into a pork barrel at the local country store).[38]

Government funding of projects was minuscule by contemporary standards and perhaps in many cases warranted, but the country's citizens and its politicians of the period could hardly have imagined the extension of federal government activity today. The federal government now has a budget of $1.6 trillion[39] per year, one hundred forty-eight thousand times greater than the federal budget in Jefferson's time.[40] The appropriate limitation of power and full clarity in law that Jefferson so strove for still remains a challenge to the country, as well the propriety of ever more servings of "pork."

Support for federal appropriations for basic infrastructure continued until Andrew Jackson's presidency in 1829, but so did general fiscal conservatism. The presidents immediately after Jefferson—James Madison, James Monroe, and John Quincy Adams—all favored reduction in public debt.[41] Government debt could be bad because it drew capital out of the private sector, required subsequent taxes to be paid out to bondholders in interest instead of paying for government services to citizens, or created a liability that made future borrowing, if needed, more difficult. Madison's words indicated a cognizance of and responsibility for that which was not the state's but which was in trusteeship by the state to be returned to the people at the most opportune time. He wanted his administration *"to liberate the public resources* [italics inserted] by honorable discharge of the public debt."[42]

Perhaps one of the most interesting administrations from a historical perspective of government finance was the one under President Andrew Jackson. Jackson was a "man of the people," and popular among frontiersman in new states on America's western frontier. But the former political elite in Washington considered Jackson's entourage coarse and his ideas radical. One might suppose a man of the people to be in favor of substantial increases in government service to the common man, but Jackson was considered a "progressive" for his time in a manner that was exactly opposite the meaning it would have in political life seventy years later.[43]

Jacksonians—the President and his followers—were strongly in favor of limited national government and even opposed federal expenditures for public works. They believed appropriations for civil infrastructure primarily benefited the Atlantic coastline states instead of those near the frontier, and that capital that was kept out of the government's hands and preserved in the private sector would mean higher wages.[44] They also believed public debt was bad because interest payments were a form of redistribution from poor people (general taxpayers) to rich people (bondholders).[45] Again, the historians' description:

> In their [the Jacksonian's] view, the economic freedom that political liberty depended on was best assured by eliminating the artificial privilege that government introduced into the natural equality among men.[46]

Jackson's was a strong, even radical free-market advocacy. At the end of the nineteenth century "Progressives" of that later era, and contrary to the Jacksonians, would argue that if the above concept was not incorrect in Jackson's agrarian society, it was surely incorrect in a time of the new industrial capitalism where powerful corporate interests could easily swallow up the common man, and that extensive government involvement and management in the economy was needed as a safeguard.

But this later popular view by scholars and economists—that is, the need for decided if not substantial involvement of the government in the economy—may have assumed several things that weren't necessarily true. The first was that people's working and living conditions—however limited they were after entering the industrial working community—were worse off after than before;[47] second, that people had fewer life choices after entering the industrial working community; third, that restrictions in commerce and on personal liberty in the implementation of government controls would, in the long run, be more beneficial than harmful to the people; fourth, that workers are incapable of developing, organizing or advancing their interests without government intervention; fifth, that government knows better than workers what action is needed; and last, perhaps most controversial, that it is always fully appropriate in a legal and moral venue for the government to even make such socioeconomic interventions. If all the assumptions just listed are false, could Jacksonian democracy have continued and functioned effectively into the Industrial Age?

The danger to the Jacksonians was not pure capitalism but an effective collusion between favored private sector interests and the government (a despotic policy of specified benefits for the privileged few) at the expense of the common man, or general taxpayer. This is what all early American leaders seemed to fear and what prompted their great caution in developing and implementing fiscal policy for the federal government. It was just that Jackson took the concept of government limitation to the wall, so to speak.

Jackson and his successor in 1837, President Martin Van Buren, opposed both debt and surplus, with President Van Buren claiming revenue surplus would foster national extravagance and lead to a vicious cycle of increasing expenditures.[48] Presidents John Tyler and James K. Polk in the 1840s either railed against owing money or advocated debt reduction to strengthen the nation's international standing.[49] Gross annual federal expenditures, including Civil Administration, War and Navy Departments, Indians, Pensions, and Interest were $10.8 million in

1800 and just $63.1 million sixty years later in 1860, despite the great expansion of the country to the Mississippi, the Rocky Mountains, and finally the Pacific.[50] President James Buchanan (1857–1861), after applying federal surpluses to retire the debt and to reduce revenues to the level of spending, would only allow expenditures clearly warranted in the Constitution, such as military construction.[51] As commented on by Webber and Wildavsky:

> These presidents [Polk and earlier] did not believe government spending should redistribute the nation's wealth from the rich to the poor; to the contrary, they feared it would take from the ordinary man and give to the affluent. "Melancholy is the condition of the people," President Polk wrote, "whose government can be sustained only by a system which periodically transfers large amounts from the labors of the many to the coffers of the few."[52]

This philosophy, that government redistribution was a danger to the common man, would be held by many giants of political and economic philosophy and national political office in the twentieth century to be either just plain wrong or part of a basic policy by very small government in early, bucolic America that had little relevance to modern realities. The new guard with the slide rules and ideas on social management knew best. Or did they?

◆

The primary effect of taxation to taxpayers is the loss of capital for home or business (the funds in principle taken to finance the government). This means that immediate productive capacity or purchasing power is reduced for the taxpayers after tax remittance.

The secondary effect, depending on the tax and economic conditions, can be a general or specific disincentive to further production of various goods and services;[53] in other words, the secondary effect means increasing costs (the tax liability) can influence shifts in or lessen or stop production. This can have rippling effects throughout the economy and actually decrease tax revenue, thus creating additional tax liability for remaining taxpayers.

Taxes in modern society are just one part of the equation, however. Government benefits, specifically benefits provided directly to individuals (as opposed to general government services like national defense), are the other part, and are also going to influence production.

The complexity of the tax code, variance in individual income, and the award or exclusion of services paid through state subsidy make it difficult to identify the actual tax/benefit break-even point. But, theoretically, it can be done. Ignoring all secondary effects (defined earlier) and looking only at the direct cost of taxation, do average- or low-income people benefit from government redistribution? The answer for each individual is, of course, they might—at least in the short run. But the answer doesn't end here.

The efficiency in providing an economic benefit is apparent in a normal, non-governmental, economic exchange where a private buyer exchanges value with a private seller. But when a government agency intervenes, the cost of operating that bureaucracy is added to the costs of the original economic transaction and, depending on the activity, the incentive for higher productivity can be lessened for those recipients being subsidized. The non-recipient taxpayers—the third parties in the equation—may then have to absorb not only the tax costs for the subsidy but also higher prices resulting from a less competitive marketplace.

The interlaced scheme of modern government taxation and subsidy for social service interests, industry, and agriculture will be explored more fully in Chapter III, but an example of the consequences of subsidies is given here from Walton and Robertson's description of modern agriculture in their *History of the American Economy*:

> Clearly, government agricultural policy has been based on an attempt to redistribute income to farmers. In doing so, food production has been curtailed, higher prices have been imposed, and taxes elevated. . . .
>
> Unquestionably, farm programs have helped operators who were well down in the income scale, but it is just as clearly true that the lion's share of assistance has gone to those who were already at the top of the heap. The biggest direct subsidies have gone to the biggest producers; . . . Studies indicate that inequality of incomes in agriculture is greater today than it was three decades ago.[54]

By the 1990s agricultural payments were averaging $10 billion per year in direct payments alone.[55] Some government contracts are not only linked to an assumption of regional economic benefits but are constructed, perhaps cleverly, to appear as needed or *entitled* benefits to other citizens, such as the use of farm surplus purchases by the government in federally subsidized school lunch programs.[56]

Assuming some or even all of government appropriations for special services are appropriate avenues of government expenditure, relative return of value to the general taxpayers or serviced citizens compared to private sector service can be very low. Many federal programs today, whatever laudable intent existed in their conception, may in actual implementation be little more than pay-outs to special interests. Federal assistance to private businesses alone, or "corporate welfare," was estimated at $85 billion a year by 1995.[57] Early American administrations were exactly right in their concern for and prediction of abuse in the expansion of federal spending or "assistance" through federal redistribution.

Economic favoritism or economic inefficiency, however, may be irrelevant concerns for proponents of redistribution through federal tax policies. The final justification by proponents of federal-government redistribution *is* redistribution. They believe that whatever wastes or inefficiencies exist in governmental fiscal policy are less important than the fact that higher-income taxpayers are subsidizing those with lower incomes and thus providing a net benefit to the "common man" or average citizen. But there is a problem with even this position.

The problem has to do with the secondary effect of taxation (described earlier). The greater the level of taxation the less capital is retained in the private sector. This lower level of private-sector capital can mean a corresponding decrease, immediately or over time, in productivity. Lower productivity can mean lower income and a smaller tax base, *and thus less tax revenue or wealth to be redistributed.* A person in a particular occupational circumstance may receive much aid (redistribution) in a socialist country where there are high taxes, for instance, and still be much poorer than another person in the same occupational situation in a capitalist country where there is no redistribution of income and little or no taxes.[58]

The construction of the ideal redistributive "formula" of taxation and spending to allow redistribution and maximize productivity and benefits has long been attempted by economists. But the question with respect to individual rights remains. Is the construction of this theoretical ideal a laudable attempt to manage the economy or a threat to basic economic liberty?

◆

Government's, and to a large degree society's, disposition toward fiscal conservatism in early America was gradually to change during and after the American Civil War. Advancements were occurring in science and industry, and with that, changes in society. The Industrial Revolution had arrived in full swing and America grew. Technical advances allowed people to increase production and create wealth to an astonishing degree. Society benefited. Consumers could benefit incrementally from each new or improved product or service with no financial or development risk to themselves, and inventors, entrepreneurs, and businessmen could benefit (profit) commensurate with their service (sales) to the buying public. Business ventures could mean high profits but could also entail substantial investment and risk.

Increasing economic disparity between successful businessmen and most of the general public in the Industrial Revolution prompted social critics to question the accumulation and concentration of created wealth. Commercial success had not been considered a problem before in America, and commercial and tax law had supported individual property rights of the producer. The assumption in early America had always been that the industrious and innovative could pursue their own private business ventures at their own risk, and with the resource (product or service) they created could engage in volitional trade with others and retain the profit (or wealth increase) from their transactions. A shopkeeper, for instance, would hardly begrudge his neighbor if the neighbor invested his own labor, capital, and risk in a business venture and made a thousand dollars. The shopkeeper might even applaud the neighbor if he turned around and spent a hundred of it in the shopkeeper's store!

The acceleration of commerce and change in industrial America, however, introduced new variables that suggested to many this laissez-faire principle was no longer acceptable.[59] Corporate and business expansion and commercial success were becoming increasingly associated with unwarranted industrial hazards, lack of sanitation and control in food and drug production, consumer product dangers, stock and bond manipulations, environmental pollution, ruthless business competition, child labor, and general worker exploitation.

The role and responsibility of government in addressing these conditions had to be defined. Government could, as a possible solution to the industrial age problems, enforce existing statutory and common law principles, which it was not doing, and create prudent new civil and criminal law applicable to these new economic times and thus move toward protecting laissez-faire tradition. But if the problem was the creation and concentration of wealth, these improvements would not be enough and laissez-faire would have to be abandoned. Government management of the economy and redistribution of resources would be necessary.

The added advantage (or disadvantage) of government control of the economy meant traditional mechanisms of redress or legal protection could be legally and practically overridden, and traditional business planning and contract law in the courts would become less relevant. Indeed, with government management of the economy, any act of commerce or level of profit could be changed merely by imposing regulations and tax mechanisms to remedy perceived inequities in business or society.

◆

The Civil War in 1861 brought the first big expansion of the federal budget. And with the increased spending came increased taxes. Both the Union government and the Confederacy passed income tax laws.[60] The Federal income tax was a graduated tax from 1 to 10 percent and accounted for as much as 25 percent of internal revenue collections.[61] Citizens in both the North and South tolerated the income tax and higher taxation because of national emergency,[62] just as citizens had tolerated higher taxation in the War of 1812.[63] The Civil War precluded attention to and scrutiny of the new tax, and it was not until after the war ended that increased focus returned to fiscal controls and taxation.

Americans might sustain sacrifice for war reasons, but whiskey excise tax—or income tax—in time of peace could be another matter, especially when strong philosophical leanings went elsewhere. An illustrative view of the political and ideological opposition to the income tax in this period is provided again through Webber and Wildavsky. Senator Justin Morrill of Vermont commented in 1864 that in the United States "we make no distinction between the rich and the poor man . . ." and that "The man of modest means is just as good as the man with more means, but our theory of government does not admit that he is better. . . . It [the income tax] is seizing the property of men for the crime of having too much."[64] And the historian Davis points to an 1869 *New York Tribune* editorial that denounced the income tax "as the most odious, vexatious, inquisitorial, and unequal of all our taxes."[65]

The federal income tax law, politically unpopular for the era, was repealed by Congress in 1871. The Civil War Debt of $2.5 billion at the end of the war[66] was paid off in the twenty-four years after 1870 by surpluses from import duties on consumer goods.[67] Presidents Abraham Lincoln, Andrew Johnson, Ulysses S. Grant, and Rutherford B. Hayes all wanted wider distribution of the debt or to pay it off over time, with

Grant even in favor of cutting taxes to induce economic growth.[68] Fiscal restraint was embraced in the 1880s under Presidents Chester A. Arthur, who condemned government surpluses because he believed they corrupted morality and led to rising expenditures,[69] and Grover Cleveland, whose similar opinion was reflected (in a remark prescient of exploding special-interest demands later in the twentieth century) that public extravagance "begets extravagance among the people."[70]

But the inherent attachment in the American psyche to limited federal government and primary economic liberty was changing, ever so slightly. A premonitory event, contrary to the fiscal conservatism of the time, occurred in 1885. Many members of the House of Representatives, eager to expand spending in the face of surplus revenue, succeeded in establishing a separate Appropriations Committee away from the Ways and Means.[71] *Close procedural relationship between taxation and spending was beginning to come apart.*

Appropriation bills in the new system could now be channeled to legislative committees made up of spending advocates. This reinforced what is known today as "the Iron Triangle," a relationship between special interests, administrative bureaus, and the Congressional committees concerned with the bureaus' affairs, and a pork-barrel collectivism called "log-rolling," where Representatives vote for each other's individual projects.[72]

It was obvious government would expand to some degree with the nation's huge growth in people, land, and industry. Western civilization was now in the age of the Industrial Revolution and America was a chief player. Heady national expansionism in the United States and its territories was the order of the day, whether in westward settlement or new industrial development. But careful attendance to law and principle might be limited. The existing nebular definitions in the political arena for both federal government obligations and the proper revenue mechanisms to finance those obligations didn't help.

Businesses of the late nineteenth century, in a parallel to those of the twentieth century, could also be more opportunistic than truly capitalistic and trumpet free enterprise only so long as it suited their immediate agenda. Then it was time to run to the legislature or courts for special favors. Farmers, for instance, could not successfully sue the owners of burgeoning new factories polluting their air and water because the courts held—in a denial of basic common law property rights and a nice touch of collectivism for the industrialists—that the common good (industry and jobs) were more important to society than adjustment or compensation to the farmers. Of course, with culpability for damages removed and no economic incentive not to pollute, the stage was set for a hundred years of pollution problems in the country.[73]

Federal tariffs, favored by those guiding the industrial growth in cities along the Eastern seaboard, had been passed to protect American business. But however tariffs may have protected industrial growth and domestic jobs from foreign competition, many viewed them as undesirable and as discriminatory toward farmers and consumers, and a subsidy to domestic manufacturers because they raised the purchase price of manufactured goods.

Substantial economic power had come into the hands of the industrial giants. This caused a response from political opponents—the new Progressives advocating reform of corporate excesses and Populists representing the farming interests—who moved to counter the Eastern industrialists.[74]

Believing rudder movement on the ship of state had been pushed far right by the industrialists,[75] the Progressives and their allies pushed for a course correction to the left by advocating major changes in fiscal policy with increased governmental controls. The position of minimum involvement in the economy by the federal government that had been characteristic of earlier America was changing. And the move for many major players would be from principles to pragmatism.

The growth of huge personal fortunes in the 1880s along with Democratic and Populist reform advocacy from the southern and western states and a Treasury deficit after the depression of 1893 all created favorable political conditions for federal income tax advocates, and they grabbed their chance. The pro-income tax Democrats were successful in adding a clause to an 1893 tariff-reduction bill, levying a 2 percent tax on incomes over $4,000.[76] The income tax had returned to the national scene.

There was no war going on, however, as there had been when the last federal income tax had been implemented during the Civil War, so the new law divided public opinion and heightened political protest. Heated debate emerged from such principles of the era as William Jennings Bryan of Nebraska, who supported the new tax, and opponents who claimed the measure was the first step toward socialism.[77] There would be a climax in this immediate contest and the income tax temporarily taken away, but it would not be the mighty Republican industrialists and their political allies in Congress who would do it. It would be the Supreme Court of the United States—and a stockholder dissatisfied with the new tax encumbrance on his financial investment.

One Mr. Charles Pollock sued Farmers Loan and Trust, a company he held stock in, claiming the income tax was unconstitutional. The suit eventually went to the Supreme Court and in April of 1895 the court ruled that the portion of the income tax that was based on income from real estate was unconstitutional because it was a direct tax under the Constitution, and direct taxes by the federal government on the states had to be proportional based on population. They also ruled that the portion of the law that taxed interest derived from state and municipal bonds was unconstitutional because it violated the separation of powers provision in the Constitution.

The court then struck down the rest of the law in May 1895 because it held that the voided provisions were inseparable from the rest of the law, and thus the whole law was void.[78] The Supreme Court, the nation's last protective rampart against potentially suppressive and constitutionally inadequate legislation, was concerned about the new role legislators believed the federal government should be taking in managing private enterprise. Justice Field wrote, "The present assault upon capital is but the beginning. It will be but the stepping stone to others, larger and more sweeping, till our political contests will become a war of the poor against the rich."[79] The Supreme Court was concerned, but political focus, even among Republicans, would become increasingly pro-income tax.

Opponents of the income tax were now relying on a fine technical interpretation of one law to preclude any recurrence of the tax system they dreaded. But the anti-income tax politicians seemed incapable of either articulating a strong enough argument against the tax or to convince their colleagues if they had one. The nation's economic policy looked to the Democrats and Populists to be skewed toward elite, opportunistic capitalists—in particular the Eastern industrialists—whom they believed had benefited unfairly and should be forced to cut a bigger slice of the pie for the working man. That the income tax could be against the long-term interest of average Americans was not accepted, if ever considered, by the new Democrats. Andrew Jackson's Democratic-Party philosophy of very low taxes and limited federal government was behind the view of the modern Democrats, who were now marching to the tune of governmental activism.

Political conditions were becoming increasingly turbulent by 1908 as Democrats, Populists and insurgent Republicans—often representing mid-western or western farming, ranching, logging, or mining interests—protested the high protectionist tariffs. Republicans were now in a fight among themselves about tariff policy as well as battling the Democrats and Populists. The Republican traditionalists believed high tariffs protected American industry, and Democrats, Populists and the

Republican reformers believed the high protectionist measures unfairly cost western industry, farming, and American consumers.

The political conflict was also confused because some interests—Democratic as well as Republican—supported protectionist measures for particular regions or industries and opposed others. The situation was an inducement for many in Congress to look for other means of government revenue acquisition, and the income tax was increasingly championed as a remedy.

The advocacy for an immediate utilitarian solution to fiscal management problems at the turn of the century has a very strong echo in today's proposals for tax reform. The focus was, and is, not on how individual economic liberty can be protected, but how parochial political interests can be satisfied while minimizing social instability.

Tariffs, though, and not income taxes, were the initial and immediate focus of much of the debate in 1908, centering around the Payne-Aldrich Tariff and amendments to it. Republican President William Howard Taft believed tariffs had been set too high and had promised a revision,[80] but active reconstruction he left to Congress.[81] Amidst much debate and political strife, a bill was finally put together in the House Ways and Means Committee under Republican Chairman Serano Payne that increased seventy-five and reduced over four hundred tariffs.[82] Republican insurgents, the Republican progressives, were not completely satisfied, but the bill passed the house and was sent to the Senate anyway.[83]

The chairman of the Senate Finance Committee was Nelson W. Aldrich, an Old Guard Republican supported by the Eastern industrialists. Aldrich, considered an adept and cunning politician, took the bill and bottled it up in Committee. When it came out it had over six hundred tariff increases.[84]

The Republican progressives were outraged and they publicly renounced Aldrich's party leadership. Aldrich then read them out of the party.[85] Pressure had been building in Congress to reduce the high tariff burden by passing new inheritance and income tax laws and Democrats, who were also allied with radical remnants of the Populist Party, now seized the opportunity and approached the disaffected Republican moderates on a plan to embarrass Aldrich.[86] They offered to attach an income tax provision to the tariff bill. The Republican moderates agreed.[87]

An unusual twist in events then took the horse of political direction from a bucking half turn in the direction of the income tax system to a flat-out run directly toward it. The political subplot is an interesting tale on how mechanizations in a legislative forum can bring just what a politician wanted—and didn't. The result for the United States of America would be a new multi-trillion dollar federal tax system that would bring economic management directives of the federal government from the simple setting of tariffs and excise taxes to an extensive regulation and control of citizens' earnings, and the intrusion of the federal government into every facet of economic life.

Chairman Aldrich, realizing things were getting out of hand in the Republican Party with the rebellion of the Progressive Republican insurgents, met in May of 1909 with President Taft to discuss the threatened passage of the Democrats' and insurgents' income tax bill.[88] Taft actually supported the concept of an income tax but was concerned about both Republican Party unity and public criticism of the Supreme Court if the Court had to rule again on constitutionality of another income tax law. Aldrich, like the Old Guard Republicans he represented, opposed the tax but was faced with the possibility of its immediate imposition anyway from what would be a triumphant political opposition.[89]

Taft and Aldrich came up with an extraordinary scheme. They would first support a 4 percent excise tax on corporate profits.[90] This was actually an income tax, but it would apply only to incorporated businesses and not to individuals and was expected to meet the legal technicalities that had been established by the courts, and thus pass Constitutional muster. Taft would also support an income tax amendment to the Constitution that, if passed by Congress and later ratified by the states, would permit the passage of personal income tax laws. The political momentum of the Democrats and the Republican insurgents for an immediate income tax law and substantial reduction in the tariffs could then be deflated.

The President surprised everybody and shocked the insurgents by making his proposal public in June of 1909. The plan worked. The wind was knocked out of the sails of the political opposition and the original, personal income tax proposal died. The corporate income tax law proposed by Taft was then debated and passed both houses of Congress almost unanimously.[91] The income tax amendment was also passed by the House and Senate by early July with another astounding level of support—60 to 11 in the Senate and 317 to 14 in the House—laying the groundwork for Constitutional change.[92]

An income tax statute to tax *corporations* now existed. But the income tax amendment that had passed in Congress and that would permit the creation of income tax statutes to tax *individuals* meant nothing unless that amendment was also ratified by the required number of states and brought into Constitutional law. The ratification process could be a lengthy one as the amendment was debated state by state, even if the amendment was eventually ratified—and income tax opponents could hope or believe that would never be the case. Senator Aldrich, through the assistance of President Taft, had successfully defeated the Democrats, subdued the Republican insurgents, and prevented the personal income tax from becoming law—for a while.

If the United States could construct elaborate protective tariffs, why could it not counterbalance or replace those taxes with a federal tax on personal income? The ineffectiveness or lack of philosophical or practical argument against the income tax again provided an excellent opportunity for pro-income tax forces. The overwhelming support of the income tax concept by Congress in its vote for the income tax amendment should have given Senator Aldrich and his supporters pause for—if they hadn't already divined—the eventual outcome of personal income tax legislation.

The fierce sense of independence embraced by early Americans—from frontiersmen to shopkeepers to the intellectual elite of the day—had found legal fruition in political rights ensconced within the Declaration of Independence and ultimately the United States Constitution. But what was originally coded into the Constitution by the Founding Fathers under a limit on federal powers—the basic right of the individual to peacefully produce, keep, and utilize the fruits of his labor—was about to change.

The income tax amendment that had been passed by Congress in 1909, and previously disregarded by Republican conservatives, was approved in four years by various states and accepted as ratified by the required number in 1913,[93] and the Sixteenth Amendment was added to the Constitution.[94] The new Congress that year, with a Democratic-Party majority and President Woodrow Wilson in the White House, would then dismiss any political remnants of income tax law opposition and pass this century's first federal income tax statute for individuals. The modern federal income tax system in the United States had become reality.

———— ♦ ————

How did the Democrats, coming out of a Jacksonian heritage, and Republicans, elevated in a climate of free enterprise that was making America a world power, come to implement a fundamental Constitutional change and embrace such a potentially severe impediment to individual economic liberty as the income tax system?

The answer is Democrats and a substantial number of Republicans did not view the income tax as a threat to economic liberty. The major players in both parties, whether they supported or initially opposed it, increasingly came to see the income tax in a utilitarian instead of a philosophical light. They viewed it as a tax tool that might benefit their political policies and their constituencies' immediate social or economic needs.

The Democrats wanted a counterbalance to the tariff favoritism and big profits of big business, and the high prices to farmers and low wages of workers. The inherent Republican resistance to the income tax was mollified by what acceptance of it meant to both the Democrats and Republicans—a tantalizing prospect of increased political power.

The goal of the new twentieth-century politicians, Democrat and Republican, however, was not raw power for their party in the construction of an autocratic state. The goal was one of efficiency. Could not government leaders redirect resources in the nation to what they believed were appropriate, needed areas without the traditional, cumbersome process of debate, spending justification, and traditional methods of taxation?

Government efficiency in the direction of citizens and their resources in order to create a better nation has been the goal of ruling institutions throughout history. *But this is exactly what the nation's founders fought against in the creation of the new American state and what other early leaders strove to prevent for over one hundred years after Independence.* The country's early leaders didn't want an efficient subjugation of citizens and expropriation of their resources, and so held dearly to limits on federal power in the administration of national government. The new national leaders at the end of the nineteenth century moved toward increased government management of the human condition instead of universal protection of basic economic rights. They believed old policies were no longer applicable when in fact, universally applied, they could have been the basis for the most effective resolutions to the problems of the time.

Practical examples today are limitless. Businesses that are free of arbitrary regulation and government subsidy maximize their productivity, while only costing those buyers purchasing their products or services—not third-party taxpayers. Businesses do not damage the environment or other private resources without suffering civil liability, but neither is their capital and development hamstrung if they are prosecuted for only real violations and not encumbered with controls and arbitrary expropriations by the state. Workers or investors can form partnerships, unions, cooperatives, corporations, and associations, where even the lowest paid laborer can reinvest in the equity base of an enterprise and rise, exponentially, to great wealth.

These things are all possible with economic freedom. But when the state assigns arbitrary seizure to the creation of wealth, all bets are off. The fight becomes not one for better production and service in the economy but for the creation and manipulation of tax law and redistribution of resources to benefit politically favored interests. The philosophy of taxing personal production merely because production occurs and then assigning arbitrary, politically related conditions to that assessment is offensive to many who understand basic economics and value personal liberty.

The significance of the Sixteenth Amendment and the conditions it provided for has been totally underrated by economists, historians, and sociologists. What occurred with the passage of this amendment was an effective transfer of all new properties (income) received in trade between citizens, including each yearly Gross National Product (GNP)—or precisely—*the right of transfer of all such properties,* to government supervision to be managed or dispersed at the statutory whim of the political power base currently in office. The original Constitutional protection afforded the individual with respect to his economic foundation, the fruits of his labor, was now gone, and state and national governments could arbitrarily seize resources or assign huge liability to individuals, organizations and businesses conditionally and retroactively. In other words, just because a man earned something the government could take it.

The United States had now come full circle. What started out as a fiercely independent America dedicated to the protection of individual liberty now abandoned a basic property right in favor of increased government action to redistribute wealth for a promise—or an illusion—of a better society.

The gravity of the situation under the new Sixteenth Amendment, however, was certainly not apparent to many immediately after its passage. The average personal income in 1913 was $621 and the new federal income tax that went into law that year taxed only people who made over $3,000 ($4,000 for a married couple)—and that was only 2 percent of the population, and the maximum rate was only 7 percent. Ninety percent of federal revenue was still coming in from customs and duties.[95]

Exemption limits on the income tax were dropped to $1000 to increase federal revenue when World War I arrived, and the percentage of federal revenue from income tax climbed to 60 percent, but the income tax was still primarily a tax on the better healed. Between 1917 and 1919 just one percent of the taxpayers who filed an income tax return paid over 70 percent of the income tax collected.[96] The wealthy were finally supporting what many politicians and citizens considered a much fairer portion of federal expenditures.

Cordell Hull, draftsman of the 1913 income tax law, stated the tax was sure to exceed "in its justice, flexibility, and productiveness any tax law on the statute books."[97] The income tax seemed to be a painless mechanism for the country, or at least for the vast majority of citizens in it, to finance the government. Unrestrained, arbitrary government seizure of personal production had been formalized under the Constitution and assessment of personal income implemented under new statutes. But irrespective of this, the early low-assessment ratios for most Americans and the high revenue acquisition from a smaller, wealthier elite suggested to many the new income tax was nothing but a boon to the country—and could *never*, of course, be a threat to the common man.

III. A Century for the Economically Disoriented

Every social system is based, explicitly or implicitly, on some theory of ethics. The tribal notion of "the common good" has served as the moral justification of most social systems – and of all tyrannies – in history. The degree of a society's enslavement or freedom corresponded to the degree to which that tribal slogan was invoked or ignored.

Ayn Rand in her analysis of modern political and economic systems; from *Capitalism: The Unknown Ideal.*[98]

The passage of federal income tax law after the closing of the nineteenth century laid the base for dramatic changes in government fiscal policy for the twentieth, but those changes would still take decades to evolve.

An early impetus for expanded federal expenditure came with the entry of the United States into the World War I in 1917. Total spending by the federal government rose from 2.3 percent of GNP in 1905 to 24.1 percent in 1918,[99] but old traditions of fiscal conservatism die hard. After the war, spending dropped back to 3.4 percent of the GNP by 1924,[100] even as government regulation of the economy began under the newly established Federal Reserve Board.

Despite the wartime tax increases, 70 percent of the American war debt for the World War I had been financed by government borrowing, and the elites of the day, including President Warren G. Harding, pressed for reduced public spending, minimal taxes and a balanced budget in concert with debt reduction.[101] Volunteerism and limited local public relief continued in America as a mechanism for relief to the poor. Veterans' pensions remained the only federal service program until the federal government—along with forty-one states by 1920—adopted workmen's compensation.[102]

America had implemented a new method of revenue acquisition, the federal income tax system, but was still using that new system in the 1920s for traditional revenue needs and at limited levels. The income tax, although becoming more complex with various deductions, was reduced in 1926 to 1.5 percent on the first $4,000 of income and rising to 5 percent on amounts over $8,000.[103]

Progressive and labor movement advocacy for labor reform legislation, child welfare, slum clearance, urban housing programs and social insurance was active but emphasis was not necessarily on federal action—both state level and matching grant programs were being considered.[104] Although little change had occurred at the federal level during the 1920s, the Progressive intellectual base that rose at the turn of the century would be ready for action, and for massive federal policy change, when the next great national economic calamity hit.

The arrival of the worldwide depression in America with the crash of the domestic stock market on October 24, 1929 was an impetus for consideration and acceptance of new measures of social service activity at the federal level. But the sense of individual independence, personal responsibility and buoyant optimism in the American character remained endemic during and after the 1920s and carried American society through a depression, another world war, and to the relative contentment of the 1950s; and was not seriously altered until later, during the confusion and cynicism surrounding the Vietnam War.

Today modern leaders have not successfully addressed modern fiscal problems and also have not recognized underlying attitudes in American culture that further supported the modern expansion of federal involvement in the economy. The substantial shift in that direction started during the 1930s.

A new president, Franklin D. Roosevelt, came to power in 1933 in the midst of the Depression and initially pushed for governmental spending reductions and a balanced budget. The House of Representatives passed the Economy Bill in the first Hundred Days of the Roosevelt Administration that reduced civil service and Congressional salaries, cut other federal expenditures, and even halved the pensions of disabled war veterans.[105]

Roosevelt, though, pushed expanded federal activism in other areas with his New Deal. The National Recovery Administration (NRA) was started to set price-fixing codes designed to equalize competition; the Public Works Administration initiated to promote heavy construction projects such as dams in the western states; the Labor Relations Act created to deal with labor relations; the Agricultural Adjustment Act passed to subsidize and stabilize agriculture. Unemployment was addressed by passage of the Federal Emergency Relief Administration (FERA), the Civilian Conservation Corp (CCC), the Civil Works Administration (CWA), and the Works Progress Administration (WPA). The Social Security Act became law in 1935 to provide work retirement benefits.[106]

Federal expenditures increased from $3.3 billion in 1929 to $8.9 billion in 1939, with the federal expenditure of GNP going from 3.2 percent to 9.7 percent in the same period.[107] Aid to agriculture, welfare, work relief, and public works were over fifty percent of the federal expenditures by 1939. By 1940 social welfare spending alone was 37 percent.[108] The income tax, which had fallen in the 1920s, was adjusted with the Wealth Tax Act of 1935 to increase estate, gift, and capital-stock taxes, and an excess-profits tax was also created.[109]

Roosevelt's policies were dramatically new to America but not draconian. The job programs sponsored by Roosevelt were not intended to interfere with private industry,[110] and Roosevelt, although conferring with the noted economist John Maynard Keynes in 1935, disagreed with Keynes' theory on using massive government spending to stimulate the economy and maintained his preference for a balanced budget.[111]

Roosevelt may be lauded, of course, for the hope and confidence he inspired in the electorate during the Depression, for his preparation before and moral leadership during the Second World War, and for the fact the nation remained both politically free and fundamentally capitalistic during an era of rising, fanatical socialism in the world. But both the immediate and long-term economic effects of the New Deal programs may not be so positive.

The NRA, with its price-fixing mandates, was ruled unconstitutional by the Supreme Court during the Depression, and other programs, while being heralded by many, have been criticized by others as slowing economic recovery.[112] The economic efficacy of the New Deal may be less important, however, than what it brought at the political and sociological level: public acceptance of extensive federal involvement in the economy.

Federal involvement in social services could now be mixed with an unlimited income tax to produce a very potent cocktail. Unlimited drinking began at the government's revenue bar, but one question could not be avoided: Who, ultimately, would pick up the bar tab?

◆

Federal government expenditures would grow substantially in the last half of the twentieth century. Calamitous as well as momentous world events arrived at the doorstep of America with the arrival of World War II in 1941; then the Cold War, Korean War, Third World expansion, Vietnam War, collapse of Communism in 1989, and finally the current technological revolution. It would be expected that during this period of history, expansion of federal government activities—especially national defense during time of war—would occur, and it did. The social service and subsidy expenditures of the federal government also grew substantially, but how could the overall expansion of government spending be justified or explained?

Federal spending had reached $1.56 trillion[113] per year by 1996—and the national debt was close to $5.5 trillion.[114] The nation had indeed grown, and with it, the fiscal requirements of the federal government. But did it cost more than one and a half trillion dollars to run the national government each year?

The cost of general federal government services and law enforcement in 1996 was $29 billion, or only 2 percent of the year's $1.6 trillion budget! National Defense—including veterans and foreign affairs—was $316 billion, or another 20 percent of the total. Both general government and national defense total only 22 percent of the $1.6 trillion, so where was the other 78% of the budget being spent?

The other areas of expenditure were all related to some type of social or economic service or subsidy—Social Security, Medicare, and other retirement benefits ($597 billion, or 37 percent); social programs such as Medicaid, food stamps, housing assistance, and public health ($287 billion, or 18 percent); physical, human and community development, including economic, financial, scientific, or educational subsidies ($127 billion, or 8 percent)—or interest on the national debt ($241 billion, or 15 percent).[115]

Utilization of the income tax as a primary revenue source to finance expanded social service spending can be seen in tax receipts. Tax revenue in 1996 from the traditional, historical excise and custom (tariff) taxes, plus estate, gift, and miscellaneous taxes was $115 billion—or more than three times the amount needed for general government and law enforcement ($29 billion). But the 1996 revenue from income tax was $828 billion; and Social security, Medicare, unemployment and other retirement taxes were an *additional* $509 billion.[116]

Twentieth century income tax had begun as a tax on corporations, but corporate taxation no longer held primacy. Tax receipts from the personal income tax were now 79 percent of the income tax revenue total and corporate income taxes only 21 percent. Tax conditions and federal expenditures had radically changed from the beginning to the end of this century, and the reason for that change needs to be explored.

◆

Production of regular goods and services and their distribution—the question of humanitarian relief aside—are almost always more efficient in the private sector, as almost all economists will almost always testify.

So why was the American government, with an apparent support of most of the American populace, spending over $1 trillion a year in human services and subsidy? Was this a prudent, warranted investment in human social service support through the federal government? And beyond that, and perhaps separate from it, what was the relationship between appropriations and the *mechanism* of taxation?

Serious discussion may ensue on how much direct government expenditure for social service spending (spending beyond basic government administration and national defense) is socially desirable, politically acceptable and economically sound. National fiscal policy involves more, though, than the question of effectiveness of direct social service *spending*. There is a convolution of influencing factors in modern government and finance.

Recipients of governmental appropriations are beneficiaries in governmental fiscal policy. But under the current federal system benefits are hardly restricted to direct spending by the government. Extensive allotment or subsidy is directly or indirectly awarded to beneficiaries through the tax code. And to complicate things further, statutory law, as will be explained later, is used to implement regulatory expropriation—another type of benefit for some and an effective tax on others.

The mechanics of these operations will be reviewed, but first the underlying philosophy that exists in tax policy today and the psychology of modern American tax makers, taxpayers, and beneficiaries needs to be looked at and compared with historical values and concepts. An explanation can then be ascertained as to why the country is in its present fiscal situation and why many popular remedies to current fiscal problems may or may not work.

The first big policy question examined here and the one facing federal policymakers and the public at the end of the nineteenth century was the role of the federal government in directly providing services previously offered only through the private sector, including those designated as government social services. The debate that ensued in the 1890s on government involvement in the economy was vigorous and has continued into modern times, with substantial federal policy change along the way.

Should the federal government limit the scope of its activity in American life to foreign relations, national defense, police, the courts, and the general administrative duties on government lands? Should it provide just immediate emergency humanitarian assistance in time of regional or national emergency or long-term federal welfare subsidy to states, cities and individuals? Should the government control and subsidize banking; manipulate the money supply and interest rates for economic management; guarantee and provide primary, secondary, and higher education; provide assistance and subsidy to farms and businesses; guarantee and provide health care; give care to legal and illegal immigrants; regulate businesses on internal operating procedures; implement policies to guarantee good housing and good paying jobs; and support art and cultural programs in the country? Is it the obligation of the federal government to provide not only basic governmental infrastructure but to guarantee various economic services to citizens who are unable or unwilling to acquire those services through the private market? Is government an agent to collect, manage, and disburse resources?

The answer is that over the past hundred years Congress has increasingly chosen to define government as a social service agent and an agent of economic redistribution, although this has caused many problems because government outside of its service status does not *produce* wealth, it merely *reallocates* it. State and later expanding federal control of the education system helped induce expanded teaching of statist ideals and the belief that economic basics and economic opportunities for people are authorized merely by legislators voting for those conditions, and the actual physical redistribution of resources to provide for those conditions is not to be construed as a trespass on the original producer or owner but *a duty to which the original producer or owner must submit.*

Naturally, the anointing of one's interest group by legislative pen as a chosen benefactor rather than as a payer became a very big concern for individuals, organizations, and businesses. Appropriately inculcated with the neo-socialism of our time and not wanting to be seen as gauche and provincial by protesting a newly expanding government being hailed as compassionate, virtually everyone was on board, or trying to get on board, the government benefit train. Everyone's cause was noble—education, children, commerce, small business, big business, industrial development, environmental preservation, agriculture, family, religion, science, and medicine—and everywhere there were caring legislators.

People could obtain grants, subsidies, advantageous legal regulations and directives, and tax deductions and exemptions. Everyone (perhaps with only an adequately compensated lobbyist) could claim more rights and be happy! And there might always be modern, socially active courts yearning to be New Age legislators that could create new law for new rights if none existed before. That the bounds of the Constitution had been exceeded in this new, popular definition of rights may not have been so correct as the idea of a Constitution turned upside down—an involuntary servitude of some being transmogrified into the "rights" of others. But ultimately implied in these new tax policies was—legally at least—the national interest. And that is the cloak that Congress could sit under and others strove to be covered by.

There was only one problem. This great increase in government service could be very expensive. This is unlike the original free enterprise system based on volitional trade, where two parties each create a product or service and trade value for value *and both parties are better off.* The farmer trades some of his wheat for the carpenter's work and the farmer has a chair and the carpenter has bread. They only make a trade when both will benefit.

Gradually American legislators had become less like these traditional, figurative, independent-minded Americans and more like medieval barons constructing their own command economy with a resultant economic retardation associated with that type of political and economic environment. A mandate or grant by Congress for a particular interest group meant the receiving party received benefits *without making an economic contribution,* and the party paying, the taxpayers, *were doing so without economic compensation.*

The trick for Congress was to flip the ratio as much as possible so those that were taxpayers could be receivers for other benefits, and vice versa. This may not be efficient economically, but it tended to allay complaints from an electorate increasingly conditioned to view the American government as a rich Uncle Sam who had better give *them* stuff. Firmly held, one might suppose, in the bosom of many legislators was the idea that if enough benefits are dispersed and advantageous directives and regulations created on the one hand, and enough money seized from people on the other, Congress could take care of everybody.

The award of benefits to citizens by Congress would be easy—but not the assessment for those services, especially when the receivers of benefits were different from the payers. Even when receivers were payers it could be difficult to impose the high costs of expanded government services on a populace that had historically prospered under less government and on more personal responsibility and economic discretion. A situation where individual citizens were faced with stark, repeated and increased seizure of their earnings could more easily lead to public protest or revolt, and thus trouble for the government in assessing and collecting revenue and imposing economic policies.

Citizens that were fully conscious of the relationship between taxation and expenditures, and could easily measure such, would turn to avoidance, changing their economic activity in the face of increasing taxation to minimize assessment and loss of their resources. The ultimate result of such grass roots economic repudiation would be a reduction in tax monies and benefits controlled by the government, as well as reducing the government's ability to manage private resources and the economy. What tool could government, politicians, and bureaucrats implement to influence and control individual economic activity as well as redistribute vast quantities of private resources to achieve their political goals?

The income tax, in its present form, was the answer. It was the perfect vehicle under which to manage the economy and redistribute resources while reducing the chance of widespread protest or revolt, as long as citizens were conditioned to believe in the income tax system's efficacy and fairness, where fairness was defined, in good collectivist mold, as equity of condition financed by *someone else's* conscripted resources.

The social managers under the income tax system, the legislators, could thus regulate and redistribute resources and only have to deal with the limited, interested lobbyists for each tax condition, specifying taxes or benefits *indirectly* in the form of deductions and exemptions—instead of providing direct subsidies. Tax law was so complex that full income tax law analysis was usually not possible except for highly paid specialists representing their private constituents. Legislators would thus be able to construct elaborate controls and assessments on citizens in the economy more easily while dealing directly and separately with individual, private power brokers.

Problems and conflicts in resource acquisition became endemic in the twentieth century, but politicians and much of the electorate viewed the problem *not* as one of economy and production. Rather, the problem was thought to be either a lack of proper manipulation of the tax code or proper redistribution through government allocations—or both. Hence, heavier investment was made by legislators, the electorate, and even foreign interests—directly or through lobbyists—in constructing or changing fiscal preferences by the federal government, *thus effectively increasing the power and control of that government.*

If the reasons for the expansion of federal government power and the limitations on personal freedom were not always understood by the electorate, the consequences were still felt. By the last part of the twentieth century many Americans had become increasingly uneasy about activities the federal government had become involved in and the direction national policy was taking.

Federal subsidies and tax breaks for individuals, organizations and businesses had expanded to bailout requests for businesses, cities, and foreign countries—contemporary examples being Chrysler Corporation, New York City, Mexico, South Korea, and Singapore. Even North Korea, a Communist country repressing and starving its own people, was being aided with $100 million in fuel oil, as well as nuclear technology, from the United States.[117]

The federal government was continuing to subsidize, directly or indirectly through agricultural support, the production of grain based ethyl alcohol and tobacco, both associated with widespread health problems in America, and then at the same time taxing or suing those industries for revenue.[118] Billions of dollars were being spent to "protect" responsible Americans from illicit narcotics they wouldn't buy from people they wouldn't associate with, in a "war" on drugs that seemed more a violation of civil liberties and increased assessment of the taxpayer than a protection of public health. Even basic medicinal use of pharmaceuticals directed by licensed physicians was being threatened by a federal policy of home and doctor office invasions to force submission to an irrational—but politically correct—venue of personal medical treatment.[119]

Perhaps one of the more bizarre events was the undeclared, international warfare waged in 1989 against the tiny country of Panama by the United States and the kidnapping of the Panamanian head of state. The federal government was also setting dangerous precedent in using the U.S. military for domestic, civilian police actions in its drug war.[120] The supposition of citizen protection in America through limited government was belied by new, unusual government policies.

Statutory tax laws were not even necessary, in some cases, to expropriate citizens' property, nor was due process in a court of law required before confiscating property in alleged criminal activities. Federal asset forfeiture laws, as well similar ones existing in states, allowed law enforcement officials to seize a person's property without notice or hearing merely because of the government's belief they had probable cause that the property was somehow involved in a crime. The government did not need to file criminal charges against the owner or anyone else.[121] The amount deposited in the federal Department of Justice's assets forfeiture fund increased from $27 million in 1985 to $556 million in 1993.[122] And the assumption of judicious application of forfeiture law is oppugned by examples of government charades on the high seas: The research vessel Atlantis was seized off the coast of Massachusetts because a *single* marijuana cigarette was found in the ship's crew quarters, and a Scripps Oceanographic Institute research vessel was seized because a marijuana cigarette was found in the locker of a sailor who had been *previously fired.*[123] A prominent U.S. Congressman wrote in an independent book that in more than 80 percent of asset forfeiture cases, government officials can and usually do keep property even though the owner is not even charged with a crime.[124] Yet amongst the American people, few seemed to consider an unprincipled application of tax law as a policy precedent for a growing extension and abuse of federal power in other areas; or perhaps, unfortunately, to even consider principle at all—trusting instead in the belief of growing state power to give them increased material benefit and physical security.

Regulatory roles of the federal government were in fact being expanded—not to protect rights but to limit them. Private landowners, for instance, were coming under increased federal regulations and could no longer use their private land for chosen private purposes, but in many cases had to maintain it for the public interest—like open space, environmental or species preservation.[125] This was a maintenance activity for the "public" good at no cost to the public or compensation from the government, of course, but at extended investment, maintenance and tax cost to the property owner.

The effect and costs of regulation as an effective, secondary tax system in the country should not be minimized. It can be a substantial "tax," as great as any other excise tax. A prime example of the degree to which secular interests have mated with the expansion of federal powers and have decreased personal liberty in the country has been the story of the modern American toilet.

The federal government, although possessing no Toilet Clause within the Constitution, became increasingly obsessed about the thorough flush of water that occurred when people used their standard, appropriately engineered toilets.

Now, most citizens were confident enough that there was a good purpose for a full flush, and perhaps felt flushed that the government should be questioning their privies. But Congress in 1992 passed a law anyway requiring every new residential toilet made in America to use 1.6 gallons of water per flush instead of the old standard 3.5 gallons.[126]

The reason federal legislators should suddenly become concerned about water conservation was curious. Federal legislation for the commode would be, to many citizens, a leap from federal jurisdiction to state jurisdiction to local jurisdiction to, well, private jurisdiction. It was as if Congress felt America's citizens didn't have a proper pot to . . . take care of things in, and government central planning could divine a remedy.

Further, Congress for decades had subsidized water supplies, especially for western agricultural interests, and thus introduced economic incentive *against* water conservation. Water is also a genuine renewable resource, and no matter how many times one flushes a toilet, nature keeps dumping water back into rivers and reservoirs every winter.

The immediate availability and cost of transporting water to the tap and toilet, of course, was an issue. But conservation occurs naturally as customers, preferring not to flush their money down their drains, so to speak, minimize consumption in response to increased price (real value). Plumbing improvements, or a toilet that functions better with less water, can certainly be sold as an advantage to consumers as long as it can be justified as such in the free market.

But of what consequence was saving a couple of gallons of water (and a few pennies) in a corner of the lavatory when citizens joyously took thirty-minute showers, swam in their lap pools and hot tubs, and watered their huge front lawns and golf courses? Shouldn't Congress, if it was really concerned about forced conservation, regulate shower times, pool size, lawn type, golf course size, dishwater depth, number of house plants, ice cube tray size, and so on? Government legislators did not seem interested in either free-market justifications or, curiously, a universal application of water conservation measures. So what was the real issue if these others were not relevant?

The answer was that new "water efficient" toilets which might require multiple flushes of water, extra tons of cleanser, and man-hours of labor to maintain, would not find acceptance (or, of course, sales) unless Congress could institute a "Friends of the Toilet Industry" policy and impose a citizen Toilet Mandate where new dwellings were required—that means forced under federal law—to have the new machines.

What was the real world economic result to disaffected taxpayers and toilet consumers? Possible increased lavatory purchase costs, recurring adherence or blockage of various "materials" to the sides or interiors of their new "efficient" commodes, and a black market in used, original style toilets.[127] One might wonder what Andrew Jackson would have said about this situation.

Another example of conflict and contradiction is taxation and citizenship. The federal government, charged with protecting U.S. borders and the citizenship process, has had substantial problems in enforcement, despite the vast growth in federal bureaucracy. Even if federal government activities, such as immigration or naturalization, are not being managed effectively, it might be expected that citizens would at least have the right to vote on state and local issues in a democracy and have the will of the people for state or local functions implemented. But this is not necessarily the case.

Citizens in California early this decade had become concerned about the influx of illegal aliens in that state, and in 1994 passed a state measure, Proposition 187,[128] to prevent illegal aliens from receiving non-emergency state services without charge. The federal government stepped in—on this *state* law—to prevent implementation of the measure, and Proposition 187 has been bottled up in litigation ever since.

Now, the question here is not about the measure itself. It is about the right of the electorate to settle the issue democratically—taxation, as it were, with representation. One side of the Proposition 187 issue may argue, and has, that it is better, even if only for practical reasons, to provide medical and educational services to people rather than to have sick people or truant children, while the other side may argue that distribution of limited government services to illegal residents affects legal residents as well as encouraging and expanding illegal immigration.

Such a policy dispute is normally settled in law, which is what occurred when Proposition 187 passed. The state's citizens apparently did not believe state government should force California citizens and legal residents in the state to pay for non-emergency state services for people illegally in the country, nor encourage indirectly illegal immigration. The federal government's legal response to that was somewhat chilling: The citizens of California *cannot* vote to *not* be taxed to pay for social services for people who are illegally in the country.[129]

Foreign corruption and suppression can be a large incentive for the disaffected to leave foreign countries and migrate to the United States. Is the U.S. federal policy, in forcing Californians to subsidize illegal immigration, providing a social "safety valve" for foreign despotism and effectively taxing U.S. citizens to subsidize foreign tyranny? The consequences of federal fiscal policy are not limited to local influence.

Many Americans are concerned about the economic and political direction the country is taking, and some perceive the original American social contract is being broken by America's leaders who are abandoning a true American heritage in favor of an increased state control that is the hallmark of second-rate countries and low-level despotism throughout the world. And the predicate for this change is the unwarranted fiscal power operating in the national government.

It is important for a nation to be specific and consistent in its social and fiscal organization. A nation choosing a form of government should specify and establish what benefits and services it is going to provide citizens and how it is going to finance them. Leaders in a nation like the United States, whether turning the nation toward more government controls or more free trade, have an obligation to codify and stabilize both the level at which government services are to be provided and the means and rates of taxation.

This has not been done in this country. Rather, legislators have continued to expand government services, bureaucracy, and expropriation of citizen resources without providing a principled rationale nor a cohesive plan. Unprincipled redistribution of resources by a government will ultimately be met by increasing complaints from those desiring even more from the government and contempt and cynicism from those expected to pay the rising bill. The final end can mean bankruptcy and social disintegration.

Additionally, the mere type of tax a government employs, irrespective of government spending habits, can have a stabilizing effect or destructive impact on the economy and in society, as will be evidenced in the following chapters. This is the most important point made in this treatise, that irrespective of whatever expenditures are made for whatever purpose, the government revenue base must rest on a sound tax system that citizens trust. The big question with respect to this goal remains: Can effective tax reform be realized within existing tax systems underneath the Sixteenth Amendment, or is a substantial functional change—and perhaps even Constitutional revision—warranted?

IV. The Income Tax—Shooting Yourself in Both Feet

Let me tell you a story. It is about a native seal hunter who, on January 1st, is out hunting off the northwest coast of Alaska. He is paddling his kayak through some gently rolling swells when he notices a spot on the horizon. He stops paddling and pulls out his binoculars, and under a sky of gray cloud and wafting fog he peers through the magnifying device and watches as the spot on the horizon gradually grows larger. Then another spot appears. Then a third one. Some things are approaching America.

Time passes and the shapes on the horizon grow larger. The seal hunter can now make out the subjects of his study. They are three vessels, and he suspects they are followed by more. And by the flag that they are flying and the appearance of the men on deck he knows *who* they are and *what* they want. "Damn," he mutters under his breath, "They're coming!"

The seal hunter turns his kayak toward shore and paddles quickly toward a small fishing village on the coast. Saltwater spray bounces off the bottom of his water-resistant coat and rolls down the sides of his spray skirt as his craft splits the swells and glides toward a distant, sheltered bay. A small wooden pier abutting a vast tundra plain finally appears in the distance as he comes within sight of land.

Reaching the pier, the seal hunter barely stops to tie up his kayak before he climbs to the upper wooden concourse of the dock and bounds down its snow-covered planking to a group of wood-sided houses and outbuildings. He enters the second building, a yellow-painted work shed with an aerial extending high in the air from its sheet-metal roof.

The seal hunter pushes some furniture aside and moves to a table with a radiotelephone on it. He turns it on and selects the appropriate frequency for a civil alert station in Fairbanks. The radio static is finally broken and he establishes contact: "Alert! Alert!" he shouts into the mouthpiece, "Three vessels of invasion party sighted. Advise you notify coast watchers on all coasts immediately!"

Soon reports are coming in simultaneously, not only from Alaska but from all over the country. From southern Alaska: "Thirty-four invader vessels sighted multiple fishing grounds. Fishermen stripping gear from own vessels and heading inland for safety." From Hawaii: "Eight boats coming in northwest of Maui, two merchant vessels attacked!" Down the Pacific Coast: "Invaders blockade Puget Sound entrance—sixty others moving on Seattle!" . . . "Regular Columbia River traffic in panic as invaders approach merchant ships and docks." . . . "One hundred eighteen invader boats approaching San Francisco Bay!"

Then the Gulf Coast: "Shrimp boats are run down by the invaders in Gulf of Mexico. Unidentified individuals boarding off-shore oil platforms." And the East Coast: "Florida vacationers desert beaches as launches approach in formation from offshore." . . . "Lighthouses and fishermen in Carolinas report phalanx of assault vessels passing barrier islands and harbor entrances." . . . "New Yorkers abandon waterfront and ascend high rises to escape expected invasion parties." . . . "Port commercial districts from Boston Harbor to northern Maine shut down as business owners and workers flee marine shorelines." And on the decks of the invading boats, prepared for mischief and mayhem, are pirates and brigands—smoking, spitting, and yelling obscenities with guns, explosives, knives, and swords dangling from their jackets and pants—and the pirate Skull and Crossbones flying at the top of the masts!

All state and local government officials are notified and the President, Congress and state governors are briefed. But no orders go out to stop the invasion. Local civil authorities are told to stand down. The Coast Guard is denied permission to intercept the vessels. The Navy is kept in port and the Army confined to its barracks. The Air Force is grounded. Local, state, and national government leaders advise the people not to get too excited and to stay clear of the invaders. Some citizens rally, "We must not allow this!" But other citizens accept the invasion. Most of the press is either passive or severely critical of the protesting citizens and the protestors are effectively silenced.

The pirates and brigands dock their boats all around America's coastlines and disembark while anxious men and women grab their children and run for safety. The invaders head inland and lay siege to anything of value. What they can't steal they destroy or ruin. Homes, schools, offices, businesses, farms, crops, hospitals, roads, bridges and highways are damaged. Agricultural harvests and deliveries are stymied, scientific and medical research is interrupted, and industrial production and general commerce is cut back.

The raucous bands of pirates move farther and farther inland, going through state after state until they reach the center of the country. The invaders arrive in the middle of some trampled Kansas farm fields on April 15th after causing $538 billion worth of property loss and damage, their lust for property and destruction finally satiated. The invaders pause, regroup, and then return eastward and westward, heading back to their respective boats, dragging what booty they can. After loading their spoils onto the decks and into the holds of their boats they sail off over the horizon. And then the following year, the following January 1st, they come back and do it all over again.

◆

The preceding story is one of loss and waste. But it is *not* an analogy for any current or past government expenditure, nor with any federal income tax monies actually paid or due the government. And, of course, America's leaders would never actually let a physical invasion occur. And we, as a nation, would never permit such great economic loss and waste. Right?

Well, the $538 billion figure of lost resources in the story is the same amount as the yearly compliance and other costs incurred by American taxpayers operating under the federal income tax system.[130] And what do these costs consist of? They include the direct compliance cost, or what it costs people to prepare (what they hope is) a proper tax filing and remittance; enforcement costs of the government, including audits, litigation and forced collections; disincentives to production (people limiting their economic activity because of assessment liability and tax-code complexity); and the *economic* cost of both tax avoidance and evasion, which is the extra cost in the economy to the taxpayer to construct and manage personal and business affairs to minimize federal taxation.[131] The compliance cost alone of the federal income tax system is estimated at $202 billion, or 9.1 billion business and personal man-hours.[132] These costs are *in addition* to any taxes paid. Compliance with income tax law can cost individuals and businesses in preparation and filing costs many times the amount they actually pay in taxes! The government has also, like the story, not taken any action to remedy the situation but has stood by while resources are lost. The country is not physically invaded every year under the income tax system, but the storied economic loss described above is commensurate to the costs of operating the federal income tax system *exclusive of collected tax revenue.*

There is a real impact on lives when resources are wasted in society. The $538 billion figure represents the base amount of goods and services—everything from new housing and education to new inventions and medical cures—that were never produced because the physical and intellectual energies expended were *not* for those items, but for compliance to a difficult and confusing tax system.

This operational cost of the federal income tax system is nearly two-thirds the amount of total income tax revenue collected.[133] What if other economic transactions in society occurred in the same manner? Citizens would be flabbergasted, for instance, if they purchased a brand new $20,000 automobile and afterward were told another $13,000 was due to process the sale's paperwork—and that they would be fined and jailed if they refused remittance!

Additional significance of the $538 billion figure should be noted. This amount is $431 billion more than the 1996 deficit of $107 billion.[134] The government has moved severely into debt yet the average annual cost of operating the federal income tax system is *over four times the annual federal deficit* alone! To look at it another way, the Vietnam War, lasting over a decade, cost the taxpayers (in taxes only) $150 billion.[135] Ten years of operational costs at 1996 levels is approximately *five trillion, three hundred eighty billion dollars*! That is the equivalent of spending taxpayer money for thirty-five Vietnam Wars. Again, this is a cost in addition to the amount of actual tax monies paid.[136]

The economic cost is high.[137] But problems with the federal income tax system are not just monetary. Societal questions have arisen related to planning, assessment, collections, enforcement, and civil rights protection of taxpayers. The basic framework in which people live and work has been affected.

Nearly everyone, of all social and political persuasions, believes something should be done to correct the tax system in this country. But what is the solution? Could effective remedies be implemented to modify, reform, and save the current income tax system?

The vast political, business and academic arenas have not been entirely idle. Real concepts and plans have been put forth by politicians, businessmen, and academics to address the current federal income tax problem. And real adjustments and substantial modifications continue to occur to the tax system, with many more pending. How effective will recent income tax modifications, and some of the proposed reforms, if implemented, be?

♦

First, a clear definition of the income tax. The income tax is a charge on the net income of a business or individual. People participate in the production of goods and services (they create wealth) and distribute those resources to others in society, the buyers or employers, for a return payment in sales or wages for a total compensation, or gross income. Authorized expenses, or deductions, are subtracted from gross income to give the net taxable income—the legally defined profit taxable by the government.

The recent popular view of America and taxation has very often been that of a country with accumulated resources that need to be divided up for the people by elected government officials under the guidance of economists and social planners who will all have enough wisdom, compassion and technical expertise to accomplish this challenging task in an expeditious and prudent fashion. The designers, though, need a theoretical basis from which to construct the income tax system, and they have certainly chosen one. The central precept on which the modern income tax system has been based has been that of *progressive* taxation. Under this theory, the more income people have the more tax they can be liable for.

The federal income tax is also so configured that as income increases the *rate* of taxation on that income also goes up. For instance, a person or business earning $20,000 a year might pay 15 percent of that income ($3,000), earning $30,000 a year they would pay 20 percent of that income ($6,000), earning $40,000 a year they would pay 25 percent ($10,000), and so on.

Thus, progressive in modern lexicon means those that have more, or at least have more taxable net income, pay more, and pay at an increasing rate. Those that earn less, pay less, or nothing at all. This concept of "progressive taxation" has been a central theme of politicians, economists, and others who have viewed the federal income tax as a progressive and fair means of revenue acquisition, and as a mechanism of social management and public assistance.

Certainly, then, could not sufficient attention be given to improving the design of the income tax system by the country's leaders and their experts so that problems with the system could be resolved and the federal income tax made more simple, efficient and fair? Could not the operational problems be resolved by more efficient management? Could not one of the several modifications to the income tax system offered by current political candidates, elected officials, or economists be the solution to improving the income tax?

The answer is *absolutely not.* The popular assumptions today with regards to what is progressive, what is fair, and especially the appropriate role of a tax system in society are absolutely false and constitute, in some respects, a reprehensible perversion of what American principle and justice should be. The federal income tax system is in reality an aberrant and economically destructive tax mechanism, as will be further demonstrated both philosophically and empirically, and modifications or changes to it to make it more "fair" will not work.

Pirates debating streamlined mechanisms of extortion and adjudicating disposition of the spoils among their members and among their conquests is not a remedy for piracy, nor is tweaking the cupidity of a state married to a revenue system based on graduated, predatory economic conscription.

A discussion of the functioning of the federal income tax system and a description of its real social and economic impact in our society follows.

◆

The most contentious practical issue in the construction and application of an income tax system is the concept of net income. Net income, remember, is what a person makes after expenses. There are thousands and thousands of expenditures that reasonable people could construe one way or the other as an expense, or as a part of net income. Is a company-provided meal to employees or clients to be considered a tax-deductible expense of one business and the sack lunch of wage earners in another business *not*? Should a "business junket" to Hawaii be deductible, but an employee's transportation looking for a job not? Is the big office building of a commercial business owner to be considered non-taxable but the more cost-efficient home-business of an entrepreneur not?

Of course, Congress has *attempted* to make clarifications in law in its thousands and thousands of regulations, *but such law is arbitrary and based on no solid principle.* The food that goes into a human being, in the case of employee meals for instance, is all the same, whether paid for by an individual or business. *And the level of human biological benefit is the same.* Why does the government threaten one individual with tax liability for the value of the meal and not another, merely because of the form or rate of compensation or type of legal entity purchasing the product?

The concept of net income is further complicated in income tax law by the fact that arbitrary pronunciations of business or personal expenses are not necessarily made in any attempt to meet a universal applicability of "expense," but may incorporate specific aid or benefits to specific individuals, industries or groups under particular conditions. Rather than just a mechanism for correlating general liability conditions in routine business and personal transactions, deductions and exemptions can be incorporated into the tax system as a mechanism of social and economic management.

The question of the validity of the deduction and exemption process is one the current political power base has not acknowledged. The answer to the question, though, is this: The legal definitions in tax law of net income, gross income, and the income tax law itself—no matter how carefully defined—are aberrant exercises in tax construction and resource control and not relevant to a just and sound tax system. The manipulation of tax rules is a facade to imply concern for economic fairness while doing just the opposite—employing a backhanded attempt at economic favoritism and economic redistribution.

Benefits through tax code manipulations are harder to define and less subject to fiscal planning and accounting controls than direct appropriations. What has been ignored in the construction of the income tax system has been the true social, economic and practical ramifications of the state denoting some economic activities as tax exempt while applying the penalty—the tax—to other activities every time they occur.

The great concern of a legal entity being taxed—be it individual, business or organization—has been to lobby for a law and implement into practice various tax conditions and deductions so as to lessen the amount of income recognized as taxable. The ongoing objective is for taxpayers to shift the real cost of government service elsewhere, irrespective of what that liability shift will cost others immediately, or what the income tax system will cost the taxpayers themselves in the long run.

◆

The relevance of arbitrary liability assignations in the income tax system can best be understood by examining some other examples of deductions and exemptions. Only then can the psychological manipulation of voting citizens and the wasteful manipulation of private resources be more fully understood.

Whatever the real social benefit of a particular deduction or exemption is, it is important for the deduction or exemption to *appear* beneficial for greater public acceptance. One example is the educational tax credit for college tuition. A family, for instance, may *not* have to pay any taxes on $10,000 of income received that it then spends on a son going to college because of an income tax deduction-credit permitted by the government for that purpose.

This educational assistance may seem at first view to be a wonderful service that the government is accomplishing, "helping" a family and promoting higher education. Yet, the honest and perceptive man sees it for what it is. The government is saying that the family spending money on higher education doesn't have to pay what it normally would have to in taxes because of the college-tuition expenditure. This does not, however, have any impact whatsoever on government services provided to the family—national defense, courts, police, and so on—*nor on the total cost for these services to the government.* Government services still have to be paid for by *someone.*

So this means, logically, that if the family sending their son to college is not paying what they normally would have to, *other people will be forced to pay more—either directly or indirectly, through other taxes, monetary manipulation, or deficit spending.* A man who works two jobs and his spouse who works and have never gone to college, and never will go to college, can be forced to indirectly subsidize another family and their son's increased economic position during *and* after his higher education. It is unlikely the average wage earner jumps for joy upon hearing of fraternity parties during college or of Junior driving his new BMW after graduation, and the fact that it was subtle government seizure of the worker's own labor that helped pay for it.

Education, of course, is not the only popular, widespread tax deduction. Politicians have traditionally championed tax conditions relevant to voter demographics, and a good example is home ownership. Pride of place has always been an important facet in American cultural lore, and home ownership has been associated with both economic security and stability. Stable people tend to own homes and stable people tend to vote, so it comes as no surprise that a homeowner mortgage deduction has long received support from a Congress recognizing that relationship.

But exactly what is the mission and justification of federal-government involvement in middle class private-sector housing subsidy besides the generation of middle class pork? No one seems to consider who *doesn't* get a homeowner's mortgage deduction—those renters who in many cases can't afford to own a home. So how does it make sense to have renters—or poor people, if you will—pay a relatively higher tax rate effectively subsidizing, through a loop in the Federal Treasury, property investments of the landowning class?

Homeowners may cry they pay higher rates in other areas, including higher income tax rates than some lower income renters, so compensation assistance in maintenance of their familial abodes is certainly warranted. But if there is an effective wash in costs and benefits for both the higher-income homeowners and lower-income renters, whose backs are really being scratched other than those of the vote-getting politicians? Whatever fiscal absurdity the homeowners' mortgage deduction is in practice, one certainly shouldn't minimize its political importance: The current Senate Minority Leader in a recently proposed tax reform package advocated a flat income tax with at least one notable exception—the inclusion of that little touch of middle class housing-tract socialism, the mortgage deduction in question.[138]

But special-interest conditions in the tax code are hardly limited to *personal* income taxation. Businesses may operate in the hundreds of millions of dollars and receive an implied, commensurate government service for the size of their operations yet pay no taxes whatsoever, depending on their allowable deductions and reported profits.

Then there is the serious problem for personal and business taxpayers *and* the government of just determining what the applicable income tax should be for a given situation. This is because of the arbitrary and *subjective* nature of the income tax system itself.

Subjective construction of tax laws occurs, of course, by *legislators* when they create the income tax law with its myriad special-interest conditions. It also occurs when a *government agency* such as the Internal Revenue Service (IRS) tries to interpret and implement the law, and then again by the *personal or business taxpayer* when they attempt to apply conditions of income tax law to their own unique economic situation. But even if income tax regulations are clearly defined by Congress, correctly interpreted by the IRS, and correctly applied by the individual or business taxpayer in his particular economic situation (and accepted as such by the IRS), it does not mean there is any uniform or objective application of tax law.

Practical problems in the application of income tax law abound. A noted columnist and author and his writing partner, for instance, once submitted a movie script to a major studio that was rejected.[139] They were surprised later on to find their plot in a new movie up on the silver screen. The two ended up successfully suing the studio for a share of the profits for using their script. But although the movie grossed $150 million, the studio claimed there was no *net* profit—thus no taxable net income. It was therefore asserted by the studio that no commission on profits was due the authors.

This claimed lack of profit—if justified—could have been because the movie was a financial failure (it actually didn't make any money) or the studio had excellent tax planning by tax accountants to take advantage of asset and expense classifications to eliminate *tax* liability, and they based their legal position on that accounting basis.

The income tax is like a blackjack table where everybody that works is forced to bet in a game they can't win. The big players have their boys on the sidelines counting cards, but even if they minimize their losses to zero the government, as dealer, just keeps everybody playing until the house gets the take it wants.

The entire non-objective federal income tax system tax code is subject to and rife with individual subjective interpretation, legal ingenuity in tax avoidance, or outright tax evasion. The fact is that society is full of imaginative or manipulative individuals and businesses who may regularly ensure a minimum or absence of reported income. Legal or not, this can mean other people—the little guys not allowed to count cards—are forced to pick up the tab of relevant government service for everyone.

The political cries of legislators, however, to "close the loopholes" and make the income tax code more objective and understandable is nothing but contemptible obfuscation. For even if objective application and interpretation of existing income tax law were possible—which it is not—the net income scheme of taxation still provides little or no relationship between the level of service provided by the state and the amount assessed the taxpayer.

◆

The net income scheme of taxation also imposes an effective penalty on efficient individuals and businesses and forces them to subsidize the inefficient. A business selling goods or services is a vendor, in accounting terms, to other businesses, organizations or individuals. A regular private sector vendor, for instance, servicing two other businesses at the same rate is going to bill each of them the same amount. The vendor is *not* going to somehow assess the first business more for being profitable and exempt the second business because it was poorly run, while advising the first business it is their social obligation to pay the bills of their inefficient competition!

Yet the federal government does just that. It excuses liability of incompetent or inefficient enterprises—businesses that claim they made no profit—by reducing or eliminating their taxes, effectively transferring the cost of government service to other, productive entities in society—the businesses that report a profit. The businesses that report a profit must then assume an increase in immediate general tax liability in whatever form to balance government expenditures, or assume the liability for deferred payment of government debt with the associated increase in governmental interest charges, another effective tax.

The counter argument of taxes not being warranted for failed or no-profit enterprises, because such enterprises don't have the revenue to pay the taxes, is spurious. A poorly operated or inefficient enterprise is liable for their gas, electrical, and water bills; for paying their employees, suppliers and landlords; and for property taxes—and federal tax assessment should be considered no less important. Immediate inability by any taxable entity to meet its federal tax obligations can be addressed just like any other liability in American commerce and appropriate civil law and regulations applied. The federal government is in reality another vendor, a provider of governmental service, and the federal government should be universally respected just like other vendors.

This is not to suggest at all, however, that an income tax assessed a failing *or* profitable business is warranted, or that any federal tax liability based on income is a proper assessment. Rather, any valid tax system (in place of the income tax) when applied should be universally applicable.

———— ♦ ————

Politicians interested in the extension of their political image as supporters and benefactors of society have included certain deductions and exemptions in the tax code for a special category of economic activity. This category consists of "non-profit" organizations, including educational, fraternal, professional, and charitable organizations, and religions.

But should this category of human activity be any different than other areas with respect to an objective application of tax law? Do educational, fraternal, professional, charitable, or religious organizations deserve special treatment? The specific application of preference for religious institutions will be examined later in this section, but first we'll discuss the "non-profit" concept in income tax application.

The reality is that there is no "non-profit" human activity. Citizens and residents in a free society engage in that activity they think *will* profit them or their interests. Whether they themselves profit personally in an immediate, material sense is not the appropriate question. There is a "profit" in their activities to someone.

Human activity and physical infrastructure requires, in our current civilization, service by the government. The fact is that the organizations just identified, and the people they service, benefit directly and indirectly from general government services—national defense, police, the courts, the national highway system, and so on. These are services and—just like other goods and services in the economy—*must be paid for by someone.* If individuals and organizations receiving the benefit of government services do not pay for them, who will? The answer is that others *not* in those organizations will be forced to do so.

Charities, churches, and other groups classified as "non-profit" take into account the real cost of goods and services every day they are in operation. They pay for construction costs, wages, supply costs, transportation costs, and utilities. I doubt it would ever enter the minds of people involved in these institutions to pull out a gun, march to the homes and offices of their neighbors that are *not* in their particular organizations and say, "This month you will be helping us pay our gas bill." Yet it seems to have been very convenient for politicians to appear benevolent leaders and exempt the organizations from payment for *government* services, forcing that tab to be picked up by someone else.

It is not the province of the government to denote certain activities or organizations as better than others in a tax code. Should the neighborhood boys' club receive a tax exemption but not the father who takes his children to the park on Sunday? Should those meeting in a big church receive a tax deduction while those meeting for home prayer not? Should there be no tax on people receiving free meals but an increasing, graduated penalty on those working two jobs?

Many government preferences do not in reality portend beneficence—in many cases quite the opposite. A politician grandly denoting the activities of one group of citizens as eleemosynary while forcing other citizens to assume the relative cost of government service suggests not so much the philanthropist, as it does the bully boy in grammar school, strongly suggesting that you share your ice cream cone with the bully's little sister—or else.

An argument may be put forth by charitable organizations that they are carrying services that might otherwise have to be borne by the government if the charities did not. This argument implies, however, that an obligation exists with the state in the first place for payment or provision of those services. *This can be challenged in principle, and is certainly not axiomatic for tens of thousands of special interests claiming a special tax exemption status under a manipulative tax code.* Whatever government social service expenditures are accomplished should *not* be accomplished through a complicated tax code but rather in the daylight of objective, direct appropriations. And if private social service contractors are utilized for dedicated government expenditures, the government has an obligation to the taxpaying public to offer service contracts through competitive bids.

The non-profit income tax designation for religious organizations deserves special attention because of the importance of separation of church and state in American society and the importance the nation's founders placed on that principle. Throughout history, suppression has often reigned when religious infrastructure and dictates were integrated with the operations of the state, and this condition is evident in other countries in the world, even to this day. But when civic functions are separated form private activities and religious freedom is protected, social and economic success has blossomed.

The problem with the current tax system is that Congress, prohibited from supporting *one* particular organized religion by the Constitution, decided to support *all* organized religions through the federal income tax code! The income tax system has lent to politicians the pole necessary to vault those original, bothersome barriers of Constitutional limitations on federal powers, and they've used their new tax pole to vault everywhere. One ought not be surprised when they then, subsidy and exemptions in hand, crash through stained-glass choir-loft windows and land in the grateful and caring laps of local church congregations that are surely mindful of such funding acrobatics later in the secular voting booth.

But why should the government support any business, any industry, any activity or any philosophical group just because it claims metaphysical tenets and can plug its religious description into a tax code pigeonhole of a "properly defined" religion? Indeed, which is more spiritual and positive—a benign, contemplative Henry David Thoreau contemplating humanity and personal social responsibility in the quiet New England woods, or a wildly expostulating Jim Jones—previously subsidized through tax exemptions—organizing a cyanide-laced grape drink death party for men, women and children in the South American jungle after murdering reporters and a U.S. Congressman?[140]

There can be severe social as well as economic costs in the application of a poor federal tax system. These can be substantial, direct costs to the economy, as previously identified, but there can also be indirect costs such as a small-business person who does not expand his operations and hire additional employees because of costly tax compliance requirements. This may mean a businessperson, his customers, and existing or prospective employees may be less able to financially *support* so-called non-profit organizations, and instead actually place an increased financial *demand* on those very institutions for social welfare assistance. Thus charities, churches, synagogues, mosques, and temples—instead of gaining increased resources for limited needs—may receive *reduced* resources for *expanded* needs.

On the other hand, a sound and stable tax system supports a stable economy; productivity can thereby increase along with wealth and private charitable support—as well as having the overall *need* for that charitable support go down. Thus, *greater* economic support will remain for those that still *do* require assistance.

The truth is the best protection for serious religions and private charities, and in fact all free human activity, is a limitation on the fiscal powers of the state. Religions, charities, and all other organizations currently "tax exempt" under the income tax system may be financially much better off without such exemptions if the income tax system is changed and objective principles of taxation are applied.

◆

The income tax system incorporates mechanisms that suggest the government possesses a supreme economic cognizance and enlightened benevolence that in reality do not exist. Rather, income tax law actually inhibits economic productivity, limits personal choice, and can be an unfair penalty on lower-income individuals. Such is the case with tax credits allowed individuals for accumulated savings.

Again, the surface appearance is one of the government helping individuals and businesses save and retain capital by allowing tax deductions for revenue retained and not spent. But what is revenue not spent? The consumer makes his valued choice of spending in basic honesty in the absence of government interference. But when the government interferes, an artificial inducement is created to hold capital in reserve. A reduction in tax liability to the would-be spender occurs when he does not spend, but again, this does not relieve the government's (and ultimately the general taxpayers') liability for the cost of government.

Where is this liability shifted? It is shifted to those who either choose to spend, *or those who cannot afford to save.* But the scenario gets worse. An immediate beneficiary of these artificial economic mechanizations may be financial institutions who acquire increased capital and, of course, the taxpayers who are saving. However, since purchases are *not* being made (for the given amount of capital withheld or saved), businesses and individuals who would receive revenue for productive economic activities do not. Sales can go down, business development can slow, and unemployment can increase—and the available tax base can be reduced, shifting even more burden to remaining taxpayers!

A specific example of a tax savings scheme embraced by modern legislators is the "assistance" given to the Americans in securing retirement capital. Congress has created the Individual Retirement Account (IRA) system whereby taxpayers can deposit income into a retirement savings account and defer taxes on that deposited income until they later withdraw the funds—presumably in retirement years when their yearly net income may be less and applicable tax rates are lower. This program allegedly encourages savings and helps people ensure future financial security during their retirement.

But what is really occurring with this program? First, it must be pointed out, like all mechanizations in the income tax system, Congress is not *producing* anything for anybody. No new wealth or capital is created. It is true that *some* people *may* benefit from IRAs, but a net benefit is a surety for no one, and those that are lucky enough to benefit may be doing so by *suppressing working class and poor people who share no benefit from the IRA program.*

But wait. Wouldn't working class and poor people be automatically helped by a retirement program like the IRA system? The answer is no, but let's leave an analysis of the working class position to last and look at financially secure people who normally, and prudently, save for their retirement. The truth is, people financially secure enough to build a private savings account for their retirement should be doing this anyway. A government aid program is hardly appropriate for people in this category. It is true that a second group of people, those on the financial margin, may be induced to move some of their limited capital to a retirement savings account for an expected tax savings. But will the financially secure and those on the margin, the two groups that have the discretionary capital to invest in a retirement account, really accrue a net benefit by participating in the IRA program?

A liability for the IRA program to the individual is the loss of full liquidity, where the taxpayer can be assigned taxes, interest, and penalty for early withdrawal if a taxpayer's funds are needed by him prior to retirement. So a citizen entering the IRA program suffers immediately from a liquidity penalty—which can be severe depending on personal economic circumstances were the dedicated assets to be needed for emergency or even basic living expenditures. A citizen's retirement savings are effectively locked away under duress by the state and cooperating financial institution for some hazily promised future benefit.

Then there is the astounding position implied or stated by the authors of this law that people who later withdraw funds from their retirement accounts after the legal retirement age will be in a lower income bracket, and hence will not have their former, higher tax rates. This is the benefit? Less income means (in the real world) a lower standard of living. So, is it a calculated arrogance by the authors of this law that people must lock up their capital for up to forty years and then lower their standard of living when they retire (at a time when they should be enjoying what they earned in life) to get any benefits? Of course, this assumes that tax rates will be the same. What if tax rates increase? Wouldn't it be a cruel joke to retire and pay *more* taxes because of one's tax "savings" plan?

But let us go on. Assuming there is a net benefit to *some* individuals during the decades of administration of the IRA program, who has benefited from the program? Well, of course, only those or some of those who participated in the program will benefit. Remember, Congress did not create any new capital by the tax law authorizing IRAs. The law merely reduces, temporarily, the tax liability of IRA participants. *The current and following years' fiscal liability of the federal government, the government's spending that has nothing to do with taxation, has not changed.* So if the government denotes a group of people as not having to pay as much as they normally would have to in taxes, in this case the IRA participants, then who is going to make up the shortfall in government revenue? Who is not getting IRA benefits? The people who did not participate in the program. And who are those likely to be? *The working or poor people who can't afford to participate!* A net tax advantage to the more financially-secure indirectly financed by the less well off.

And there doesn't seem to be any benefit for the country as a whole from the IRA system. Studies as early as 1984 showed overall savings by taxpayers did not increase—they simply switched funds from other sources to IRAs, and in 1984 the IRAs resulted in a $9 billion annual loss of revenue and corresponding increase in the federal deficit. In fact, savings actually declined as a percentage of GNP.[141] The IRA system has continued, though, as another vested interest program now integrated into the tax system. The government has created nothing, levied limitations and constraints on capital, and penalized the working poor in another shell game. Yet the body politic continues to support IRAs as an important function of government management and beneficence in personal financial planning.

There is an argument that non-participants to a tax-deduction benefit do not assume the cost of that deduction when it is taken by others, as just suggested in the above example of IRAs, and that the people actually paying for them are people with the higher incomes who not only pay more tax but pay at a higher rate.

This condition of higher-income liability for new tax costs may or may not be true. Assuming all things remain equal—tax law, incomes, government expenditures, and benefits—when a program like the IRA is implemented, non-participants are net losers, however little or great, as tax liability is lessened for everyone except them, thus raising their own relative liability as citizens for overall government spending. If tax rates are raised elsewhere, unexpected government revenue is received, or other taxes like excise taxes or tariffs are altered to bring in increased revenue, then the program may not alter the net cost to non-participants, or their relative benefit/liability ratio may actually improve.

But this brings up an interesting fact. No matter what special benefit a particular taxpayer thinks he is getting in the tax code, there are thousands of other conditions that exist (or that can disappear or be added in) that affect a taxpayer's actual cost or ultimate liability as a citizen. Add to this the other variables like the amount of correct and incorrect tax returns and payments, legal tax avoidance, tax evasion, proper tax enforcement and changing government spending and benefit amounts, and the fact that actual cost can also be deferred by the government through monetary manipulation or deficit spending, and it can be quite difficult to make a valid value assessment. A taxpayer never knows where he stands in this shell game. Perhaps that's why many politicians like it.

◆

The income tax is an impediment to domestic businesses where the industrious are taxed multiple times for creating and working with the same capital: The citizen is first taxed when he earns money to invest. The corporation he invests in is then taxed on the profits it earns from that investment. Afterward, the citizen is taxed on those same profits if he takes any of the profits out in dividends, and then taxed once more if he makes a profit on the sale of his securities. And finally, when the citizen dies, the government may tax the same money again in the form of an estate tax.

But this is just the surface impact of cumulative taxation and the effects actually are much greater—the income tax system is also a serious liability to American industry and American jobs. Corporate income tax and payroll tax costs in the United States create substantial increases in product cost to Americans, and also impact the United States in the global economy by creating a more costly export product for prospective foreign consumers.

European nations, on the other hand, that have implemented a Value Added Tax (VAT) on their domestic production instead of an income tax have provided an advantage to their own industries in international trade when competing against Americans that operate under the income tax system.

The VAT is essentially a sales tax at each level of production and resale, and VAT tax rates and assessments are relatively easy to identify and track. A VAT is recorded on each sales document (the sales invoice) and can be easily audited. European countries have allowed VATs on their domestic industries to be deducted or credited at the time of product export to the United States. This can substantially lower the selling price and increase gross sales over American domestic products as well as boosting the profits of foreign companies, because American companies operate under the income tax system where cumulative tax costs must be incorporated into the sales price of their products.[142]

Take, for example, an American tractor company that purchases parts from fellow American suppliers in the assembly of its machines. Incorporated into the tractor company's sales price will be the company's total production cost, including the cost of components from suppliers. The sales price of the suppliers' components will ordinarily incorporate the *suppliers'* total costs, including the related income tax expenses for any sales profit.

Say the tractor company sells its tractor to consumers for $150,000 each, and the total production cost to the tractor company is $125,000—$25,000 for internal operating expenses and $100,000 to suppliers for parts. If it costs the suppliers, collectively, $60,000 to produce the tractor parts for one tractor, the suppliers' gross profit before income taxation would be $100,000 minus $60,000, or $40,000. If the income tax rate is 30% then the income tax on the suppliers' profit would be $12,000 (30 percent of $40,000). The net profit to the suppliers would be $28,000 after subtracting the income tax liability.

The gross profit to the tractor company would be $25,000—the retail sales price of $150,000 minus the internal production and parts purchase cost of $125,000. The tractor company then must pay the 30 percent income tax levy on its own profit of $25,000, which would be $7,500, leaving a net profit of $17,500. The total embedded income tax in the retail sales price—the total of the tractor company and suppliers' income tax cost—would be $19,500 (and this is not even considering the other embedded tax costs from subcontractors of the suppliers; or from payroll, Social Security, or other taxes on all suppliers and the tractor company).

A foreign company producing an equivalent tractor with the same production and tax cost under a VAT is allowed to deduct the tax amount for overseas sales. The foreign company would thus be able to realize a $19,500 greater profit than its American competitor while selling the foreign tractor at the same retail price.

Obviously, though, foreign competitors are very willing to take advantage of market conditions and could sell their tractor for substantially less, even below the cost of the American tractor, and still realize a profit. What is left is jobless Americans and empty manufacturing plants—poorer Americans because of jobs that never were because of American plants that were never built because of suppressive taxation.

This is not necessarily a recommendation of European tax systems, and one shouldn't consider jumping into an American VAT just yet. What is important here are the effects on trade under the federal income tax, which are not good. The federal income tax—Sixteenth Amendment notwithstanding—effectively violates Article I, Section 9, Paragraph 5 of the Constitution that prohibits taxes on exports.[143] But so successful has the pro-income tax political base been in conning the American populace into demanding increased tax rates on successful companies that people, even as they lose jobs to foreign competition, continue to insist on a graduated income tax with its inherent penalty on production. Efforts to increasingly assess the productive—those that dare make a profit—are attempts to choke ever tighter the necks of the economic geese in American commerce that would otherwise be laying the golden eggs of national prosperity.

◆

A political and ideological claim that the income tax is "fair" because it is a graduated tax on wealth isn't even true. The income tax is not based on wealth, it is based on net income that can be identified in interpersonal or inter-business transactions in the applicable tax year. Existing wealth (money, investments, or property) previously acquired in another year is not taxable. And income earned during the tax year outside of the United States can be deductible.

Self-generated, or *imputed* income—wealth developed or generated by and for the same legal entity (individual, organization or business) and not the result of an economic transaction with others—is also not covered under income tax law. This is because it would be difficult or impossible to quantify.

Examples of imputed income include a man who paints his house himself instead of earning money and then paying a professional house painter to do the job, a woman who derives pleasure from flowers and grows them herself instead of earning money and buying flowers from a florist, or a business that builds its own assembly line instead of hiring outside engineering experts.

In each of the imputed income examples above it might ordinarily be easier and more productive for the primary individuals involved *not* to do the work themselves but to contract out to more efficient experts. This would also benefit businesses (and their employees) that contract and sell to the buyers, as well as the economy in general.

But the prospective buyers, or consumers, of others' economic products and services can be dissuaded from engaging in commerce with them if there is a tax—an effective penalty—on the personal earnings that the buyers would need to *initially* generate in order to make those later purchases. Considering an income tax liability as high as 39 percent,[144] plus Social Security and Medicare taxes plus state taxes, it might be far less expensive to attempt some sort of domestic construction, production, service or repair—even though other people in the economy cannot then benefit, and businesses and consumers end up with less-efficient production or service in their operations or home.

Individuals or businesses thus have an incentive to hold land, agricultural resources, mechanical assets, finished goods, personal skills and localized labor to provide for themselves internally and thus minimize or eliminate outside economic transactions and related income tax liability. This can work to the advantage of a large corporation in the transfer of service and commodities between the corporation's divisions where there is no identifiable economic transaction and no tax is due, whereas small businesses that rely on external trade are effectively penalized.

Imputed-income favoritism under the income tax system is an attack on small businesses and places them at a competitive disadvantage while effectively dampening competition and raising prices for consumers. But the income tax system can also work to the detriment of larger businesses by creating disincentives toward more efficient inter-business trade at that level, too.

A basis of wealth, productivity, and economic security in modern society is the division of labor and free economic trade in products or services that are the result of that labor. Trading enterprises are unfairly penalized and the economy is damaged when trade is artificially discouraged by tax regulation and when people turn inward to marshal and conserve resources. The implementation and operation of the income tax system in society and its slighted advantages toward imputed income is an attack on the very basis of modern, productive economic intercourse: the basic right of Americans to engage in free, productive trade with their fellow citizens.

The condition of favoritism toward imputed income, the fact that existing wealth already created is not taxed, and that income earned outside the United States may be deductible can mean globe-trotting millionaires can pay little or no federal tax. But the favoritism for imputed income under the income tax system does *not* mean government legislators do not want to tax imputed income for philosophical reasons, only that it may be impossible in accounting terms to track and assess that activity. And considering the complexity of classifying and then enforcing imputed-income tax regulations, there might be social upheaval if the government ever attempted it. Similarly, if the government attempted taxation of earnings made by Americans residing in foreign countries, there would be less of an incentive to bring any earnings back into the country.

This variance in income tax applicability demonstrates another inimical characteristic of the income tax system. The income tax can have less to do with any objective assessment of real net income (actual production) than with an expeditious seizure of citizen resources based on ease of extraction.

◆

One principle seems to have been heralded above all others by proponents of the income tax. This principle has transcended almost all political parties and has been embraced by major political factions to one degree or another, and is popularized by many academics and professional economists. This principle is the *ability to pay*.

Ability-to-pay rhetoric may have an appealing political twang for speaking politicians and listening constituents, but the legal definition—the only definition that counts—has been rather imprecise and ever changing. And this is in no small part linked to the difficulty in defining deductions and net income. But the question of properly defining deductions and net income aside, there are still two more problems with incorporating the ability-to-pay concept into a tax code.

The first problem is that two different individuals can have the same net income (where net income is defined exactly the same for each) and have a dramatically different ability to pay. Net income does not mean discretionary income. In other words, a taxpayer may use the taxable portion of his income in whole or part to pay for necessaries (non-discretionary items) like food, rent, clothing, transportation, medical care or other required living costs where these expenses were in whole or in part *not* deductible, depending on the taxpayer's situation with respect to the given year's tax code. Living costs can vary in different parts of the country, and even vary dramatically within different parts of the same state, so this can mean different levels of discretionary income and thus different levels of ability to pay, even for two taxpayers with the same gross *and* taxable net income.

One taxpayer, for instance, may have unforeseen auto repairs or housing damage, multiple relocations, longer work commutes, liability for other taxes or fees, or other costs not deemed deductible that a second taxpayer—with the same personal income and tax liability—does not have. So taxable net income is not necessarily an indicator of ability to pay nor of the wealth of the individual.

The second problem with the ability-to-pay principle incorporated into the tax code is more fundamental. It has to do with the nature of economic transactions, liability for service, and the role of government in social and economic management. Should a tax system be primarily an assessment for government service or an agent of economic redistribution?

Theoretically (but not always actually) people who earn more pay more in the income tax system. There is no economic relationship, though, between level of government service to the taxpayer and his personal production or income. A citizen who works harder and is more self-reliant, in fact, may actually represent a decreased need for and decreased receipt of actual or implied government services. People that work harder and raise their incomes may pay more and receive less.

There also is no justification for attaching an unlimited liability to a person's potential earnings. Government expenses are, in the end, finite. A man may go to a hardware store, for instance, and buy a lawnmower for the full sales price of $300.00. But he would be incredulous if the proprietor from the hardware store returned to his doorstep every week thereafter, demanding another $25.00 when the man brought home his weekly paycheck because the man's "ability to pay" had increased. A hardware store wouldn't do this, of course, but the government does it all the time because it has divorced the concept of relative cost of government service from individual tax liability and substituted the ability-to-pay condition.

A tax based on ability to pay can provide an incentive for individuals to *reduce* productivity, or least to reduce tax exposure of that productivity, and also to lobby for and *maximize* tax charges on others to gain additional government benefits funded by those other people. One segment of the population can be rewarded for being less economically efficient, while lobbying for the economic suppression of their fellow citizens.

A relatively larger level of actual or implied government service to areas of wealth generation can be a basis for assessment, but merely taking wealth because it is produced is not a sound basis for a tax system, even if the goal is social management and redistribution. Proponents of collectivism could, theoretically, still achieve higher levels of revenue acquisition in standard assessments rather than trying to assess income.

A tax based on standard-rate assessment of fixed quantities, as opposed to ability to pay, has the advantage of consistent and relative liability. All taxpayers pay the same rate, only those with an increased resource base (more to tax or greater wealth) would pay more. An increased levy to expand government expenditures is thus felt proportionately in respect to the interest (percentage of the tax base) each citizen or taxpaying resident has. This is not the condition, though, of the income tax.

Butter and 1040s don't mix. Social service needs, if addressed through government, should be handled through the appropriation process. Application of the ability-to-pay principle—especially when associated with the plethora of special-interest deductions in income tax law—is irregular at best and even then irrelevant to a sound tax system. The holding of an immediate ability to pay as a prime criterion in a tax system is nothing but an attempt to turn a tax system into a federal aid program.

———— ♦ ————

Scheduling of financing for government spending under the income tax system is beyond anything imaginable in the private sector. An enterprise in the private sector will identify the cost of a project and then assign precise (to the penny!) financing of it to appropriate individuals or institutions (and, of course, through volitional contracts). All parties in a normal private sector transaction know exactly what they can afford and exactly what they would pay before any transaction is finally agreed upon and before any billing and spending is actually initiated.

The government, however, has chosen what could be described as the "Blind Man With A Shotgun" or "Carpet Bomb 'Till They Scream!" approach with the income tax system. Spending is completely separate from tax liability under federal fiscal policy and income tax assessment. Government costs are essentially dumped into one big bucket, and then (after the input of national and international lobbyists) an extremely long

(75 million words) federal tax code is modified. At the time the new tax code is implemented the "Shotgun" or "Carpet Bombs" of individual tax liability are fired or dropped. But most people still don't know if they're going to be hit by the tax buckshot or shrapnel until they later try to complete their tax return. Who will be the tax liability "casualty" on April 15th?

The really unfortunate thing about this system is that citizens cannot give informed feedback to the legislators when spending proposals are made. People may have a general disposition for or against particular governmental spending. A lot of citizens, obviously, are for particular governmental spending that directly benefits them. But on any expenditure, citizens, in order to give a responsible viewpoint, must know their own individual tax liability with respect to the proposed spending measure.

A citizen, for instance, might like to see an improvement in the federal highway system that included expanded access and rest stops for interstate travelers. But if the expense for that, in conjunction with other government expenses that must be paid for by taxes, created a tax burden the citizen, his family, business, or employees could not sustain, then it would be imprudent for him to support such a capital outlay. On the other hand, if he and other citizens could see immediately that the relative expenditure was sustainable and the relative benefit worth it, they could then confidently choose to support the expenditure.

But there are differences between private and government financing. Considering the fact that an appropriation or budget may be passed months or even a year or more before taxes are due, would it not be difficult for a citizen to know his exact tax liability *before* the tax year ends? And would it not be especially difficult, if not impossible, to determine relative, individual liability for line-item expenditures in a proposed budget?

The answer is no, it's not impossible. It's easy. A detailed description of an alternative tax system that provides this function begins later in Chapter VII. But for now, an examination of the dreadnought of modern federal revenue acquisition, the income tax, continues: Is this tax system plowing through the economic waters of the nation finally better at protecting and servicing our shores . . . or sinking friendly merchant vessels?

◆

There are many deductions, conditions and exemptions in the income tax system that people take advantage of and in doing so effectively shift the cost of government to others. But besides legal mechanizations such as direct legislation and personal financial strategies in tax systems to minimize tax liability, there is a very large amount of direct tax evasion.

The black market economy in the United States, or that portion evading taxation, had been estimated in 1980 to be from $159 billion (6.1 percent of GNP) to $1.095 *trillion* (41.6 percent of GNP).[145] The IRS has put the figure at a more optimistic $80 billion, which is hardly comforting.[146] This means people who pay no taxes can receive direct or indirect government services they do not pay for. This is nothing but an additional burden on those who *do* pay taxes and who must make up the difference for the cost of government.

There is the question of implementing an equitable tax system in the country and what that system should be. However, any system that is chosen should reflect objective and effective enforcement practices. Gross lack of accountability and inequitable enforcement by the government should not be accepted by conscientious citizens already paying their fair share. Responsible citizens should not be forced to pick up the tab for others because government leaders have chosen to operate a bad tax system where evasion is rampant.

The resulting and rising concern and even cynicism toward government has been met with little action by legislators who seem to ignore the relationship between the income tax and the social as well as economic problems facing the country. The fact that bad law may breed contempt for general law should arouse concern not only for immediate economic stability, but concern for future prosperity and long-term civil order as well. Law is what civilized society is based on, and corruption of law leads to the corruption of society.

◆

The government has made it extremely difficult for many, including responsible people who—though finding the income tax system convoluted, confusing and grossly unfair—still want to comply with the requirements of current law. Citizens and businesses can't just fill out a remittance slip. They have to contend with 6,439 pages (again, 75 million words) of tax volumes, 480 different tax forms, and 280 forms that explain the first 480 forms.[147] A tax accountant, or accountants, though, may not be the only technical assistance one might need. For there are not just tax regulations. There can be extensive tax case law that can determine how a law or regulation is to be interpreted.

Businesses and the self-employed have to contend with the possibility of several segments of accounting books. Assets might be depreciated, for instance, in one depreciation schedule for operations, and then have to be maintained in a second tax schedule to compute the depreciation expense allowed under income tax law. The lobbying in and drafting of tax law; the training of professionals and staff in a company's business; the functional mandate that includes consideration of complex tax mechanizations in the decision making process of management; and the administration, interpretation, tracking and enforcement by the IRS all make for a very complicated scenario. Add to this the fact that businesses can defer expenses and income over a period of years and the situation gets worse.

But if that isn't bad enough, federal income tax law can also be applied retroactively. The Constitution prohibits ex post facto criminal laws, so the government cannot pass a new law today and arrest a person for violating it last week. But the government can apply *civil* law under the income tax system to implement prior period tax assessment, and in doing so it has gotten around the Constitutional limitation on *criminal* liability related to those assessments.

First, the government passes civil tax law but applies it for a past time period—as when an income tax law is passed at the end of the calendar year taxing all income from the beginning of the year. Taxpayers then may owe additional taxes they hadn't planned for. Not only is an unexpected *civil* liability for taxes created, but taxpayers are also required to submit a tax return for the given tax period with failure to file, or failure to file correctly, for those taxes a *criminal* liability.

Signing one's name on the personal or business federal tax return means that whatever has been stated therein, no matter how conscientiously assembled, can be used against the citizen himself in civil and criminal court if (in the government's view) something in the return is incorrect.

The IRS can file claims against taxpayers for multiple prior years. The taxpayer can be forced to not only collect and maintain extensive financial and employment records and receipts but may have to demonstrate, when audited, correct historical compliance against the complex, ever-changing tax code. The IRS can also seize property without normal due process. It doesn't have to prove anything.[148] The taxpayer can thus be in a terrible position of having to engage in contemporary interpretation of tax regulations and complying, or trying to comply, with very confusing, current-year tax code—while having to prove reporting accuracy and personal innocence for events that occurred years ago under entirely different but equally ill-defined tax law.

The IRS can legally turn an accountant *against the citizen that hired him* in tax proceedings and is the reason professional tax attorneys are now advertising their services—so that the tax attorney (having lawyer-client confidentiality status) can have clients honestly discuss personal finances with an advisor without fear of identifying a possible error or somehow saying something that could be used by the government under an immensely complicated tax code to entrap and effectively railroad citizens to the poor house. It is indeed a sorry state of affairs in this country when one has to consider hiring an attorney just to hire an accountant.

Federal attacks on free trade and business hiring practices are evident in the government's income tax policy on the self-employed—companies can be intimidated by the IRS if they hire independent contractors. Businesses that hire self-employed people must report on them to the government (via the 1099 Form), and accountants have even been hired by the IRS to spy on their clients.[149]

The degree of complexity in tax law and the concern for protection of capital and property has led many business enterprises to invest heavily in tax accounting expertise and legal experts, making audit investigations and challenges by the IRS more involved and difficult. This has led to charges that the IRS focused its enforcement muscle in the 1990s against the path of least resistance and most easily intimidated—the dutiful working and tax-reporting small business class.[150] The IRS was also accused of focusing 85 percent of random audits in the 1995-1997 tax years on people with reported incomes of under $25,000.[151]

The focus of increased audit attention by the IRS on low-income groups, however, may not be without rational explanation—sort of. The IRS has been charged by Congress to not only monitor tax assessment and remittance but to also monitor "refunds" on tax payments to the government that were never made. Is that not impossible?

No, it is not impossible and the reason is that the government has not limited itself to just *indirect* subsidy through the income tax code. Matter and anti-matter—depending on what science fiction novel one reads—may not occupy the same space at the same time, but Congress has tried to implement within the same time/space continuum an income tax system with a tax and an anti-tax (or monetary pay-out). This pay-out—the Earned Income Tax Credit—is supposed to be a direct subsidy to help lower-income wage earners. But an indication of the functional integrity of the Earned Income Tax Credit—and perhaps the whole federal income tax system—might be taken from the fact that the Treasury Department in 1997 reported 26 percent of claims for the Earned Income Tax Credit—$4.4 billion—went to unqualified recipients.[152] This can mean one thing to low-income as well as other taxpayers who don't qualify for the credit: an average higher tax liability to cover those not paying.

Social Security recipients belong to another penalized group that encompasses many lower-income people. Social Security can be taxed twice (depending on individual taxpayer retirement income)—once when wages are earned and the Social Security deduction is made, and then again when recipients receive Social Security payments. How does this meet with the government's alleged interest in encouraging retirement savings?

The focus on small business owners and low-wage earners in audits and taxing of Social Security are examples of what the nation's early leaders feared in excessive government taxation and redistribution of resources—control and suppression of basic economic rights of the common man.

◆

Public accountability is lacking in the income tax system as well as basic privacy. Yet it is important in a tax system that all tax assessments and tax payments be made public, or remain open to public review. And the right of personal privacy should also be maintained with the personal financial standing of individual citizens excluded from public disclosure. These two conditions—public accountability and right to privacy—may seem totally contradictory but they are *not* incompatible.

The public has a right to know about the financial assessment and expenditures the government is involved in and if tax policy, in both a cumulative and specific sense, is being justly applied. The income tax system makes that all but impossible—allowing the IRS secret and wide variance in investigation, reporting, interpretation, forgiveness of debts, and assignment of penalties. One person may pay onerous taxes under complex legal strictures and still be assessed heavy penalty for accidental error on his tax return while his neighbor—already enjoying high preference in tax law from legislative favoritism of his industry or lifestyle—can have even minor taxes and penalties waived for him by skillful lawyers in administrative tax proceedings.

But the first citizen may never know this, or can't know this, because of complex secrecy regulations in income tax law. Even Congress, the institution that created the income tax law, and the

President's office, in charge of administering national tax policy, have been prevented from reviewing, overseeing or analyzing tax situations and problems![153] Strictures on confidentiality, however, have apparently not stopped internal IRS employees from rifling confidential documents of noted public figures or celebrities out of mere curiosity when their particular official duties had nothing to do with those taxpayer case files.[154]

It is in that context then that comprehensive background information accumulated and used in an official capacity by the state against the citizen could also be available for dissemination and possible use by the less scrupulous in criminal activities. How ironic for a citizen to be *legally mandated* to supply an information base that could be used against him, to be exposed to possible *illegal* internal administrative actions, and then to have senior oversight from the Congress or the Executive branch *legally prohibited.*

The public, the press, and of course, senior government officials, all need to know what's going on in the implementation of fiscal policy, of which taxation is certainly a part. The country does not need the IRS acting as a secret society and making judgments and assessments that can never be reviewed in an objective, open forum. The governmental fiscal process starts with funding appropriations and the creation of tax law, which is public and therefore open to scrutiny and to questions, but ends up in manipulation of resources and reporting by taxpayers and their accountants, in secret tax filings, unequal tax remissions, and closed-door administrative actions.

People, though, may point to a paradox in integrating the principle of public disclosure in a tax system with personal privacy rights. Wouldn't people's personal privacy and possibly their security—especially in the case of public officials or celebrities—be violated if tax returns, assessments, and IRS judgments were *not* held confidential, but made public? The answer is yes—with the income tax!

Maintenance of the current federal income tax system ensures the paradox is not resolved. But if the income tax system is discarded and another tax system is employed, both public disclosure and personal privacy can be maintained.

The conventional property tax, for instance, is based on assessed property values that may be public record. But that information has nothing to do with personal or business income or other expenditures, and thus cannot reveal private financial activities to the public. Yet official records on rates, assessments, payments, penalties, and back taxes are still available to government officials, citizens, and the press.[155]

A big problem with the income tax is that it does not share the public disclosure characteristics of a system like the property or sales tax. The lack of public review under the income tax, both for individual citizens and the press, is one more indication that this system should not continue to function in the modern American state.

———— ♦ ————

The income tax has turned the halls of American government into new, monarchical-like corridors of economic intrigue and counterplay where entreaties are made to entice or stop a legislative royalty in the anointing of favored tax conditions. Income tax law is a way for legislators to "spend" without have to face the appropriate questions and trials of direct governmental allocation.

The truth is, any benefit to a special interest that cannot be justified in regular appropriations probably cannot be justified. The income tax system is a convoluted system of resource acquisition and disbursement where legislative policymakers dictate the economic values of others and enforce their prescriptions through manipulation of a tax code. Special deductions, exemptions, and even outright payments in the income tax system are used for individual or group favoritism, welfare maintenance and social engineering purposes. The cost to the third parties to whom tax liability has directly or indirectly shifted in this system can be substantial, and the artificial construction created in the economy can affect national productivity and social stability.

The twisted and ever-changing tax code not only inhibits sound economic planning, but prompts manipulation of private resources by taxpayers to avoid arbitrary government seizure. Producers alter service or production not for consumer need but in response to changes in tax regulations. Goods and services that are desired by consumers are not provided in the most efficient manner and thus cost the public more.

The disincentive for production, and the economic cost of resource reallocation to protect from or take advantage of government tax regulations and subsidies is substantial. *This portion of the economic cost of the federal income tax system is estimated at more than $315 billion per year.*[156] And once again, this is before the cost of taxes themselves!

———— ♦ ————

People have repeatedly cried for income tax reform, have had income tax "reformed," and then lived to see what re-created fiscal corruption looks like. The famous 1986 tax reform bill under the Reagen Administration, which was supposed to be a genuine effort to reform federal tax policy, ended up with seven hundred different special-interest tax breaks.[157] Ten years later things hadn't changed.

An income tax bill that passed the House in the summer of 1997, for instance, defies justification—and explanation. That bill includes a $500 tax rebate for people who haven't paid five hundred dollars in taxes, a three-year tax break for corporations donating computers that expires in two years, seventy-nine different special interest measures that benefit one hundred people or less, including a tax break for apple cider producers and an obscure bond provision for the Virgin Islands, and a "reduction" in estate taxes that actually raises them.[158] This cannot be hailed as a grand bipartisan tax construction. It more resembles the efforts of distracted juvenile hobbyists building an expensive passenger steamship with wooden planks and water-soluble glue.

It is not surprising that problems abound in administration of the federal income tax. The IRS, the agency charged with this duty, employs over 136,000 people and spends $10 billion per year in an attempt to manage the system.[159] Even so, the General Accounting Office (GAO) has said the IRS could not account for over half of the $6.4 billion it spent in 1992 for office rental, salaries, and computers, or prove whether or not it actually holds $797 million in assets it claims it seized.[160] The GAO stated in a 1996 report that $1.4 trillion collected in 1995 and $122 billion in refunds "cannot be verified or reconciled to accounting records maintained for individual taxpayers," and amounts collected for Social Security, income and excise taxes "cannot be substantiated."[161] And yet, the situation with respect to record-keeping is even worse: Empty shelves now appear in the National Archives and Records in College Park, Maryland where historical IRS records are supposed to be maintained.[162]

Direction has been attached to Congress in this analysis, but to be fair a large share of blame must be attached to the Executive branch of government. The Executive branch is the second party necessary to sign bills into law (unless there is an override of a Presidential veto on a bill). Presidents have routinely acceded to huge appropriations from Congress or actively participated in them. Federal budgets accelerated to over a trillion dollars under President Ronald Reagen, a conservative Republican, and his successor, President George Bush, both members of a party supposedly concerned with fiscal conservatism—which highlights why citizens cannot rely on mere political review to preclude unwarranted taxation and spending.[163]

♦

The federal income tax is a bad tax system, but not just because of technical problems in its implementation. It is a bad tax system because the political and economic philosophy on which it is based is fundamentally anti-American and aberrant. The income tax is based on the theory of the master and the servant, where the traditional American role of government as servant is reversed and the citizen becomes the servant of the government, submitting all economic activity to the inspection and approval of the government master.

Irrespective of the level of public expenditure, the essence of the federal income tax in funding those expenditures is a constant leveled attack against productivity. This concept of incremental and constant seizure of the fruits of a free citizen's labor is so egregious, so contrary to basic American ideals, that the almost visceral 1894 response in the Supreme Court to its attempted implementation is not surprising. A Constitutional change was required to reverse the original, pre-1894 protection found in that document, and the result was implementation of the Sixteenth Amendment—which truncated the Fourteenth Amendment, made a mockery of the Fifth, and left the Tenth impotent.[164]

The reason for assignment of increasing personal liability, an effective penalty, by the government under the income tax system is, ironically, that a citizen is responsible and productive and creates wealth for himself and society! The citizen, under the income tax system, may then only keep an arbitrary percentage of his or her earnings that the government dictates. Just because a citizen earns something the government can take it.

The more a citizen works, the more of his resources can be seized by the state without benefit or compensation—and at an increasing rate. *Under the income tax system the citizen exists, economically, at the pleasure of the state.* The elitist power base that happens to be in political office will dictate the percentage of what a citizen may be permitted to keep, as long as the citizen meets the strictures, regulations, and dictates under the secular religion of a politically imperial tax code. No matter what exuberant euphemisms exist in the political sphere, this is rank tyranny.

Proponents of the income tax will claim the income tax is not involuntary servitude. They will say no one is forced to work. Think about that. We have truly passed the year 1984 and entered the realm of doublespeak when under the auspices of the state a costly, confusing, and destructive tax system is heralded as humanitarian, and contemporary pundits and leaders rejoin in denoting the loss of economic liberty—and the imposition of forced redistribution based on economic responsibility—as something progressive.

This concept of the income tax is repulsive to those who know and truly understand the principles and concepts that grew out of the European Enlightenment and that eventually found fruition in the establishment of law and liberty in the United States. It is interesting to wonder what war-weary Revolutionary War veterans, muskets over their shoulders and returning to their farms and villages after eight long years of fighting the British, would have said to today's legislative representatives had they been met and informed by those representatives that from then on, no matter how hard citizens worked, the percentage of what they'd be allowed to keep would be dictated by the government!

The income tax is not necessary to fund the federal government. Everything now being funded by the federal government could be funded *without* a federal income tax system if citizens so chose, and this could be done without threatening citizens' liberty, and possibly with very great savings to the country. The income tax should be replaced, and personal liberty and economic freedom protected.

The question that remains is what tax system, or systems, are the most appropriate replacement for assessment and acquisition of federal revenue in this country.

V. Other Tax Systems for Friend, Fool or Folly

No matter how hard the Slave works, no matter how much he produces for his Master, should the Slave work an additional week, an additional day, or even an additional hour, the Master shall have a claim on those assets, too, and the Master shall dictate to the Slave the percentage of what the Slave has produced that he, the Slave, may, perhaps, keep, so long as the Slave meets all the Master's dictates and regulations, which are contained in voluminous Journals containing the conditions of Slave reward as authored by the Master's Counselors, and which provides for the Master's favoritism and support for certain Slaves over others in those industries he thinks most prudent, and the Slave may not claim he has no time to know these Journals but must abide by them always, and the Slave must provide written documentation for his payment to the Master and testify to the correctness of his submission to the Master under the Journals, and shall sign such Declaration, and if ever after such Declaration be found or merely suspected of being in error by the Master, the Slave shall be exposed to seizure of not only any suspected arrears, but of such interest amounts for that time period to the benefit of the Master, and then amounts taken for penalty in punishment of the Slave, and finally the Slave shall be subject to criminal jail where he may greatly suffer. For be it known, that on this land it is for the Master to decide how wealth created will be spent, and this is for the benefit of all the Slaves, as each Slave must understand his position for the good of the estate, and that what a Slave produces is not his—the fruits of his labor are to be harvested as directed by the Master, as this has been agreed to by all, and if the Slave be good and tend greatly to the Master the Slave might be given favors, and maybe even great favors taken from other Slaves. And so accept this and no more talk of this thing called Liberty.

— "Alice in Wonderland Revisited" The Author, 1998

Two criteria have traditionally been considered by legislators in the creation of new tax law for revenue acquisition in this century. The first of the two criteria is the existence of actual revenue in the entity being taxed—that is, a person or business must have money before it can be taken. The second criterion is ease of extraction—how difficult or easy it is, politically, to expropriate the particular tax entity's resources. The formula for ease of expropriation is

(Wealth - Effective Lobbying = Tax Assessment).

Assuming the revenue need of the government is valid, are the two criteria identified above the only conditions that should be considered in the creation and implementation of a new tax? How do other taxes work and what are their advantages and disadvantages? Following is an analysis of various taxes, some generic and others specific, that are in use or have been proposed.

Excise Tax

An excise tax is an internal (domestic) tax on the manufacture, sale, or consumption of a particular commodity or service. Federal excise taxes in the United States have included taxes on oleomargarine, adulterated and renovated butter, processed cheese, coconut oil, diesel fuel, sugar, firearms, narcotics, slot machines, bowling alleys, billiard tables, phone communications, safe deposit boxes; transportation of persons by rail, motor vehicle, water, or air; transportation of property (except coal), transportation of coal, pipeline oil transfer, entertainment park admissions, cabarets, roof gardens, table wine, music machines, wagering, cigarettes, cigars, photographic apparatuses, film, appliances, club dues, tires, beer, electric light bulbs, lubricating oil, passenger automobiles, auto parts, trucks and buses, musical instruments, gasoline, and other items.[165] Tax rates for each type of item can vary. Articles sold to other businesses for further manufacture or resale can be, but are not necessarily, exempt from an excise tax.

An excise tax, unlike the income tax, is usually certain. There is an item, an exact tax rate for the item, and a specified regulation or condition under which the tax is due. Excise taxes can be implemented for one or more reasons of social management (i.e., sin taxes), government economic management (suppressing one industry or product to promote another), funding general government fiscal obligations, and funding specific government services related to, or not related to, the particular taxpayer remitting the excise tax. The first two reasons for implementation of an excise tax are dubious at best and will be discussed at length later in this chapter.

The third condition, funding general fiscal obligations, has probably been the chief reason governments have implemented the tax. Government sees areas of the economy where wealth (money) is being generated and attempts to capture it at a transaction point (point of sale) where it can be easily identified, quantified and retrieved.

An excise tax funding general government services, however, is for a revenue appropriation for the general good (general fiscal obligation), but assessed through a charge on a specific product or service. This can burden, perhaps unfairly, the merchants and consumers trading in the particular product or service being taxed. An example would be an excise tax on television sets dedicated for general revenue needs. People who didn't buy television sets would not have to pay the tax, but would, theoretically, still be benefiting from the tax revenue that was collected to finance general government services.

An excise tax that is certain and stable, however, can influence commerce in other areas of the economy where costs can be, at least in part, indirectly transferred from direct taxpayers to non-payers. For instance, buyers of the television sets paying more for the sets because of the excise tax, have a given inducement (however incremental) to set higher prices in their businesses or demand higher wages in their jobs where non-payers of the original excise tax (those who didn't buy the television sets) can end up paying, in the end, higher charges for those goods and services, and thereby indirectly supplementing the tax base. But the farther removed one neutral economic transaction is from other taxed transactions, the less likely costs will be disbursed, and this is even more so if the excise tax is unstable (changed often in rate or condition).

A relatively low excise tax rate and greater individual applicability of an excise tax (i.e., most families own television sets) means the tax can be more politically palatable. The whiskey excise tax resisted by Pennsylvania frontiersmen in the 1790s Whiskey Rebellion was perceived by the tax opponents as an attempt by urban elites (Hamilton and the Federalists) to fund government operations at the expense of the settlers,[166] and is an example of resistance to a particular tax creating strong political—as well as fiscal—repercussions. The complexity of modern tax law and plethora of special interest subsidy today, however, makes it much more difficult to question the service to assessment ratio of a particular tax, let alone protest it.

Excise taxes can be dedicated to particular appropriations instead of supplementing general revenue needs. A dedicated excise tax itself, though, does not necessarily fund any benefit (appropriation) for *payers* of the tax, and *recipients* of the related appropriation, although being beneficiaries of the tax assessment, may not be taxed at all.

For instance, the government could create an excise tax on fertilizers of 10 percent and dedicate the proceeds to college agricultural training. Citizens who buy neither fertilizer nor take the training have no direct cost or benefit. Farmers who buy fertilizer are taxed, but have no direct benefit. Agricultural students have no assessment but enjoy the funded training.

Of course, a rationale for linking the training appropriation to an assessment on fertilizer is that farmers who pay the tax ultimately benefit by having a trained work force—the graduates of the college agricultural training. Theoretically, and on average, the farmers may benefit. But any link for some excise taxes between assessment, payers and beneficiaries can be tenuous, to the point there is no link at all and the excise tax is just an arbitrary element for the collection of general government revenue.

The best excise tax is that which has a service to cost relationship, where the assessment is related to the amount of government service and the beneficiary: An automatic increase ensues—in assessment to the particular taxpayer and revenue to the government—in relationship to the increased level of service to that taxpayer, and vice versa.

An example is a gas tax where the excise tax funds that are collected are dedicated to road construction and maintenance. Increased highway travel by citizens means a greater need for highways and related maintenance, and as more driving occurs the purchase of gas also increases. Since the excise tax is tied to the sale of gas, more tax is collected to pay for the increased highway use when it occurs.

With a dedicated gas tax, a business that efficiently uses in-house manufacturing and minimizes transportation costs is going to be using the roads less, and thus would be liable for less tax than individuals or businesses that choose more highway travel. Road construction and maintenance funding automatically expands or contracts with gas purchases and relative road use. A good excise tax, such as a dedicated gas tax, is a sound tax and part of a rational economic exchange.

Tariff

A tariff is a duty, or charge, on imported goods. Tariffs are imposed to raise revenue, and to protect domestic businesses and manufacturers from foreign competition by increasing the cost (through the duty) of imported goods. Tariffs can be targeted against specific foreign industries that are competing against domestic companies.

Tariffs can create higher prices for the consumer and impede free trade. However, political conditions and social standards around the world are not the same as in the United States. Worker protections, civil rights, pollution controls, environmental protection, and internal free trade all can be lessened or abandoned by foreign regimes intent on leveraging power for larger, nationalistic purposes.

Foreign industries in collusion with their governments can participate in orchestrated price fixing and product dumping to economically break domestic companies and remove them from competition, clearing the way for later market control and price hikes to consumers. Foreign economic and political suppression in the pursuit of international market advantages by foreign political and economic oligarchies can also be an impetus for social dislocation and illegal immigration or other problems that directly affect the United States. Modern political conditions are complex but cannot be divorced from economic planning and protection of U.S. economic interests.

Tariffs, the source of a large percentage of federal revenue in early America, may be a positive and even necessary economic tool in some circumstances. Citizens incur the liability of tariffs in the same manner as domestic excise taxes—higher prices. But they also enjoy the same benefit—government receipts to the Treasury, and the country may benefit from tariffs in the protection of key industries. A high degree of economic caution is warranted when considering tariffs, but their implementation may be necessary under certain conditions to protect American consumers, industry, or national security.

Stamp Tax

Stamp taxes are payable by the purchase and use of stamps and have been required in the issuance, sale, or transfer of stocks and bonds; conveyances of real estate, sales of playing cards, and issuance or renewal of foreign insurance policies; and even in silver bullion transfers. Payment of stamp taxes can be evidenced by placement of the appropriate stamp on the stock, bond, or memorandum of sale or, for instance, on the back of playing card packs.

Stamp taxes are very certain forms of taxation, and proof of payment is demonstrated by the physical stamp or memorandum. Stamp taxes are really just another form of excise tax, and their individual validity can be adjudged the same way.

Sin Tax

Sin taxes are excise or sales taxes levied against items and activities deemed less "moral" or desirable because their misuse may cause social or health problems. Gambling, alcohol, and tobacco taxes are examples. Citizens, advocacy groups, and politicians may lobby for sin taxes because they believe special assessment against the items or activities can serve as an economic disincentive to their use.

Another reason politicians may give for the taxation of items like alcohol and tobacco is that the cost from misuse of the substances—the cost of medical treatment—may be borne directly by the government if the individual lacks medical insurance or becomes indigent. This argument becomes questionable, however, when politicians use the funds for general-purpose expenditures instead of applying them to relevant health care needs. Tax revenue acquired from sin taxes can, in policy and practice, have no relation whatsoever to any government services rendered to producers or consumers who are paying the taxes (for instance, casinos and gamblers, or tobacco companies and smokers), and revenue collected from the assessments can be used for all manner of public funding.

Concern about rationality and consistency in the application of tax policy, including arbitrary assessment on tobacco, is not new. Early twentieth-century economist Henry Simons poignantly noted:

> . . . [I]t seems a little absurd to go around arguing that poor people could or ought to do without tobacco, especially if it is taxed, in face of the fact that they do not do anything of the kind, that the commodity was selected for taxation because they are not expected to do so, and that the government would not get much revenue if they did. The plain fact, to one not confused by moralistic distinctions between necessities and luxuries, is simply that taxes like the tobacco tax are the most effective means available for draining government revenue out of the very bottom of the income scale.[167]

The real reason government may levy taxes, sometimes substantial, on sin tax items is because they are viewed as the "cash cows" of revenue production. In fact, in the case of tobacco, state and national governments have recently been working toward block settlement moneys in abeyance of punitive civil action against tobacco interests, which may leave one wondering where civil litigation and effective taxation begins in this country.[168]

The supreme irony of sin tax implementations is they can end up neither reducing the purportedly unhealthy activities nor increasing the desired government revenues—nor in enhancing the country's social conditions. Canada, for instance, doubled its cigarette tax between 1984 and 1993, but underage smoking failed to decrease. What did occur in Canada was an estimated black market for 40 percent of all cigarette sales in the country—the tobacco contraband being smuggled into Canada over the U.S. border.[169] While do-gooders and bureaucrats enact legal dictums for "the good of the populace," they do nothing, in some instances, but lay a fertile ground for organized crime associated with black market activities.

Most activities in life are associated with some degree of risk. Individual choices and individual actions are the responsibility of those individuals who indulge in the behavior, for good or bad. Government policy should not be implemented to penalize a legal industry or all the consumers thereof in an attempt to control the potential personal excesses of some.

The sin tax smacks of behavioral control by the state. It first implies the adult individual is not fully responsible for his or her actions, then implies the state must discourage certain behaviors—yet profit from them! The state apparatus that can imbue this convoluted philosophy into minds of the masses and have them accept it may well have less trouble in controlling those citizens and limiting their freedoms in other matters.

Luxury Tax

A luxury tax is an excise tax, sometimes substantial, on particular products or services (specialty items) in the economy, usually associated with a higher amount of wealth or discretionary income. Examples of luxury taxes are special tax assessments on gems, furs, or yachts.

Luxury tax rates on specialty items can be much higher than regular sales or excise tax rates on more common items that are considered non-luxury, such as gasoline and petroleum products. Food, rent, and transportation can either be considered necessaries and excluded from *all* taxation—sales and excise included—or considered a luxury and taxed as such if associated with any degree of special comfort or opulence. An example of a food and transportation luxury tax would be a special assessment for meals and travel on a vacation ocean liner.

The assumption by policymakers has been that purchasers of luxury items have a relatively higher level of discretionary income and can thus afford, and are willing to pay, an increased tax levy on the specialty items they desire.

A luxury tax is not implemented under any social-management pretext like sin taxes are. The purpose of the tax is *not* to discourage purchases—just the opposite is hoped for. The goal is the pure acquisition of revenue, and government officials are quite happy, officially and unofficially, when a lot of the luxury-taxed items are purchased.

The luxury tax may seem to many an easy way to obtain a lot of government revenue from those who can most afford to pay. But the luxury tax is in reality based on arrogant government assumptions. One of the assumptions is that people who are wealthier are less concerned about increased cost when they consider a purchase. This of course is absurd, and it is often the rich who are the ones most concerned about cost.

Another assumption is that government can effectively identify that which is luxury and that which is not. But preferences and priorities can be different even for people who have the same amount of wealth. One person may take his disposable income and spend it immediately on multiple purchases while another will save his money and buy one large high-value item later.

An example is the purchase of a thousand vanilla ice cream cones over a couple of years, or the purchase of an emerald bracelet once in the same time period. Proponents of the luxury tax cannot argue one is more "luxury" than the next. A person could make a rational choice based on personal preference to enjoy a daily ice cream cone, or forestall that pleasure over a given period of time to save for the bracelet. There is no rational reason for a third entity—in this instance government tax legislators—to deny choice or lay penalty on either purchase.

The disregard for individual economic freedom can also be bad economic news for many people who never purchase so-called luxury items but are involved in the production or sale of them, or are related to individuals and businesses dependent on sales of the host (taxed item) industry. For example, in 1991 Congress looked around for another way to boost federal tax receipts and decided additional revenue could be acquired by applying an assessment to the sale of boats that cost over $100,000. Certainly (it was assumed) those people who could afford to pay that amount of money could well afford—and would pay—the luxury tax. However, several economic realities occur in such a situation. One is the realization by a potential purchaser that later market value of an item—a boat in this instance—can be much less than its original purchase price because of the added new-purchase tax levy. Financing a purchase can be more difficult and later resale can mean substantial loss, especially in the competition with previously built used boats where the luxury tax didn't apply.

An older domestic boat can be purchased and refurbished instead of buying a new boat and the boat tax thus avoided by the purchaser—but to the artificial benefit of those who refurbish used boats, the effective loss of tax revenue to the government, and the sales loss to craftsmen and merchants who would otherwise produce and sell new boats. And then *total* loss to American industry could occur when a buyer purchases a foreign-built boat through a foreign port that has no such new-boat purchase penalty.

There is, too, the assumption by legislators that people buying a boat must be rich when in reality a boat, even an expensive one, can be far less expensive than a regular house, and that many people live on their boats. And, of course, other people might decide boating had just become too expensive and their money could be better invested in one of innumerable other forms of outdoor or indoor recreation.

So what is the net effect of a "luxury" tax imposition? Industry workers, investors, and others businesses in the towns where manufacturing and sales occur can lose money or jobs. Lower sales can mean a possible increase in the trade deficit (from lack of domestic but increased foreign purchases); a possible increase and cost in social service demands from unemployed workers; loss of capital investment and thus loss of national wealth and security by the investors; new relocation and retraining costs as businesses are liquidated and workers are relocated; reduction of consumer choice by buyers who no longer can afford the increased cost of the taxed commodity (new boats); and finally, lower net taxes to the government even though tax charges and tax rates had gone up.

A luxury tax may only mean slightly less convenience to those who avoid the tax and spend their money elsewhere. But for others it can be a serious impediment to commerce and harm to their livelihood. And if luxury item sales slow and net tax receipts decline it can also mean less revenue to the government. Congressmen from both parties blamed the 1991 boat tax for a decline in boat sales and repealed it in 1993.[170] The tax apparently had not worked as intended and correction had been made.

But no one seemed to address the real principles under which the tax was applied, only that this particular luxury tax on boats was viewed as not successful in recovering tax revenue without destroying the tax base.

Despite the boating lesson in 1993, Congress afterward continued to have difficulty floating effective tax policy. Poor tax planning and unprincipled tax construction in innumerable other forms would be luxuries the national legislature would continue to indulge in at the country's expense.

Fines, Interest, and Penalties

Government revenue can be acquired through fines, interest, and penalties, but a couple of factors make the reliance on these sources for regular operating revenue undesirable. The first is that the purpose of fines and penalties is to induce potential violators not to violate the law and to punish people who do. Therefore, government policy is set, ostensibly, to discourage the activities (violations) that generate the revenue in the first place, and reliance on the revenue from violations for regular government operations may create a conflict of interest between governmental economic and social policies.

Fines, interest, and penalties can also be relatively small, only mitigating costs associated with enforcement or administration. Interest charges, for instance, may only cover the cost of the government's temporary loss of liquidity (through the lending or extension of capital by the government) and provide little or no increase in net governmental income. Fines, interest, and penalties may provide some gravy in governmental fiscal policy but little revenue meat.

Direct Service Charges

Direct service charges by government agencies are similar to private-sector transactions in a fee-for-service situation. Relative charges for government services are directly charged to the serviced entity. For instance, a U.S. Forest Service campground may charge a fee to campground users for overnight camping to finance operation and maintenance of the campground.

Direct service charges, especially when funds are tied directly to the serviced operations, can be an excellent method in certain situations for financing government activity. The Forest Service campground example is a good one. An undeveloped campsite in the backcountry used infrequently by a smaller number of people might have little related service cost and thus there would be no user fee, or a very limited one. Another campground where water, restroom, and trailer hookups were provided and a much larger number of visitors serviced might charge a slightly higher fee, but would also garner a much greater amount of total revenue to service those visitors because of the volume.

As use of a particular government service financed through a service charge increases, so does the needed revenue and payment to support it; as use decreases, revenue and expenditures decline. There is an automatic link between operation, cost, and financing. Direct service charges may be limited in their applicability, but where appropriate should be one of the first revenue systems considered in financing government services.

Environmental Tax

An environmental tax, also called a pollution tax, is an assessment on individual taxpayers based on the environmental damages or impact each of them has caused, or a general assessment of the tax base (all taxpayers) to finance environmental repair, maintenance or improvements. An environmental tax can be an excise, sales or other type of tax.[171]

Taxation occurs for many purposes in society. But environmental taxation (like environmental legislation) can have a special allure in modern culture because it suggests, by its very name, that there is a commitment by the state to protect or enhance life-conditions in the country and that a remedy is going to be applied by the state with the strength of law. Some questions, though, should be asked before environmental taxation is implemented:

- Could the environmental issue in question be resolved between private parties instead of by government action?
- If new government action is warranted why is teaching, communication, regulation, subsidy, or litigation not appropriate, and taxation is?
- Why has existing civil and criminal law—and perhaps existing taxation—not been successful in preventing pollution, or in recovering pollution-damages if pollution has occurred?

- Who is going to benefit economically from the revenue generated under the new environmental tax?
- What is the *new* environmental impact caused by people that change their economic activity to avoid the tax?
- What are the expected direct and indirect benefits to society under the tax, and have these expectations been scientifically validated?
- If the benefits to be funded have been validated, what is the total cost, short and long term?
- What is the relationship and level of liability for those bearing the environmental tax assessments and those enjoying the expected improvements?

Assuming these questions are satisfactorily answered, how should taxation be applied with respect to environmental issues?

One approach is to use a Piqouvian tax[172] to meter or measure the level of pollution or impact of individual taxpayers to determine their liability, and then assess them accordingly for relative costs. An example of this type of tax would be an assessment (excise) for every ton of waste discharged by a company from its factory smokestack to compensate the local community for a reduction in average air quality.

Next, there are mutualization taxes where an assessment is applied to a collective group or region but where the funding so collected is spent to the overall, or mutualized, benefit of the group.[173] This situation would include, for example, an excise tax on riverside businesses to fund policing and protection of the river that the businesses depend on for their water supply and commerce.

Finally there are general assessment taxes where individual tax liability is not correlated to the activity of the individual and monies are expended for projects not necessarily related to those that are assessed. An example is a sales tax for environmental repairs or improvements on all businesses in town whether the businesses have polluted or not, or whether the businesses enjoy any environmental improvements funded through the tax or not. General-assessment taxes tend to remove the relationship between cost and accountability for the individual and thus are conducive to irresponsibility in the private sector, and unwarranted assessment and spending in government (Government does not have to demonstrate relative culpability or liability in tax assessment).

Protecting environmental resources is important. But the question is not just "getting the mule to water"—it's whose fields you walk over to get there. Piqouvian-type and carefully-crafted mutualization taxes make sense generally and their application in environmental protection means liability is apportioned to those causing the environmental pollution or impact, or in the case of environmental improvements, those enjoying the related tax-funded service. Hence, where environmental taxes are warranted, those types that are more closely tied to the conduct of the taxpayer should be considered as a preventive measure and inducement for people not to pollute—and a charge to those who do—and should definitely be preferred over general-assessment taxes. But the potential tax *mechanisms* that could be used as environmental taxes—excise, sales, or other systems—still need to be fully examined.

Sales and Use Tax

The sales tax is a charge on all, or most, economic transactions at the retail level. It is basically a blanket excise tax with certain products, like food, excluded from assessment. Services or labor may also be excluded from a sales tax, depending on the particular sales tax law.

Businesses that buy inventory or components for construction of inventory can have those purchases excluded from tax liability under sales tax law as long as the inventory or assembled products are resold. A retail auto parts store, for instance, may pay no tax when it purchases parts from a manufacturer (But the store can still be responsible for *collecting* a sales tax when purchased parts or assembled components are later resold to retail customers).

A business that does not pay tax on its inventory, however, may still be liable for paying a tax for products that are not resold to retail consumers but are used internally by the business—even if the original sellers did not assess a sales tax when the products were sold to the business (as can be the case in business-to-business or out-of-state purchases). A sales tax with this condition is referred to as a "sales and use tax" because of the government's attempt to capture value at final product disposition (where the final product is "used"). Businesses under a sales and use tax law must remit both the use tax for purchased items that are used internally (that were not previously taxed) and the sales tax they collect from their retail customers.

Sales and use taxes have been very popular with local and state governments in the country. One reason is that rates in most sales taxes are not graduated, so the same rate is applicable to every transaction. This makes initial calculation and later totaling and checking of a day's tax receipts mathematically simple.

Another reason is that government collection and auditing is applied to business concerns, as opposed to individual consumers; businesses usually have an effective internal organization for processing and recording economic transactions on a regular basis, including taxable retail sales. This is much easier administratively for the government than taxing consumers directly.

Detailed and involved accounting measures required under the income tax system are not usually required with the sales tax, so sales tax filings and audits, at least at the retail level, are relatively easy to accomplish. Collection and remission of taxes is relatively routine and reliable for the state.

But perhaps the most important advantage to the government is blanket assessment. Virtually every time an interpersonal economic transaction occurs the government lays legal claim to a portion of the resource in trade. This is not only means the government can seize a portion of new-production items whenever they are traded, but also when the same items are later re-traded. The sales and use tax is a very powerful tool for revenue collection, and it is easy to see why politicians and legislators are attracted to it.

But the sales and use tax—from another perspective—has some major problems. The first is a practical one involving the classification of finished goods and retail sales. The sales and use tax is normally assessed only on items at the point of final sale or use, whether in business-to-business transactions or in sales to retail customers. Businesses buying pre-assembled inventory for later resale may have no problem claiming an exclusion from the sales and use tax when a wholesale purchase is made from their suppliers; the products are easily classified as resale inventory and the business pays no use tax. The sales tax in this circumstance is only applied later at the time of retail sale, and the sales tax is collected directly from the customer.

Developmental or manufacturing industries that assemble raw components, however, may have more difficulty in classifying parts and supply purchases as use-tax exempt. Components, chemicals, and supplies utilized in the assembly or manufacturing process may or may not be excluded from use-tax liability, depending on the legal and bureaucratic interpretations of the state taxing agency and the courts. Businesses may have to pay a use tax on certain items, even though the items, in conjunction with other resources, ultimately represent a finished product or service to the retail buyer who also pays a sales tax—effective double taxation by the government.

The sales tax also ignores imputed income. An individual or business that creates wealth and does not engage in economic transactions with others assumes no tax liability. But the person or business entity that specializes in a particular economic activity for increased efficiency and trades in that commodity *is* taxed just because of that—even though society benefits from such specialization. This is an artificial discrimination and suppression of commerce. The foundation of modern economic prosperity is the division of labor and free trade, and the sales tax—like the income tax—effectively penalizes that.

And the sales and use tax is not always as simple as it may first seem. There can be a large practical variance in the application of law. For instance, one manufacturer might pay a use tax for the same product that another doesn't have to pay (a solvent used in one manufacturing process might be considered part of the final product and nontaxable in one business, or a business-supply item—and taxable—in another); retail foods might be untaxed when sold unprepared and cold, but have a sales tax applied when sold prepared and hot (cold caviar wouldn't be taxed but cooked beans would); and labor charges might be exempt in repair or installation, but would be taxable if one desires something newly constructed (an effective penalty on original production).

Again, lack of rational construction in the design and implementation of a tax system leads to the irrational construction of arbitrary conditions. The California Sales and Use Tax, as an example, has special regulations or classification for enterprises such as cleaners, launderers, bootblacks, taxidermists, licensed hearing aid dispensers, dentists, gun clubs, microfilmers, summer camps, beauty shop operators, barbers, and circulating libraries![174] And if property is purchased or sold for use by an aircraft common carrier, a merchant can be required to provide a schedule that shows where the property was sold or used.[175] The degree of complexity in state sales and use taxes do not nearly approach that of the federal income tax, but the principle of arbitrary assignation of liability remains.

There also can be a great incentive under a sales tax to engage, legally or illegally, in economic activity outside of the taxed locale. Consumers will make a point of making purchases while traveling outside their taxed communities to the detriment of local businesses. And businesses will focus manufacturing and sales in areas away from locations that are taxed to the disadvantage of local workers (jobs) and to consumers (product availability). People may focus energies on the generation of less-efficient imputed income and then participate in off-the-books (black market) economic activity to avoid or evade taxation.

Of course, with implementation of a *national* sales tax, the incentive would be to push American capital and jobs completely out of the country and, depending on conditions, create a huge black market economy. Anyone doubting the negative effects possible with a national sales tax should examine Canada's GST tax on commodities and see what it has done to the Canadian economy and consumer (and why Canadian citizens may be making more frequent over-border visits to their American cousins and U.S. shopping malls).

State governments that employ the sales tax may attempt to utilize out-of-state companies that receive business from the taxable state's consumers to collect their state sales tax (as in out-of-state or mail order purchases) in an effort to implement assessment on those domestic consumers who would otherwise not be paying the tax on their out-of-state purchases. Operation of the sales tax today involves a fundamental question of state sovereignty when one state tries to force businesses in another state to enforce and collect its taxes for out-of-state purchases. States should only be allowed tax assessment within their own borders, and if this is less convenient to accomplish directly, then that is the problem of the state employing the tax and not businesses residing in another locale. One state should not be allowed extra-territorial coercion of out-of-state enterprises. Nor should the U. S. Constitution be violated in the construction of artificial domestic tariffs.

There is also no direct relationship between the actual revenue needs of the government and a sales and use tax. There are only macroeconomic revenue estimates based on expected retail sales. The total amount of revenue collected by the government can vary dramatically, depending on total retail sales. The government may have a shortfall in revenue if there is a downturn in the economy. It may have a surplus of funds if there is an unexpected increase in retail sales. Surplus revenue amounts that are not dedicated funds and that are not rebated to taxpayers (which would be very difficult to do with a sales tax anyway) provide nothing but a slush fund and an opportunity for unwarranted spending by politicians, while a deficit is just rolled over as a future liability for taxpayers (delayed taxation) with the additional liability of debt interest.

But the greatest flaw in the sales and use tax may the same as one found in so many other bad taxes—the lack of relationship between government service and individual assessment. Individuals and businesses that are very productive for themselves and society (produce and trade more) don't necessarily receive any more government benefits. Quite the opposite. Because those individuals and businesses are more independent they may have less need for government services, but must—conversely—pay ever-higher taxes for the lower amount of government services they do receive. Socially and economically responsible enterprises thus endure increased punishment or penalty for being productive.

Ironically, those that engage in little or no outside trade with society, or produce little or nothing, may be the biggest beneficiaries of state services. Thus, individual tax liability under the sales tax can shift dramatically between citizens just because of the particular type of, and amount of, economic activity they engage in.

But however questionable in principle to those who eschew arbitrary assessment by an omnipresent state, the sales tax still appeals to political and economic pragmatists interested in powerful but easy revenue acquisition. The sales tax is a visible tax and a (basically) simple one, and this has been looked on as its advantage. Despite Canada's experience with their GST (national) sales tax, rising support has occurred in the United States in recent years for a national sales tax to replace the federal income tax. A formal campaign for a specific national sales tax, The National Retail Sales Tax, was recently initiated and has been gaining momentum.

The National Retail Sales Tax is described and analyzed with some other specific taxes offered by various reformers at the end of this chapter. But before that, a review of some more general tax types, including a philosophical dip into the VAT—the super, multi-tiered sales tax.

Could the VAT, with its special conditions, improve on the regular sales tax? Could the VAT be filled with the wine elixir of tax salvation, or is it a fiscal container of tax vinegar? Perhaps a nice PET, a Flat course, or going stylishly Retail will do. VAT or otherwise, please look carefully at package contents before taking home. There is a big difference between a rattling box of candy and a rattlesnake.

Value Added Tax (VAT)

The Value Added Tax (VAT) is a consumption tax similar to the regular sales tax, except that a commodity is assessed at each stage of production and sale—whether by manufacturers, wholesalers, or retail outlets—instead of just at the retail level. The VAT rate is applied on the value of the item at each sale, and the seller remits the tax to the government.

For instance, when iron ore is mined and sold to the smelter, a tax is charged; when the smelted ore is processed into metal ingots and sold to a components manufacturer, a tax is charged; when metal components are produced and sold to an appliance manufacturer, a tax is charged; and when a finished appliance is finally sold to the consumer, a retail sales tax is charged. For each new sale in the production process, however, the tax amounts paid from previous sales are subtracted from the gross VAT to give the amount owed for the last level of production (in other words, a credit is taken for the previous taxes—only the "value added" portion is effectively taxed at each level).

VAT taxes (popular in Europe) may incorporate exemptions or deductions on such items as capital investments, food, or health services. VATs can also have flat or variable rates. Sellers in the VAT invoice method retain receipts or documentation for each sale to demonstrate previous tax credits on items, or in the subtraction method, aggregate expenditure categories are used.[176] The theory behind VAT is that each business is taxed and therefore pays their relative share instead of taxing just the consumer at the retail level, as in a regular sales tax.

But the VAT is not any improvement over the regular sales tax. VAT suffers from all the limitations of the regular sales tax plus one major addition—multiple levels of assessment. The problem is the assumption in VAT that sellers at each level are paying a tax to the government. This assumption is only true if a seller is remitting what would otherwise be part of his profit. But it would be foolish to assume merchants won't incorporate increased costs, if they can, into the sales price of their products. In that case VAT ends up being nothing but a super sales tax on the consumer while creating increased accounting and management costs for producers and wholesalers.

Another major problem in any U.S. transition to a VAT would be older Americans who have already remitted taxes via the income tax and would have to pay taxes again on the *same money* through the VAT—a consumption tax—whenever they spent their savings (their accumulated earnings) that had *already* been taxed under the income tax.

The VAT is in reality just another mechanism of wanton state expropriation implemented for one purpose—to collect the maximum amount of immediate revenue from all levels of economic intercourse. The irony is that multiple assessments under the VAT that are expected to produce high tax revenue may do nothing but the opposite. Under the VAT inefficient imputed-income activities by businesses can increase, more of the population can move to barter or black market activity, and tax reporting and management costs can go up; thus, taxable sales can go down and the VAT collected can be less than expected. This may lead to an even higher VAT rate to compensate and more tax avoidance and evasion to compensate for that, with the consequent social and economic debilitations.

Inventory and Personal Property Tax

An inventory tax is a charge on the amount of unsold items a business has in stock. It is usually based on product cost (how much it cost the business to acquire it) and is levied periodically or annually. A personal property tax is similar, but is levied against individuals instead of businesses and is based on the retail value of products minus depreciation. An inventory tax can be based on any materials a business has to sell (supplies or assets), but personal property taxes are usually levied only on assets--items such as vehicles, furniture, art, books, sporting goods, clothing, and so on. Excise or sales taxes are assessed only at the time of purchase, where inventory and personal property taxes can be a recurring assessment as long as a business or individual retains ownership of the taxable items.

Major problems exist with the inventory and personal property taxes. The first is accurate accounting and enforcement. Business must expend extra effort to maintain tax records and to accomplish physical inventories at tax time to provide tax assessors with accurate information. Physical inventories by businesses to properly report tax liability and physical audits by the government to verify them can mean more downtime and cost in a business as well as indirect or direct inconvenience to customers. Since inventory and personal assets are highly transitory, taxes on them are subject to error or fraud. Items can be accidentally miscounted during an audit or deliberately moved prior to one being started.

Inventory taxes can also be great impediments to the proper functioning of business transactions in an otherwise free economy. Inventory taxes introduce an artificial inducement to sell or discard merchandise prior to tax assessment. Businesses cannot manage inventory on the basis of customer need under an inventory tax system, but must factor in the delivery and possession time of products based on tax assessment periods.

An annual 15 percent tax on retail inventory on April 1st, for instance, can prompt artificial discounts by a business to sell merchandise before the tax-assessment date, hold off delivery of new merchandise until after April 1st, or manage transactions and delivery outside the tax zone. There would be strong inducement to discount all sales prices up to the tax amount to remove the existing stock and thus relieve the inventory tax liability. With a 15 percent inventory tax, a 10 percent loss to the business through a sales-discount would still mean the business would be saving 5 percent over retaining inventory items and having them taxed.

Even customers who are recipients of discounts from price fluctuations, however, wouldn't necessarily receive any real discount over time because total sales costs, including taxes, are often transferred to the consumer by businesses through a hike in the base sales price (untaxed retail price). What customers can receive is fluctuation in service, price, and availability as businesses reduce and delay inventory to minimize taxes. Both businesses and consumers are hurt under the inventory tax system.

The inventory and personal property taxes can also penalize the prudent and careful, and exempt and thereby effectively subsidize those who spend money on immediate consumption. The person who wisely invests in inventory or personal assets is punished with annually recurring tax charges by the government, where the person who spends his resources immediately, and perhaps recklessly, suffers no such penalty.

The biggest problem of inventory and personal property taxes may be the same as many other poorly constructed tax systems—the tax can be an arbitrary assessment and not related to the relative level of government service provided the business or individual. Personal property taxes can also mean home inspections as government assessors delve into, count, and evaluate citizens' furniture, appliances, clothing, and trinkets. This tax may be the most immediately galling to working class citizens who recall only too well grammar school history classes on British invasions and searches of private homes during the Revolutionary War and arbitrary tax assessment of that period. This may be the reason local, state, or national politicians have moved away from personal property and excise taxes and toward more powerful but distant forms of taxation like the sales and income tax. Politicians understand that under the right circumstances and applied with the right finesse a 40 percent tax on income, for instance, can be much more palatable to citizens than a threepenny tax on tea ever was.[177]

Employment and Contractor Taxes

Employment taxes include direct taxes on both the employer and the employee, where the level of total assessment is related to total employee income; as the employee becomes more productive (earns more income) a greater tax is assessed. In addition, the employer is responsible for withholding a portion of the employee's wages or salary for payment towards the employee's estimated end-of-year tax liability, and for remitting the amount withheld, as well as the employer's tax assessment, to the government.

The direct employer taxes include Social Security and Medicare payments and the Federal Unemployment Tax (FUTA), and are calculated and remitted for each employee. The direct taxes on the employee (that are withheld from his paycheck by the employer) include a matching charge for Social Security and Medicare, and a federal income tax assessment based on the employee earnings minus declared dependent allowances. Businesses are required to forward the total—the direct employer taxes *and* the monies withheld from employees' paychecks—to the U.S. Treasury in daily, semi-weekly or monthly payments, depending on payroll size and operating conditions.[178]

Various federal regulations exist on how different types of compensation are treated in the assessment and payment of direct taxes and withholding amounts. Employee expense reimbursements, per diem or fixed allowances, wages not paid in money, moving expenses, meals and lodging, health insurance plans, medical care reimbursements, fringe benefits, sick pay, tips, family employees and supplemental wages all have regulatory interpretations.[179] Employees must submit information to the employers on dependents and other conditions, and information reports by businesses must accompany their tax deposits to the federal Treasury. Businesses can also be liable for reporting on, and sometimes withholding from, non-incorporated independent contractors doing business with them, and must report their dealings on IRS Form 1099 at year's end.

Employment taxes, effective parts of the income tax system, can be summarized this way: It has allowed the government to

- dictate an employer/employee or customer/contractor relationship between private citizens.
- force a third party—the business—into individual worker tax collections for future *estimated* tax liabilities.

- arbitrarily define what a business or individual must report and claim as compensation.
- expropriate money from workers just because the person (the employee) earns it.
- seize a worker's money before he even receives it.
- withhold, in some cases, money not ultimately due the state—without interest to the taxpayer.
- force workers to pay into government controlled retirement and medical insurance (Social Security and Medicare) instead of a fund of their choice.
- force a second party, the employer, to match and subsidize government insurance programs for the first party, the worker.
- seize worker and employer deposits in those insurance programs and spend the monies for general-fund purposes (Congressional expenditure of Social Security Trust Funds).
- inflict huge administrative costs on businesses and large inconveniences to workers.
- generally interfere and subvert the freedom of labor and capital in the marketplace.

Employment taxes are control mechanisms in the worker-state currently tolerated by much of the proletariat. Many have acceded to this grand worker collectivism only because of a belief that those who are more productive—those that earn more income—shall forfeit more than they themselves have.

This philosophy of mindless personal envy and government control was a characteristic of foreign governments that are now gone but whose populations still languish.[180] But so considered, is this a rational tax policy for funding a government intended to, among other things, protect American liberty?

Property Tax (Conventional)

The conventional property tax is based on the assessed market value of privately held real property. Real property is the legal term for land and permanent structures attached to it such as buildings, sidewalks, parking lots, and so on. The property tax is considered a direct tax that cannot be avoided and that must be paid directly by property owners—unlike excise taxes where people can, theoretically at least, decide not to buy the particular commodity being taxed. The tax has been a prime source of local and state revenue to fund general government services at those levels and to finance public schooling. Prospective real estate purchasers commonly examine current property tax rates to evaluate the ultimate cost of maintaining land ownership.

Property tax rates are usually not graduated and are the same for all assessed valuations. This makes the tax objective, simple to compute, and easy to account for in financial planning.

Other advantages of the property tax are that a substantial portion of the electorate is directly assessed any rate increase, it is very clear who is paying what, and the commonality of interest among the residents being taxed affords a basis for a unified response to excesses in government expropriation.

This is in stark contrast to the income tax system—where politicians can play taxes, deductions, subsidies and exemptions for and against various interest groups to increase seizure of private assets while indulging in political favoritism for selected groups. It can be much more difficult for citizens to analyze and oppose myriad income tax law specifications with an ever changing, complicated formula of tax exemptions and liabilities than with a relatively straightforward property tax.

However, the conventional property tax, while embracing some sound tax principles, also has some limitations and cannot be lauded as any replacement for the income tax. The ease with which legislatures have applied property tax rate increases have in many cases led to substantial increases in tax liability to the point that some people—especially those on fixed incomes—have faced bankruptcy and loss of their property.

Failure of state legislatures to provide property tax relief to citizens of California after skyrocketing property taxes there in the 1970s prompted a citizen initiative, Proposition 13, to change the California state constitution to require voter approval prior to major bond spending increases by local and state governments. The initiative passed and became law and taxes stabilized, despite apocalyptic warnings from opponents claiming that government services would be severely cut.[181]

But statutory or even state constitutional adjustments are not a panacea for conventional property tax inequities. There are underlying problems with the basic design of this type of tax, and the first problem is the basis of assessment.

Property is assessed on the basis of market value in the conventional property tax. But a current assessed valuation by a government assessor for any property is only an estimate of market value at the time of the appraisal, and that official appraisal can turn out to be different than the actual market value in current or later conditions. This occurs because of the inexactness of some appraisals, and the fact that general economic conditions—and the market value of property—can change before properties are re-appraised. Absolute value of real property, like all assets, is only demonstrated at the time of sale. Further, government resources must be spent tracking and inspecting property and in some cases fighting contests from property owners on official assessment valuations.

Irrespective of the value property is assessed at, however, conventional property tax assessment may have little to do with the level of government service to the property or to the landowner. Two identical private homes on the same sized lot, for instance, may have substantially different purchase prices. The home on the one side of town—say the East Side—might cost $50,000, and the same size home in a more exclusive neighborhood, say the West Side, may cost $250,000. But the property tax assessment, based on the indicated values and a uniform rate, would be five times greater for the home on the West Side than on the East Side—even though the relative level of state and local services for both locations does not differ. The available police, fire, and social services for the residents in both houses would be the same.

Property tax is not usually viewed in the context of wealth redistribution, but it can function as this, as well as being an easy source of money and a basis for spending proclivity among politicians. Logically, government can probably take more money from a person who probably has more (the owner of higher valued property) than from one who is probably less wealthy (one who owns lower valued property), and that is an inducement for many in government to implement and maintain the conventional property tax system.

And, of course, the conventional property tax has no relation to total wealth. A person with a million dollars could live in a large condominium in a less-expensive area of downtown and pay lower taxes, while a family with a modest income but living in a suburban area—for required schools and shopping—would have to pay higher taxes if housing prices (and thus conventional property-tax liability) were higher in the suburban area. The family would thus be saddled with higher net housing costs plus *higher* property taxes, even though they may have the same size and level-of-development of property *and receive no higher level of government service* than the millionaire.

But the property tax system does not just exist as a penalty on those who have invested in higher-cost housing locations. It can also act as a disadvantage to lower income individuals and as a mechanism of unwarranted land development and environmental degradation by government and wealthier special interests. The property tax affords the government and powered money interests in the private sector the ability to seize the land of other less wealthy and less politically connected citizens.

A citizen, for instance, might own a hundred acres of land that he has farmed and that has been in his family for generations. But because of land development on the periphery of his property or other variables, the market value of his land—and thus the *assessed* valuation of it—is increased. The state in this instance is affording the citizen *no* increase in government services but may be increasing the charge for those services many times because of the non-service-related standard of assessment.

The citizen farmer, in the above example, may desire to keep and continue to farm his land but be unable to because the increased taxation makes farming economically less feasible, to the point where the farmer might have to sell his property—or forfeit the land to the government for unpaid taxes.

Other private interests, then, that normally could not force the sale of the farmer's land can utilize the tax code to indirectly price the farmer out of possession and acquire the land for themselves. The result can be dense areas of developed land for industry and habitation with little intervening open space. Areas in cities may be many times less livable because government tax policy has been based on the market value of property—instead of relative service liability for the property and of the landowner.

Ironically, cries for maintenance of open space in many communities have been met by another tyranny—zoning manipulation—where the same farmer can have his land arbitrarily rezoned by the government and thus be precluded from developing his land (without compensation) and still be expected to meet the cost of rising tax assessments. And in this case the farmer may also not be able to sell the land to another farmer because increased tax assessments make farming less viable; he cannot sell it to developers because it cannot be developed; he cannot afford to pay the increased assessments—a triple Catch-22 which can lead, eventually, to a loss to the farmer on the sale of the property or to government seizure of the land for non-payment of taxes.

It is even possible for the government—depending on political zoning pressures and a legislative whim that a property is no longer suited to open space controls—to rezone acquired land to an industrial status and sell it to developers. The government could then realize a *development* profit from the land that had originally been seized for open space. The sound alternative—the concept of purchase and trade of use-covenants for rural land and open space preservation—has been ignored by various cities and counties in the country, and governments have instead moved toward dictatorial central planning policies. This condition has been exacerbated by the conventional property tax.

Regular homeowners are also not immune from dislocations caused by property tax laws. An example has been the area in and around Santa Fe, New Mexico, where between 1988 and 1992 assessed market values of properties increased dramatically. A beautiful, relatively pristine and attractive part of the American Southwest, New Mexico has attracted artists as well as wealthy residents from California and the East looking to relocate or purchase second homes. Increased popularity of the area has caused land values to escalate, however, and county property assessments increased for residents as much as 2600 percent![182]

Many of the original residents were not the nouveau-riche looking for a scenic second home or for federal income tax shelters, but were working class residents on fixed incomes who did not want their domicile threatened because of third-party real estate mechanizations that boosted their tax rates without a desired and corresponding increase in what taxes are supposed to be about—government service.

The Santa Fe tax situation might have been tolerable to the new, wealthy residents who chose to live in that area, or to development interests looking to force out landowners who could no longer afford the increased assessments. But for the original property owners, some of whose ancestors may have owned and lived on the properties since Spanish colonial times, it was not a joyful situation—whatever paper increases in market value might now exist for their properties. From a trailer park operator whose assessment went up from $286 to $7,599 in a year[183] to an elderly woman in tears at the assessors office over an eight-fold increase in her tax bill,[184] residents were stunned or dumbfounded at the insidious consequences of a property tax system that was, unfortunately, greatly accepted by state and county policymakers not only in New Mexico but throughout the United States.

The conventional property tax system allows the government to demand increased monies from citizens and residents based on potential—not actual—wealth increase, while providing no relative increase in service to home or business owners. Whatever wealth is incorporated into increased market value may not be realized financially by the owner until he sells it. And then if the owner does sell his property any dollar profit made over the owner's original purchase-price could be meaningless in a local market of vastly increased housing costs.

The only practical resolution for the homeowners in the Santa Fe situation who could not afford the new tax levy may have been to sell their property and move to a different locale. Original homeowners could thus be forced to forego their ownership—and their land heritage—and sell their property to wealthier and more powerful interests that could sustain the larger government tax assessment. Far from the traditional American ethos of protecting life and property, government policy focused on extraction of wealth and suppression of real property rights. Perhaps the rich can eat caviar, and the poor can move into a trailer park.

Some property tax reform, as previously mentioned, has occurred, but it has generally been linked to controls on increased assessment and not on any change in the fundamental *type* of property tax, or the principles on which the property tax is based. Reforms under Proposition 13 in California, for instance, had incorporated a variety of controls and grandfather clauses. The law did apply some pragmatic resolutions to excessive tax assessments but the very nature of the resolutions—some involving preferential tax rates for original homeowners—demonstrates the conceptual closet tax reformers kept themselves in. City-state mechanisms had been and would continue to be manipulated by interest groups. Politicians remained unaware, or confident that most of the electorate would remain unaware, of a better tax system remedy.

Citizens, though, have a choice in the construction of state and national tax systems. They can defer to existing tax systems like the conventional property tax and lay in hebetude most of the year, only rising in frenetic concern when the assessor comes, denying their American heritage and pleading like slavish serfs that property and tax be adjudged the minimum. Or they can discard the conventional, the unprincipled and the simplistic, and move to a more logical and principled application of tax law.

Gift Tax

The federal gift tax is an assessment on amounts of monies over $10,000 transferred as gifts. Smaller amounts are not taxed, perhaps because effective compliance, auditing, and enforcement would be extremely difficult if not impossible. And then too, the scenario of Junior and his eight-year-old birthday party gift givers having to retain competent accountant and tax attorney counsel when they celebrate with ice cream and cake and exchange party favors may be too much for even the most acquisitive and hardened politician.

The justification for the tax assessment in gift giving is the existence of the gift-giving transaction. There is no creation of wealth. There is only the transference of wealth. But again, the modern rationale of government taxation has been to identify wealth at a point of transaction *and just because of the transaction* lay a claim to part of the asset.

The individual who has originally and lawfully produced a resource and is giving it as a gift can be assumed to have paid the previous, relevant taxes associated with it. It should be of no practical consequence to the government whether ownership of the resource then resides with the original person or the person being given the gift. But transference to an individual means assessment for the tax collector—the condition of assessment doesn't have to be logical. The federal gift tax on large gifts is based on a philosophy of current tax legislators that ensures co-recipient status for the government at all the bigger gift-giving occasions in society.

The Estate Tax

The estate, or inheritance, tax is a charge on the assets of an individual after he dies, and also against the beneficiaries of his estate. A deceased person who previously worked hard and built capital will also have likely paid a substantial amount in taxation before his death. The capital resources thus created would already have been taxed. There is obviously no increased provision of government services to him when he is dead. But his resources still exist, and transfer of assets—from the deceased to the beneficiaries—is the physical condition recognized in tax law that permits the government's claim on, and confiscation of, part of the assets.

Enormous amounts of money are spent today on attorneys and accountants to build "Living Trusts" or special investment portfolios to protect assets from government seizure after a principal dies. This is a huge waste of resources as well as helping preclude a free-flow of personal capital in the American economy. The fact that estate taxes can sometimes be avoided in part or in full by legal manipulation of assets (via expenditure of financial and tax planning resources) makes the estate tax another part of the tax code that doubly mocks the American people.

The estate or inheritance tax is reminiscent of strangers ransacking a dead man's house while his children are held back to watch. The politicians who support the estate tax are like hyenas, jackals and vultures roaming a hot African plane, not satisfied with what they can eat that's alive, and chasing away families of tribesmen to eat the remains of the dead.

Another reason the estate tax is a bad idea? It's generally not a good social policy to have a people's government rewarded when citizens die.

Excess Profits Tax

The excess profits tax has been used in the past in the federal income tax system as an additional levy on the portion of corporate profits that were considered "excessive" by the government in that they exceeded "normal" earnings.

But calculation of excess profits taxes has not been simple. Since business profit variance is common (a business can be profitable one year and less so the next), excess-profits tax regulations have provided for income averaging over several years. Long and complex tax code defined numerous details and contingencies in which net income was computed against invested capital, which then determined the excess profits tax for the current tax year. A corporation's total tax liability would then consist of the normal income tax and an additional income tax on the portion of profits considered excessive, plus, of course, any other taxes (i.e., excise taxes, property tax, and so on). Excess profits taxes have been proposed or implemented on specific commodities, such as oil (called windfall profits tax in this case), as a kind of excise-income tax mesh.[185] The excess profits tax, whatever its particular composition or name, is an example of double taxation.

A modern equivalent of the excess profits tax is the Alternative Minimum Tax, or AMT. This complicated income tax mechanism can apply whenever a taxpayer is identified as having "too many" deductions that reduce their regular tax below a certain level. Originally implemented to close tax shelters of the very rich, the AMT may now be applicable to a growing number of Americans that just dare to be more successful than the average Joe. Tax returns showing the AMT rose from 132,103 in 1990 to 414,106 in 1995.[186] The absurdity of the income tax system is demonstrated very adequately here—the allowance of deductions for citizens in tax remittance but a penalty if they fully use them.

A free society depends on individuals expending risk and resources to develop and produce new products and services. Businesses are less likely to provide new or improved products if the increased risk they would endure is not linked to a chance of increased reward. The logical values of products are the prices consumers say they are—the prices they are willing to pay. Denial of profit is a denial of price legitimacy. And how is divergence of profit to others that shared neither development labor or investment risk warranted?

The excess profits tax and similar constructions are nothing but an additional penalty on the innovative, creative, and industrious business or individual, and another predatory effort and attempted government seizure based on people's economic success. Proponents of excess profit tax mechanisms think it's not enough to implement both tax increases *and* graduated, increasing tax rates but want to lay another layer of assessment and suppression on those who would work "too" efficiently.

Personal Expenditure Tax (PET)

The Personal Expenditure Tax (PET) is an example of a personal consumption tax, where taxpayers are taxed according to what they spend (instead of what they earn as in the income tax). Conceptually, PET is the reverse of the income tax.

Advocates envision a PET as being progressive (rates increase as spending increases), having a personal exemption, and requiring preparation of a return listing income and expenditures. The individual tax base would be equal to the taxpayer's income, minus any savings, plus any withdrawals. Borrowing would be treated as taxable expenditure and repayments as non-taxable savings. Record keeping "would be only slightly more extensive than those under a personal income tax." Financial institutions would have to keep track of deposits and withdrawals, and report this information to the government.[187]

But merely taking tax revenue when resources are spent instead of when income is earned solves nothing. Replacing the income tax with the PET would be like prying the income tax monkey off the nation's back—and then turning the little critter upside down and putting him back on. Concepts, complexities and unjustified assessment that are characteristic of the income tax would reincarnate in mutated form with PET. And how many billions would the transition from the income tax system cost? Perhaps there should be a warning with this tax: "Danger—PET may devour master."

The Fair and the FAST

The Fair Tax Act of 1983 drafted by Senators Bill Bradley and Richard Gephardt was an attempt to streamline the income tax, and is a good example of the repeated proposals or actual implementations of income tax modifications over the years attempting to salvage the income tax system. The name "Fair Tax" is perhaps a much more optimistic suggestion than objective description.

The goal of those advocating the Fair Tax was to broaden the tax base and reduce tax shelters, reduce tax rates to increase incentives, and maintain a distribution of tax liability and tax preferences associated with hardships. More specifically, the tax changes would exclude from exemption various employer-provided fringe benefits, remove some current capital gains exclusions, reduce depreciation allowances, modify tax-exempt financing rules, and generally remove or reduce various other exemptions, while boosting the standard deduction and reducing and simplifying tax rates.[188] Perceived as a collection of small, manageable steps in the improvement of the tax system, the Fair Tax was thought to be a step in the right direction.

Other proposals have been offered in the past for income tax modifications, including the "FAST," or "Fair and Simple Tax" offered by former Representative and cabinet official Jack Kemp and Senator Robert Kastin. But despite the reforms under the Fair and FAST tax proposals problems inherent within the income tax system itself are ignored, and the central issue of basic, sound tax system design is not addressed. What is the significance when the vice squad hands new music sheets to the piano player but the brothel remains open? Substantially more change in tax reform is required than arbitrary revisions of questionable validity to an already inherently poor tax system.

The National Retail Sales Tax

The National Retail Sales Tax (NRST) is a proposed national sales tax, sponsored by a group called the Americans for Fair Taxation, and designed to replace the federal income tax and all payroll, self-employment, estate and gift taxes.[189]

The initial, proposed rate of the NRST is 23 percent assessed on all goods and services at the final point of consumption (the retail level). Business-to-business purchases are not taxed—at least not for those items used in resale. Used items would not be taxed. Social Security recipients would receive a rebate in monthly advances equivalent to the sales tax they pay on projected monthly purchases. Households under the official government Poverty Level would receive a similar rebate. Products exported by domestic companies would not be subject to the tax, but imports sold in the United States would be.

State governments would have the option of combining any state sales taxes with the collection of federal sales taxes and forwarding the federal portion to the U.S. Treasury. Retail businesses would serve as primary collection agents for the federal government and both the businesses and participating state governments would receive a collection fee for collecting and forwarding revenue.

The NRST is also called "The Fair Tax," the adjective "fair" being widely applied by proponents of various tax theories, some of who like to include it in the title description of their tax. Less prominent is a consistent, underlying definition of what they consider fair.

Proponents of the NRST make many claims, and the tax might be initially appealing to some as a direct and simple solution to the income tax. NRST advocates do advance a very important point—the removal of the federal income tax system and the benefits that would accrue to the individual in particular and the economy in general from that action.

But the value of the NRST itself as a sound replacement tax is more than just questionable. All the inherent problems of the sales tax, previously identified, are present with the NRST. The tax theory incorporates the concepts of both equity of condition and ease of extraction as justifications, rather than liability for service rendered.

The NRST is completely arbitrary like all sales taxes, and punishes interpersonal commerce while imputed income remains untouched. The tax is also discriminatory toward new products, because sales of used items are not taxed. Innovation could thus be stifled in the development of new products, or extensive energies expended to ensure sales items are "pre-traded" or "refurbished" at the retail level to ensure their classification as used so that sellers could avoid the new-item sales-tax liability.

Businesses that engage in export would have a distinct advantage over companies selling domestically as there would be no tax on their export sales. The relative loss in sales volume caused by higher retail prices (because of the added sales tax) could be disincentive to both marketing and sales efforts by domestic American companies. Companies engaging in domestic sales—and general consumers in America—would assume not only regular sales tax liability but also the implied cost of government service for export businesses not paying any tax.

The severe impact of the NRST on domestic trade could provide a strong incentive for companies to locate production and sales facilities out of country to avoid the burdensome tax. Substantial industry and jobs could be lost while American consumers in the United States would still have to pay the sales tax on imported goods sold here—perhaps for some of the very goods they personally used to produce here as workers before their former employers moved production offshore.

The severe rate of NRST taxation—more than triple that of some state sales taxes—could be an inducement not only for imputed income activities or barter, but for illegal transactions in the underground economy—raising the possibility of increased law enforcement problems associated with smuggling and organized crime.

Other exclusions built into the tax, such as the exemption for Social Security and "poverty" level transactions are also a problem. Here the tax is incorporating social management functions with general revenue acquisition. Like so many other tax schemes the NRST is constructed to be "fair" by manipulating tax schedules to provide an effective, forced redistribution of resources in the economy. Taxation and social assistance are separate functions, but the proponents of the NRST imply that somehow with *this* tax the two will be successfully integrated.

A substantial amount of bureaucracy will still be necessary to track incomes and expenditures to verify eligibility for exclusions from the NRST—hence income assessment could still be a prime factor in this "sales" tax. It is also likely that a substantial amount of legislation will have to be accomplished to define income and expenses to determine that eligibility. For instance, a low-income worker might have a small side business where he receives $100,000 in gross revenue but only realizes an annual $13,000 in net profit after expenses. He would be forced to collect sales taxes on the $100,000 and then "demonstrate" his personal net income to qualify for a low-income exemption.

Complicated income tax returns may still be required under the NRST for those persons, as well as forcing business people everywhere to become tax collection agents of the federal as well as state governments. A huge number of individual economic transactions would have to be chronicled every year for the federal government. And, as previously mentioned, it may not be so easy to define taxable sales transactions in the myriad industries and types of transactions that exist in the modern economy. Ever more elaborate regulations, exclusions and rebates may occur in legislative "adjustments" to the law to make the tax more "fair," including complicated regulations to define various products and services as new or used. The NRST is in reality a less-than-simple system of sales tax *plus* income tax mechanisms that would provide both old and new problems in tax administration and enforcement.

The most serious problem with the NRST, however, is that of many other existing tax systems—there is no measure of relative service by the state and corresponding assessment to the taxpayer. Proponents may claim the NRST is a very powerful and convenient means of assessing and acquiring government revenue. But mere efficiency for the government—which is only purported of the NRST but may not exist anyway—is not enough. A sound tax system must rest on a principle of proper, objective assessment by a tax-neutral federal government.

The Flat Income Tax

Politicians, pundits, and economists over the past two decades have vocalized disdain for tax code complexity and pined to the government for effective tax reform, calling on the government to do something—perhaps anything—to make the federal tax system simpler and more uniform. Common have been complaints without any suggested remedy, or suggestions of reform without specificity. But recent, definitive tax reform propositions have occurred.

One result has been the NRST, but perhaps the idea that has received the most attention has been the so-called flat tax. The flat tax is an income tax, but it is one where the same tax rate applies to all income levels. This is viewed by many people as a universally applicable—and thus fairer—tax mechanism.

The past couple of years have brought heightened interest and debate in the concept of a flat tax, and both Republican and Democratic politicians have put forth flat tax proposals. A major Republican candidate, businessman Steve Forbes, incorporated the flat tax into his presidential election campaign platform in 1996. While some conservative intellectuals have promulgated implementation of the flat tax in speech and debate other, liberal individuals have also articulated support, implying a level of endorsement across the political spectrum.

Some of the reform proposals for a new federal flat tax, however, have been about as flat as the Rocky Mountains with one tax-proposal having as many as five new rate structures (to replace the five old rate structures) and a continuing retinue of filing requirements for interest, dividends, capital gains, pensions, social security income, and so on.[190] Surely then, for some, the flat tax means not much more than rearranging the deck chairs on the Titanic. One serious flat tax proposal, however, has been the Armey-Shelby Flat Tax.

The Armey-Shelby Flat Tax, sponsored by Senator Richard Shelby and House Majority Leader Dick Armey, is a proposed income tax system with one income tax rate applicable to all individual and business tax filers, no matter what their level of income above a personal deduction allowance. The principles on which the tax code is based, according to Representative Armey, is that first, a tax should only have one rate; second, it should only tax income once and individual economic choices should not be subsidized or penalized in the tax code; and third, families should not be assessed any tax on income below their basic living allowance.[191]

The Armey-Shelby Flat Tax would provide a personal exemption of $11,350 and $5,300 for each child. This would mean a family of four would have an exemption for the first $33,300 of income. Under the Flat Tax system income can be realized at the business level where it is taxed, but the same profit when remitted to the owners or investors (as in the form of dividends) is not taxed again. Commissions, salaries, wages and pensions are taxed as personal income. Income—whether from business or employment—is only taxed once. Social Security benefits, representing previous deposits already taxed from wage earners, would not be taxed. Businesses could deduct operating expenses and the full purchase price of assets (such as vehicles, machinery, and furniture) the year of purchase. Depreciation for tax purposes, and extensive reporting for that, would be eliminated. There would be no specialized exemptions, deductions, or investment credits—including no deductions for charities. The Flat Tax would be a replacement for the current personal and corporate income taxes and the estate and gift taxes, but would not affect other taxes like excise taxes or tariffs.

Proponents of the Flat Tax imply dramatic reform. But two big practical problems of the income tax system remain—the legal definition of net income and the exclusion of imputed income. The flat-taxers continue a merry jig with those incubi instead of facing them head on. The huge problems with individuals and businesses avoiding or evading tax by classification of expenditures as expenses and the loss of economic efficiency through artificial, governmental favoritism of imputed income would continue. The proponents of the Flat Tax also broach an alleged remedy in the immediate, pragmatic sense only, and the principles underpinning the Armey-Shelby bill do not differ much from those of the existing income tax system.

There is no relationship between service and assessment in the Flat Tax. This abandonment of American principle can lead to the creation of a tax that seems on the surface (and seemed in 1913) to be very reasonable but can ultimately lead somewhere else. The principles of social management, even if reduced, are still an integral part of the Flat Tax system. How long would it take before legislators were modifying the tax to "help" someone in a "more appropriate" manner or to make things more "fair" for their constituents?

The government still arbitrarily denotes income and expense categories under the Flat Tax and imposes tax liability merely because people are productive. The choice of a systematized, *graduated* confiscatory expropriation of income being replaced by a systematized, *flat-rate* confiscatory expropriation of income induces little confidence in Americans looking for substantive reform of the federal tax system.

One thing popular debate on flat taxes in general and the Armey-Shelby Flat Tax in particular have demonstrated, though, is the vituperation that occurs when any substantive tax reform is seriously proposed in a political forum. The Flat Tax, though still an income tax, may be less injurious functionally and an improvement over the existing federal income tax structure, and may represent effective change—even if only a change within the income tax system itself.

Opponents of any substantial change in the existing tax structure, however, are so alienated from the founding precepts of American freedom and wedded to the concepts of subjugation, manipulation and social engineering that they continue to implement through the tax code conditions formerly possible only through the overseer's lash. This means that a debate for and implementation of effective tax reform may never be won while accepting opponents' assumptions—or implied operational tenets—of current taxation. The fundamental axioms of taxation (or basis in tax theory) in current governmental tax policy must be analyzed and replaced where appropriate, and then new tax law constructed on those principles.

VI. Tax System Design Lost and Found

We are not going to get tax reform by congressional committee in Washington or in the state house in this or other states voting lower taxes or voting an improved structure of taxes. That way is hopeless. It's a way we've been trying for years on end and it has gotten us nowhere.

The only effective tax reform is tax reduction. . . . The only feasible way of stopping tax increases is via constitutional limitation on government spending and government taxing.

From a 1978 speech by Professor Milton Friedman, economist, arguing for property tax reform and a state constitutional change, Proposition 13, before the American Education League in Pasadena, California, during the period of state-wide debate on the measure.[192]

A "good" tax system must be a well-designed tax system. A well-designed tax system is based on sound principles. But what are the real principles of a sound tax system?

Some have argued in history that taxation should have less or nothing to do with real level of government service to the person billed for taxes but everything to do with social and economic management. The marginal-utility doctrine of some nineteenth-century economists said that the rich should pay more than the poor up to the point psychic pain is equalized.

Of course, one could probably not give this economic prescription to his company's Accounts Receivable department in their invoicing to customers without an incredulous reaction and punitive response from a higher executive, so it is surprising (or maybe it isn't) that the theory would ever hold in government legislatures. Anyhow, would not the theory of marginal-utility mean it would pay for a poor person to never become more successful than the point at which the poor person's wealth plus the psychic pain of the rich achieved equilibrium?

In another somewhat facetious analysis a twentieth-century author in economics, Professor Harold M. Groves, said that the theory of marginal-utility applied in actual policy today, of course, could never be equitable as, reportedly, the Republicans are more susceptible to psychic pain than the Democrats.[193] But whatever validity is lacking in marginal-utility theory has not dissuaded modern politicians from advising constituents they "feel your pain" and from responding in sympathy through federal appropriations and tax subsidy.[194]

But putting an abstruse theory on redistribution aside and turning to functional specifics, the question of what makes a good tax has not gone unexamined in political spheres. A report was commissioned in 1996 by (then) Senator Bob Dole and Speaker of the House Newt Gingrich and provided recommendations the authors believed would provide positive tax reform. The Kemp Commission on Tax Reform, as it was called, identified several things a good tax should have: fairness, economic growth, simplicity, stability, neutrality, and visibility. Are these conditions the true requirements of a good tax system and if so, how is each of these qualities defined?

The first condition identified by the Commission as necessary for a good tax is fairness. Certainly, as every child learns in his first week of kindergarten, it is best to be fair with people we learn from and play with. On the way to and then past college for many people, however, the concept of *economic* fairness seems never to have been given any attention beyond the traditional, recurrent neo-collectivist indoctrinaire popular today in our media and educational institutions.

Yes, fairness. But fairness based on what? Is fairness to be based on individual ability to pay (the harder working, innovative worker who saves and invests capital coerced to service the more profligate and less industrious); family need (the responsible individual who defers social life and marriage forced to support the procreation and familial advantages of another that chooses to be, economically, ill prepared for such activity); or amount of income received in free trade (the productive punished for being productive and engaging in commerce with their fellow man, and the less industrious or economically cloistered rewarded with subsidy)?

For various tax system exponents "fairness" has nothing to do with an objective assessment standard but is *their* divination of an appropriate equity of economic *condition* for societal participants. And this perceived equity of condition is to be enforced under dictates of the state through a tax code. Despite the popular jingoism in the two major political parties with respect to liberty and free enterprise, political players have cloyed mercilessly with collectivist policies in federal taxation. Legislators can't decide whether they want a tax system or a welfare system, so they try to integrate the two, as well as staking protections or benefits for regional and organizational interests into the tax code. "Fairness," as Alice might say, "is a word that means just what you want it to mean."

The second characteristic, economic growth, is curious. A poorly constructed tax may inhibit economic growth, but how can a good tax promote it, other than be less inhibiting? And how is it that powers in the state apparatus think they should be "promoting" anything, even economic growth, when it is their Constitutional charge to protect people's liberty, whether those people choose to engage in activities associated with conventional economic "growth," or not?

It is true that a good tax system does not interfere with economic freedom, and therefore effectively *supports that which is desired by participants in a free economy,* and thus positive economic growth where it is desired—where positive economic growth is defined as more efficient production and free trade of goods and services by free men. But if current tax architects continue to believe that the economy (really meaning *people* within the economy) can be controlled and managed through tax mechanizations "for their own good" and "for the greater good of the country" then nothing is meant by "promoting economic growth" other than the traditional, collectivist subjugation of the individual to produce economic and societal conditions desired by those in power.

The third item, simplicity, is questionable. A simple tax can be nothing more than a simple, direct means of expropriating money. History is filled with simple, but unjust, tax levies on peoples. The country does not necessarily need something simple, but something that *functions easily* (or simply).

For instance, a highway bridge spanning a chasm may *appear* simple and should be functionally so to those traveling over it, and it is true that the individual mathematical formulas and engineering precepts used in its construction, viewed independently, may be simple truths. But design and construction of the bridge is *not* in any way simple, and it results from careful, reasoned planning and skilled physical construction. A tax should be like that bridge and not simplistic, but rather properly designed and economical, or *simple to operate*—both for taxpayers *and* government tax administrators.

The next condition in a good tax, according to the Commission, is stability, and they are indeed correct on this one. Stability means a tax that is *not* often changed and altered, but is one on which consumers and businesses can base their economic planning. Without stability in governmental taxation general economic stability is lessened—which can lead to social instability and worse. Stability may be the most important concept in a sound tax, and it will be further explored later in this chapter.

Neutrality means equally applicable liability for taxpayers and lack of favoritism by the state for specific groups or individuals—yet here is where most tax reformers miss the boat when applying their artificial constructions and exemptions. Neutrality is important, but current tax legislators' definition of neutrality may be as ambiguous or convoluted as their definition of fairness.

The last characteristic the Commission identifies is visibility. Visibility means citizens are cognizant of taxes in economic exchanges and they are not hidden, as in a VAT tax. People should know what they are paying the government in any economic transaction. Visibility is an important principle and the Commission should be lauded for identifying it. But with that and all the other principles the Commission believes is important in a sound tax system, what new tax does the Commission then finally recommend?

The Commission's report goes on, incredibly, to endorse a modified *income tax*. Their description: "One rate, coupled with a generous personal exemption, together produce a progressive average tax rate. Low-income taxpayers would owe little or no tax. But everyone who earns enough to cross the threshold of the exemption would face exactly the same tax rate on any additional income."[195]

This sounds very similar to the first modern income tax passed back in 1913. And everyone knows what happened after that. Suggested tax reform under yet another commiserating commission had really come to little, but politicians could preen and promise to be "fair" and taxpayers could continue to slink like hounds hoping for the dog biscuit of a lower income tax rate, or the fallen table scraps of deductions and exemptions. The hunters and hounds continually seek their game birds of fiscal feast—only too often it is a trespass on other people's property for other people's resources through the neo-collectivist gate of wanton tax expropriation.

But it is said that action speaks louder than words. The real commitment of many politicians to their concepts of fairness, simplicity, stability, neutrality, and visibility, may have been inadvertently exhibited in the September 1997 Congressional Tax Hearings on citizen tax problems. These Hearings brought in for testimony taxpayers who had allegedly been mistreated by the IRS, and various individual incidents were detailed. The Hearings received much publicity but virtually no detailed analysis. What was the real state of federal taxation when these hearings were held?

Congress in collusion with state governments at the turn of the century had implemented the Sixteenth Amendment to the Constitution to conditionally deprive citizens of their right to property in a grand promise of wealth for all through redistribution. Then after eighty-four years of capital manipulation, wanton expropriation, and economic favoritism *directed* by Congress, members of Congress listened yet again, in a supposedly compassionate vein, to citizens alleging inappropriate behavior by *tax collection* agents. And as an answer to the immediate citizen complaints Congress promised another committee to oversee *tax collection* activities.[196]

Viewing the Committee hearings was like watching a movie where a criminal godfather listens to functionaries from the neighborhood and then in a patronizing gesture promises to talk to his people about being more polite when they make the collection rounds. Here was a situation beyond pathetic, and to many downright absurd, where the focus was on allegations of bad activity by civil servants instead of bad Congressional law—the source of the problem.

And those on the tax reform bandwagon would continue to play the tunes of tax reform with a pounding drum—if not coherent melody—through 1998. One curious song arrived in June of that year with the passage of the Tax Code Termination Act in the House, which would repeal the existing tax code—without replacing it with anything.[197] Politicians that voted for the Act could always say *they* were for reform, but not have to be specific about any *type* of reform; nor would they have to worry about practical consequences if the Senate would not pass, and the President would not sign, that piece of legislation.

The House and the Senate did get together on another tax bill in June 1998 that promised major revamping of the IRS—along with $13 billion in tax breaks for speculative investors, the restaurant industry and divorced spouses.[198] Legislation passed in the House and Senate in July 1998 that provided for additional taxpayer protections in tax cases that went to court, but this was hardly a groundbreaking recognition in taxpayer civil rights—two hundred and nine years after the birth of the United States Constitution modern legislators finally agreed that a court order should exist before the federal government confiscated a person's home.[199] And there was no replacement or even serious modification of the basic tax structure under the new law, only legislators implying they can save taxpayers from IRS excesses through more Congressional manipulation of the existing tax code.

Government officials still had taxpayers under the yoke of a costly and confusing tax system, and the officials were trusting in the abeyance of citizen demand for any more radical change.

Is this current, limited debate in the public forum, confusing legislation and paucity of substantive tax reform the best that citizens can hope for? Or could there be found, in past history and in modern reason, guidelines to a better tax system?

Adam Smith's Maxims

The positive and negative aspects of various taxes have been discussed, but the exact criteria of a sound tax system have not yet been defined. What can be deferred to historically as some kind of reference for the application of a sound tax system? Perhaps attention again should return to the Enlightenment when American and world thinkers chose to focus on the basic rights of man. Across the Atlantic some primary economic principles and concepts were being identified that would provide explanation and justification for Western economies into our century. That economic analysis did not ignore taxation.

The man considered the father of modern capitalism, celebrated eighteenth-century Scottish economist Adam Smith, stated four qualities, or maxims, of sound taxation. It is important to note here that the United States of America in the last part of the twentieth century, currently the world's biggest and only superpower and the processor of trillions of tax dollars, has a tax system—the income tax—that doesn't even meet one of those criteria.

As the United States enters the twenty-first century it is as important as ever for the country to address existing fiscal problems and base any tax system it implements on sound principles. Adam Smith's maxims, or Canons,[200] follow with a view of how they are met, or not met, in various instances by current federal tax law.

(1) ***Taxes Should be Equal or Equitable.*** Smith talked of people supporting government through taxation "as nearly possible in proportion to their respective abilities; that is in proportion to the revenues which they respectively enjoy under the protection of the state."[201] The "ability" Smith talks about here is the ability to meet a general service liability, "protection," by the state based on wealth, or revenue received. A person with greater land (increased rent receipts), or greater revenue, would normally have a greater land area or greater wealth for the state to service or protect, and taxes would be in that proportion, and it can hardly be concluded by this particular statement of Smith that he believed that taxes should be used for redistribution.

Smith did talk of progression in one of his writings,[202] but he rejected the net income tax because it would cause insuperable administrative problems.[203] His other remarks that taxes should fall on individuals "like the expense of management to the joint tenants of a great estate, who are obliged to contribute *in proportion to their respective interests in the estate*" [italics inserted][204] is an indication of support for assigning tax liability in the manner of rational economic exchange. Thus, relative tax liability for service rendered—and *not* the ability to pay theory and government redistribution that is used as an excuse for today's governmental tax mechanizations—may be the most proper interpretation of Smith's first maxim.

(2) ***Taxes Should be Certain and Not Arbitrary.*** Smith wrote

> The certainty of what each individual ought to pay is, in taxation, a matter of so great importance that a very considerable degree of inequity, it appears, I believe, from the experience of all nations, is not near so great an evil as a very small degree of uncertainty.[205]

A bad tax that is correctly administered and clearly understood by people, and who know exactly what their tax liabilities are, can be much better than a "fair" tax that is poorly administered and not understood. The income tax, unfortunately, cannot be correctly administered, is not understood by the people, they have great difficulty in determining their liability, and is not "fair."

(3) ***Taxes Should be Convenient.*** The income tax is, in a sense, very convenient for the government. A legal edict is directed to all businesses in the country and money is taken from wages (withheld in payroll deductions) before citizens are even paid. However, it is hardly convenient for citizens to lose liquidity from wage withholding or by overpayment in estimated taxes.

(4) ***Taxes Should be Economical.*** Tax preparation and remittance should not be obtrusive, obstructive, or discouraging to the taxpayer;[206] and tax administration and collection should not be difficult, costly, and discouraging to the government tax agency. Smith is commenting here from the eighteenth century, but see how applicable the following statement is to modern times:

> An injudicious tax offers a great temptation to smuggling [or evasion]. But the penalties of smuggling must rise in proportion to the temptation. The law, contrary to all the ordinary principles of justice, first creates the temptation, and then punishes those who yield to it; and it commonly enhances the punishment too in proportion to the very circumstance which ought certainly to alleviate it, the temptation to commit the crime.[207]

The fact is, the modern income tax system has been extremely obtrusive, obstructive, discouraging, difficult, and costly to citizens, and equally discouraging to many civil servants and specialists in the Internal Revenue Service and Congressional and Executive budget agencies. What would Adam Smith have said to the $202 billion compliance cost (and $538 billion *total* operating cost) of the federal income tax system? Too bad Mr. Smith can't go to Washington.

Requirements of a Sound Tax System

Definitions for a sound tax system can be refined further, beyond Adam Smith's original maxims. The following are proffered requirements for the implementation of a sound tax system, applicable in any era. A sound tax must be

1. Relative to Appropriations

Government must have a need for revenue before it imparts a tax and the amount actually assessed must be relative to the budgetary need. This may seem so obvious that it needs no written definition. But the lack of definition in funding expenditures, that is, the lack of any logical correlation between government expenditures and the particular taxes that fund them disposes government toward unwarranted expropriation and then excess spending.

Taxes whenever possible should be dedicated—like excise taxes from gas sales reserved for road construction and maintenance. Obviously, there are many general government services, like national defense and the courts that cannot be funded from a direct link to an excise tax or fee but must be funded from general assessments. But whatever appropriation (expenditure) is to be made by the government, the gross amount of taxation for the appropriation—the assessment to taxpaying citizens—*should not exceed the appropriation.*

(This is obviously not the condition with the income tax. There is only a gross, macroeconomic estimate for future expected revenue at the time income tax law is passed, and individual tax liabilities may not be known by most taxpayers until months after the end of the tax year. Individual citizens can be forced to pay and pay as they are more productive (produce more income) under a tax levy that has no relationship between their payments and commensurate share of budget liability.)

Tax law should never be indefinite but provide for automatic expiration of assessments after the cost of an appropriation or budget has been met. Or in the case of on-going government services, the law should have an expiration date that forces review and passage of a new tax law prior to any renewal of government assessments. This is in the great tradition of fiscal restraint by our Colonial forefathers.

Legal strictures should be put in place to automatically rebate tax revenue back to the citizens when excess collections occur, or have a dedicated secondary purpose for any excess funds specified in the original appropriation bill. Citizens are not work horses, and certainly not work horses to be beat when enough dirt has already been plowed. Government exists to accomplish specific tasks that are defined by the people's representatives. Taxes must be relative to actual appropriations.

2. Equitable to the Citizen

Equitable to the Citizen is Adam Smith's first maxim, and a major point if not the clear direction in his arguments for equity was for taxes to be in proportion to a person's economic interest. A cattle baron with a ten thousand acre cattle ranch has a lot more to service and protect through general and specific government services than another fellow with one acre and one goat. *Equitable in the context of tax law must be defined in rational economic terms as relative liability for service rendered (or to be rendered).*

Tax equity, or just liability for relative share of government service, has nothing to do with ability to pay for that liability, and welfare assistance or the extension of government largess through the tax code has nothing but an adulterous affect on private and public accounting and management. Temporary inability to meet any tax liability can be met like any other debt liability in commerce but the federal government cannot be discounted by denying tax liabilities before they are objectively assigned.

Assistance and subsidy can be provided for whatever reason by the state—food, housing, education, or tax remittance, for instance—but since by the action of the government such assistance is a *public* action, a separate appropriation and allocation should be made (instead of exemptions or subsidy through the tax code) so that universal *public* liability is assumed instead of liability being cloaked and shifted to a discriminated portion of the tax base. Interest (immediate tax) on public debt (deferred tax) should be assessed individual taxpayers in the same way taxes for other appropriations are—that is, relative to the individual's tax-service liability.

3. Objective and Certain

This incorporates Smith's second maxim about taxes being certain and not arbitrary. Again, this may seem to be an obvious condition and not in need of emphasis. But the federal income tax is a tax where liability can be a matter of individual interpretation; the tax has created nothing but avoidance, evasion, frustration, or cynicism in much of the public and the tax has *not* been objective and certain. Alexander Hamilton, the nation's first Treasury Secretary, wrote:

> The genius of liberty reprobates everything arbitrary or discretionary in taxation. It exacts that every man by a definite and general rule should know what proportion of his property the state demands. Whatever liberty we may boast in theory, it cannot exist in fact while [arbitrary] assessments continue.[208]

Whatever the particular design and mechanics of a tax system are, both the taxpayers and the government need to know the basis for assessment and need to be able to compute quickly and easily individual tax liabilities.

A tax to be objective and certain must be visible in current and proposed rates. It must not inhibit economic planning, stability and growth—that is, changes in tax rates and liability conditions must not occur unexpectedly or randomly and cause unwarranted dislocation or hardship. Regular citizens, the press, and the government must all be able to review assessments and collections from an open, public record. Calculation of relative liability for government appropriations down to the line-item level should be possible so that shared fiscal responsibility is both known and felt by taxpayers.

Objective and certain conditions have to be applicable from the budget process prior to law (so citizens can submit informed input on proposed expenditures), and then on through taxation, remittance, and allocation.

4. Economical to Operate

Smith's last two maxims, *Convenience* and *Economy of Operation*, are both contained here. Tax system assessment, remittance and audit functions must be practical, both for the government and the taxpayer.

The citizen should be able to accomplish record keeping, tax law review (per his personal situation), liability validation, tax remittance, and obtain government assistance when necessary all within a minimum of time and personal expense. The government should also be able to administer assessments, maintain records, employ physical and legal review, provide taxpayer assistance, and perform collections efficiently and at a low operational cost.

Definitions in tax codes should be complete and understandable before they are assigned to the government tax agency; the agency can concentrate on implementation and service instead of interpretation of tax law. Procedures should be in place to resolve questions, problems or contests internally without prejudice to the taxpayer or the government's position, or the right to ultimate resolution in a court of law.

5. Protected in Law

Civil rights and prudent application of both civil and criminal law must be the basis of tax law. Citizens should have the right to review and contest any tax law or assessment in a court of law for ultimate resolution. The status of tyrannical mechanisms of intimidation and seizure that have been implemented under the federal income tax system—where citizens can be charged and their property taken without normal due process—must be properly changed to the legal status those activities deserve: outlaw acts.

The government should be precluded from seizure of money or property of taxpayers for any alleged non-payment of taxes until they have given the citizen the right to respond to any charges and successfully demonstrated their case in an open court of law and received judgment for a claim. Non-citizens or foreign corporations in the United States should have the same obligations with regard to paying taxes as citizens, but also the same level of recourse in payment questions. Criminal law should not be used as a form of unwarranted government intimidation over the application of civil law conditions and regulations. Primary principles and conditions of appropriate governmental taxation should be reviewed, formalized and ensconced in regulatory tax law separate from appropriation law.

◆

The requirements for a sound tax system in a free and democratic state dedicated to economic liberty so identified, how can those principles be integrated into a sound, functioning federal tax system?

VII. The Real Property Use Tax—A Taxpayer's Guide

As suggested before, the construction of a sound tax system is analogous to the building of a good bridge. A good bridge is functional, structurally elegant, and users are able to engage in travel on it in a swift and efficient manner. The same should be true of a tax system. As a bridge is adaptable to traffic, a tax system should be adaptable to the requirements of citizens and government. The *Real Property Use Tax,* or RPUT, is a tax system designed to meet those requirements.

Tax assessment under the RPUT is based on the principle of liability for service rendered. Government service to citizens and taxpaying residents consists of benefits that are both tangible and intangible—everything from protection of citizens to national defense to information on weather forecasting. These benefits are provided in greater amount to those interests (individual, organizational, or corporate) that have more resource to service and protect, and the RPUT is assessed on that basis.

A good tax neither encumbers nor encompasses all possible aspects (or assets) of a physical tax base, but is based on an assessment of those elements that can be easily and accurately quantified and audited, and represent, proportionately, the real, natural liability of the taxpayer. These elements are found in real property. The variables of property size, level of development and time in use under the RPUT determine the tax status and assessment amount for a given piece of land and the development on it. The total collected assessment of all properties under the RPUT then provides the funding for government to operate.

◆

RPUT assessment is linked to land, but the concept of land as a unique or important element in taxation is not new. So how does the RPUT differ from other land-based tax theory?

The Classical economists Adam Smith, David Ricardo, and John Stuart Mill addressed the issue of land taxation in their eighteenth- and nineteenth-century economic theories. They believed that income associated with the ownership of land was different from that derived through other means. The service value of land, including rents, were viewed, at least in part, as unrelated to the personal production of the landowner and could thus be properly assessed as a unique and unattached revenue base. They also viewed a tax on land, and landowners, as less likely to discourage the production of wealth in the economy than a sales or income tax on industry and labor would.[209]

The primacy of land in tax policy was further promoted by nineteenth-century economist and social reformer Henry George who argued, in a similar vein, that rents and market land values were basically an outside economic benefit unrelated to the actions of the landowner and thus could be properly claimed, or taxed, by the state. The changing market value of land commonly associated with speculation (but not actual use value) could be eliminated by taxing land values away. The Georgists believed their tax policy would promote stability and equity in the economy as well as provide for government revenue needs.[210]

Georgist theory today has been at least partially implemented into policy in fifteen cities in Pennsylvania. Buildings and other improvements (representing production or creation of new wealth) are taxed at a reduced rate while the base land itself (representing unearned attached value) is taxed at the full rate.[211]

Most modern twentieth-century land taxes like the conventional property tax, on the other hand, probably have not been implemented under any conceptual basis of land having special value or landowners having special liability. Rather, implementations in conventional property tax systems have been linked and limited to the pragmatic and utilitarian concerns of funding government.

Under the conventional property tax, a tax rate is established against the total tax base to account for planned budgetary needs of the state. One tax rate applies to all in this system, but those who have property that is worth more pay a higher net tax—or more of the total fiscal liability. The system is public, stable, uniform, and easily audited. This makes it appealing to politicians who like a stable but easily adjusted system of tax assessment; the electorate likes the uniformity—and tolerates the assessment related to market value as long as politicians can be restrained from implementing dramatic rate increases.

RPUT theory, however, is different from the Classical theorists' and Georgists' views on property taxation and also from the utilitarian policies of state and local governments in conventional property tax implementations.

The first major difference of RPUT theory is that it does not aver land as a special asset that should be taxed just because it is land, as implied or stated by the Classicists and Georgists. The market price of land under RPUT theory is the value of the land and, economically, land value is viewed intrinsically no different than any other asset or commodity. Land size, development and period-in-use are calculated under RPUT theory to determine an assessment amount because those factors, when calculated, *best represent a relative liability of the taxpayer for the implied level of government service provided him.* Land and other real property under the RPUT are not viewed as economically unique *values.* They just happen to function very well as a *representative basis* for general-revenue tax assessment.

Another major difference in the RPUT from other forms of taxation is that the RPUT is philosophically at the other end of the political spectrum. Underpinning many tax systems in play in the United States today are *primacy of the state* and the imposition of arbitrary and collectivized liability. Assessments have been levied under the conventional property tax system, for instance, to extract as much as possible from taxpayers in general—with little or no regard for the objective application of individual service liability. Aggressive state revenue acquisition has been mitigated in some cases only by taxpayer protest and political revolt, and in cases such as California's Proposition 13, state constitutional change.

The RPUT, as opposed to many other tax systems, is based on the *primacy of the citizen and taxpayer.* The real service and liability to him is addressed in a manner of rational economic exchange and protection of his basic economic rights. Since RPUT theory comes from a different philosophical perspective of the proper role of government in tax assessment, it is no surprise that the *functional design* of the RPUT is going to be different from that found in other tax systems.

———— ♦ ————

The Real Property Use Tax legislation is statutory law passed by Congress for general federal revenue acquisition and is designed to replace the federal income tax. It is *not* meant to affect existing excise taxes, tariffs, user fees or other standing tax systems, nor budget appropriations directly related to those systems.

RPUT statutory law provides the legal conditions for assessment, but tax assessment does not actually occur until an appropriation or budget is passed that directs its funding acquisition through the RPUT. In other words, an appropriation (or full budget) can be passed in Congress but Congress has to specify in the appropriation law itself how the spending will be financed. If Congress directs financing through the RPUT for the appropriation, then tax assessment for it comes under RPUT law and regulations. If Congress specifies another tax system such as a tariff or user fee, then tax assessment is employed through one of those systems. For instance, Congress might have an 8 percent excise tax on airline tickets to finance airport management and security, and such a tax would be independent of other appropriations and other taxes, including the RPUT. While excise taxes may continue to be employed for *specific assessments* to fund particular expenditures after the RPUT became law, the RPUT would most likely be used for *general* revenue needs of the government—as well as for specific projects that are not funded by other taxes and that can be held as a general taxpayer liability.

The amount that can be assessed under the RPUT, however, is linked to the finite budget amount identified in an appropriation.[212] This is unlike the income tax, where no matter how much has already been assessed during a given tax year additional, disproportionate assessments can still continue as a person continues to work. Citizens can still be liable under the income tax system even if gross revenue receipts have already exceeded the original budgetary appropriation. The RPUT, on the other hand, is limited at both a budget and individual level to a clearly defined assessment amount.

The actual assessment (the tax due) for a taxpayer depends on the property size, the level of development, and the days in ownership and use. A larger sized property that is more developed and has a greater occupancy (in use) period will be taxed more than another property that is smaller, less developed and occupied for a shorter period of time. The applicable RPUT *rate*, though, does *not* change because of size of the property but remains constant.

For instance, a 2,000-square-foot house on an acre of land that was vacant for six months would be liable for less tax than a 10,000-square foot-apartment building on three acres that was rented out the entire year. The apartment building complex has a larger base land area, more developed space, and was occupied for a greater period of the year. So the actual tax amount due for the apartment building complex would be higher, based on all those factors even though the applicable RPUT *rates* for both properties would be the same.

The RPUT is not based in any way on market value (like the conventional property tax). The government *cannot* use the tax mechanism as a means of expropriating additional tax monies just because of an increase in market valuation of property—as is done under the conventional property tax system, where increased assessment may have nothing to do with any increase in government service. Arbitrary assessment is precluded under the RPUT, by contrast, and assessment ratios are related to the real cost of government for individual taxpayers.

Untimely application of tax law is also addressed under the RPUT. Ex post facto assignation of tax liability is specifically prohibited under RPUT operation, and there is an advisory period before an appropriation can go into effect. The government *cannot* (as under the income tax system) use *civil* law to retroactively tax people for past time periods and then use *criminal* law to prosecute them after they cannot pay what they did not know they had to pay. . . . Got it?

There is a period before RPUT law can go into effect. Feedback from professional economists, businesses, labor and private citizens can be given to legislators *prior* to enactment of budget law. So Legislators can first announce tentative budget plans, and then after comment from the electorate legislators can incorporate appropriate modifications into final budget law *before* the budget law goes into effect.

Citizens can then know ahead of time, prior to a given tax period, what their tax burden is going to be and can, like other economic conditions they are aware of, effectively plan ahead. The economic stability thus realized will be of immense value for both individual citizen and collective industry.

◆

The Real Property Use Tax is assessed non-governmental owners and renters of real property, which means the tax is representative of a very large proportion of the adult population. The system is *not* a social management, welfare, or subsidy program for special interests. It is a *tax system* based on relative liability. Local, state and federal governments and their bona fide agencies are exempt from RPUT liability, but the tax is universally applicable for all private sector interests owning or renting real property. The tax does *not* incorporate special benefits for some or discrimination toward others based on any economic, educational, religious, recreational or social condition.

Minors (unless they directly own or rent real property) are not liable under the RPUT. Children's earnings under direct, parental or trustee capacity are not relevant (as they can be under the income tax system). Thus the state imposes *no* controlled or arbitrary constraints and tax conditions with relation to dependency status, and the complex deduction and exemption conditions found in the income tax system are not relevant under RPUT operation.

People living in government subsidized housing are not liable for the RPUT—at least for that portion of the ownership or rental fee that is subsidized by the government. Renters, including transients or tourists at hotels and motels, are not *directly* liable for the RPUT if landlords or business owners do not apply RPUT liability directly in their operations. But the renter or customer can pay *indirectly* through a higher, adjusted customer price if owners choose to assume direct liability for the property-use portion of the tax and indirectly pass on the costs to renters or customers.

The Real Property Use Tax in no way precludes Congress from dispensing special service, subsidy or aid to particular parties when, as is the historical custom and duty of Congress, it believes that it is in the national interest to do so. Congress can still authorize all manner of expenditures, including educational, health, housing, transportation, science, and social welfare benefits. It must, however, accomplish that through direct appropriation (and the examination and debate process that it entails) and not through costly and confusing manipulations of the tax code.

Congress can choose other types of taxation in funding specific appropriations, and other taxes like the tariff or excise tax may be appropriate in certain circumstances. However, when the RPUT is selected as the tax funding mechanism, tax assessment is distributed evenly throughout the tax base proportionate to each taxpayer's RPUT liability status (the property-use liability he or she currently holds). Thus, when the RPUT is implemented the liability for national spending is reflected proportionately, and automatically, throughout the entire country.

◆

RPUT design is sophisticated with a linked and interrelated (consanguineous) relationship between the existing property and property-use conditions, known as the RPUT *Tax Base*; four *Basic Rates,* that are set by Congress that are related to property status; and a universally applicable *Master Rate.* (A full discussion of RPUT assessment criteria—including conditions of property liability and mathematical formulas for the tax rates—are included in "Part B: Technical Prescription" in the second section of this book. For now, the reader is provided with a fundamental description of tax system operation.)

The first two of the four Basic Rates are related to ownership assessment. The owner is always liable for this portion of the tax. The third and fourth Basic Rates are related to use and are charged the legal user of a property—the owner if he is using his property, or the renter or leaseholder if the property is being rented out. Property is considered "in use" as long as it is either actually in use or available for use. Property that is formally vacated and offered for sale or rent is not considered in use, and in that case no use-tax portion of the RPUT is due.

The owner of a house, for instance, would always be liable for the *ownership* portion of the RPUT, but would only be liable for the *use* portion of the tax if he occupied the house. A renter, and not the owner, would be directly liable to the government for the use portion when he rented the house from the owner.[213] The RPUT use portion of the tax (unlike the ownership portion) would *not* be due for any time period the house was vacated and up for sale or rent.

There is a greater implied level of government service for the use of property than for mere ownership, so Congress would probably set the Basic Rates for use higher than the Basic Rates for ownership. The smaller *ownership* portion of the RPUT, though, is always due whether the property is occupied or not.

Two other basic assessment elements are identified under the RPUT Basic-Rate structure. One is the RPUT base land area (the land area identified in the legal property title) and is called Base Land. The other is the additional developed, habitable square footage known as Developed Space. The average level of human and industrial activity (the *use-intensity* of people's property) is higher on Developed Space than mere Base Land. Hence a greater implied level of government service exists for Developed Space over Base Land (for a given area) and it would have a higher Rate.

As an example, two different five-acre plots could exist under two different property owners. We will call the two properties "Property A" and "Property B." The owners for both A and B would be assessed the same amount for Base Land because the base land for both is the same size. If the owner of Property A had some agricultural buildings that covered one acre and pasture on the other four acres, there would be only one acre of Developed-Space RPUT liability for that land. But if the owner of Property B had a ten-story office building on one acre and a parking lot on the other four acres, the Property B owner would be assessed for *fourteen acres* of Developed Space (10 stories times 1 acre, plus 4 acres of parking lot). Although the Base-Land and Developed-Space *rates* are the same for both properties, the owner of Property B (the office building complex) is liable for a commensurately larger final tax than the owner of Property A (the barns and pasture) because he has so much more taxable Developed Space (high-use-intensity areas).

Both Base Land *and* the Developed Space on it have to be surveyed under the RPUT system for proper assessment. But a survey may only have to be accomplished once in the life of a property unless the amount of Developed Space changes through construction or demolition. Many new home and business owners may in practice never have to survey their property—an original RPUT survey would likely be accomplished by builders in conjunction with original site development prior to sale.

RPUT rates can change, but that does not affect property surveys. The surveyed areas of both Base Land and Developed Space can be retained in the taxpayer's working records (including the taxpayer's business or personal computer) *and* in the federal tax agency's computers and used in subsequent tax years—irrespective of changes in tax rates. Modern property surveys can easily be accomplished today with modern laser equipment that facilitates both taxpayer reporting and verification, and when required, government audit.

The problem of interpreting immensely complex statutory law for thousands of possible exemptions and deductions—as required under the income tax system—does not exist under the RPUT. Property area can be physically measured and verified. Thus, the complexity and cost of current tax avoidance measures *and* tax evasion costs in the economy should disappear, ultimately saving many billions of dollars over time from those indirect, but very real, cost factors.

◆

The mathematical elegance of the RPUT is apparent in tax system functioning. The Master Rate is calculated from the Tax Base, the four Basic Rates and the tax period budgetary appropriations, and is universally applicable no matter what property-use conditions exist for individual owners and renters. Citizens can immediately calculate their individual liability on an actual or proposed federal budget by merely applying the Master Rate to their individual Tax Base. The Master Rate in the RPUT functions as a key part of assessment calculation and is also—at a macroeconomic level—an economic barometer for the cost of government.[214]

Calculation of the RPUT for many individual taxpayers is almost instantaneous. For people with pencil and paper, it might take a couple of minutes; for the citizen that has his individual tax base entered in his personal computer, a few seconds! Since individual Tax Base information is contained in tax agency computers, people will *not even have to file returns* unless their property status changes during the year or their land is rented or vacated. Property tax remittance can be accomplished by merely annotating a property tax ID number on the taxpayer's remittance check and mailing it in.

RPUT calculation, besides determining the total tax due for an individual, can also be applied against line items in a budget to determine the exact individual liability to a taxpayer for those items. For instance, the question of individual tax cost for a particular citizen for federally funded interstate highway expenditures in a given RPUT tax year could be answered with a few keystrokes on a hand-held computer. Citizens do not have to guess the tax burden they will have to sustain under actual or proposed governmental expenditures. The RPUT provides a solid accounting system for both citizens and government administrators in evaluating costs and determining real value and affordability of government services.

The application of tax law in a free society should be accomplished with common sense under a rational economic policy, and civil rights must be protected. Under the income tax system basic rights of citizens have taken a back seat to extremist measures by the government in trying to enforce tax compliance. Lack of due process in the seizure of citizen assets in tax proceedings and threats of criminal prosecution and incarceration have been used under the income tax system because of the inherent nature of the tax; the income tax meets none of the basic requirements of a sound tax system and thus requires extreme measures to function. Like poor government, a poor tax system requires the increased use of force, fear, and manipulation in order to keep it operating.

Complex regulation and suppressive force are not necessary to run a tax system in the modern democratic state. Regular operation of and compliance under a federal tax system should be handled under civil law, and information on all policies, assessments, collections, penalties, and official reports should be available to the public and the press. An objective tax system that can be easily audited does not require extremist measures; it can function just like any other service transaction in the economy with respect to charges, billing and collection.

The RPUT is a system that incorporates a rational tax assessment schema with the legal protection of citizens and taxpayers. Any non-remittance of required taxes under the RPUT is addressed just like non-compliance issues in other contractual relationships in the economy; the problem is first addressed administratively with ultimate recourse for all parties in a civil court of law.

Both penalties and interest can be due for non-compliance under the RPUT, but criminal proceedings are applicable only in cases of fraud or embezzlement of third-party funds (such as RPUT rental receipts taken and spent by a landlord instead of being remitted to the government). The threat of criminal prosecution *cannot* be used for mistakes, errors, or delays in filing, or even for willful refusal to file. The government can assess penalty and interest on past due amounts and enforce collection through civil proceedings, but because of the objective nature of the tax and the fact that it can be easily audited, the requirement for supplementary collection efforts should be minimal. Both citizen compliance with and confidence in the tax system should be high.

◆

A summary of Real Property Use Tax implementation:

- Congress enacts the Real Property Use Tax Law creating a new administrative tax agency (i.e., the Federal Tax Service Agency) and sets the four Basic Rates and other criteria for administration and assessment. (*The IRS would continue as a legacy agency only as long as necessary to resolve existing and past tax assessment, collection, and refund issues.*)
- Property surveys are accomplished by taxpayers, and initial Tax Base information is accumulated by Congress. (*For smaller, less complicated properties, this can be accomplished in minutes with modern laser equipment, and it only has to be done once in the life of a property unless the physical property status changes.*)
- Congress, in the budget process, makes public the proposed budget law [the law that specifies how much and in what ways government is going to spend money], and economists, business interests and regular citizens then provide feedback to legislators. (*Individual citizens will be able to calculate, almost instantaneously, their own liability and will be able to make informed comment on budget proposals.)*
- Congress takes regular citizen and professional economists' comments into consideration and passes statutory appropriation law specifying appropriate funding through the RPUT, *prior to the beginning of the tax assessment period or year.*

- Taxpayers remit taxes due. (*For property owners not renting their property under RPUT rental provisions this can be once a year; for renters or leaseholders, the Service-to-Use Fee is remitted with regular rent; and for owners that rent their property, tax receipts are due quarterly.*)
- Collections, audits, and enforcement actions under the RPUT are accomplished under civil legal code like other normal transactions in regular economic intercourse. (*The government cannot use the threat of criminal incarceration for errors or mistakes in tax filings; any legal action, civil or criminal, must be accomplished under due process. Confidence in and compliance with the RPUT by citizens and taxpayers should be high, though, with supplementary collection action by the government usually unnecessary.*)

The Real Property Use Tax is clear and direct, but it is not a "simple" tax. Rather, it is a *simple tax to operate* for taxpayers and government administrators and, when implemented, should contribute substantially to sound fiscal planning, effective management, and finally economic stability and general prosperity.

VIII. Principles and Benefits of the RPUT

How would The Real Property Use Tax specifically meet the aforementioned Requirements of a Sound Tax System? And what are some of the other potential benefits from implementation of the RPUT?

Principles, concepts and potential benefits of the RPUT need to be further explained or highlighted. What follows is a listing of the five Requirements of a Sound Tax System and descriptions of how the RPUT is designed to meet those requirements.

1. Relative to Appropriations.

All Real Property Use Taxes are related directly to specific, finite appropriation amounts. The RPUT is not a blanket general tax but one related directly to government spending. Characteristics are:

- ***Linked Directly to Appropriations.*** Tax assessment is directly related to the basic reason for taxation—funding the actual cost of government operations and spending. Unlike the income or sales tax, where the government can seize unlimited resources from individuals even if budget costs have already been met, the RPUT has built-in limitations within the tax mechanism itself; assessment is limited and commensurate with a finite liability at both the budget *and* individual-taxpayer level.
- ***Limited in Duration.*** An RPUT is not an unlimited tax (as under the income tax system), nor is it an assessment for an indefinite time period. The time period of the tax is directly specified through appropriation law. Once the budget-assessment period ends, the tax ends. New appropriations must be passed to implement new assessments.
- ***Operated Under the Daylight of Direct Appropriations.*** The back door of income tax code manipulations will be gone. Vested interests wanting government support or subsidy will have to appeal through the front door of direct appropriations, where the negative—and positive—aspects of their proposals can be publicly debated and then accounted for in clear, direct financing.

2. Equitable to the Citizen.

The Real Property Use Tax is not designed for citizen subjugation, arbitrary state expropriation, economic favoritism, or welfare or social service manipulation. Rather, the RPUT is based entirely on rational economic exchange and individual, implied liability for government service. Tax assessment of the taxpayer is based on factors commensurate with an implied level of service by the state to the taxpayer. Those interests that have more resource liability pay more – but at uniform, standard rates. Functions include:

* ***Service to Cost Relationship.*** People who have more property resource pay more, those that have less pay less. But people are *not* punished merely for earning income and being productive.
* ***Objective Relevance in Assessment.*** Responsibility for government cost is *not* manipulated through the tax code, increasing the benefits of some through exclusions and favorable tax conditions while effectively transferring the cost of government to others. Liability for government spending is reflected proportionately throughout the tax base as represented through an objective assessment schema.
* ***Proportionate Spending Liability.*** Politicians are less able to segment recipients from payers and manipulate the tax code for special interests during budget implementation. All segments of the tax base feel a proportionate increase in government spending liability whenever taxes are raised.
* ***Assessment Related to Level of Service.*** A larger, more developed property has a greater implied level of government service than a smaller, less developed property. But non-relevant, invasive government policies on personal and business operations are *not* part of the tax system.
* ***Distortion of Incentives Eliminated.*** People are no longer rewarded for not working, nor increasingly penalized if they do.
* ***Productivity Rewarded.*** People (and not the government) can keep what they earn and are not punished for creating wealth and prosperity for themselves, their families and communities.
* ***Free Trade Supported.*** Government interference in regular commerce through the tax code does not exist, and business and labor can engage in free trade without incurring additional tax liability. Imputed income is given no special preference, and division of labor, which is the basis of prosperity in the modern world, can function without penalty.

* ***Industry Preferences Eliminated.*** Special, beneficial tax conditions for some industries—and an effective higher rate and penalty for others—no longer exist.
* ***Commercial/Non-Commercial Not an Issue.*** The government doesn't say the businessman doing the million-dollar deal can eat steak and deduct it and the housewife fixing her furnace and eating a peanut butter sandwich can't. The government doesn't say an activity that can be classified as business is any better or any worse than any other human activity—the government exists to protect economic choice and personal liberty and *not* suppress it through a tax code.
* ***Freedom in Production.*** Imputed income is *not* an issue. Individuals, organizations, and businesses can make the choice of internal production and use, or trade for external production—the choice is the citizen's, free from government restriction.
* ***Savings Are Not Manipulated or Extorted.*** The current savings schemes under the income tax system promise less government seizure of citizen resources *if* citizens participate in the institutional manipulations specified in the income tax code. This is an outrageous manipulation and interference in private sector spending and investment. RPUT, on the other hand, does not interfere or penalize citizens for *their* spending, or *their* investing, with *their* capital that *they* earned.
* ***Workers Can Keep What They Earn.*** *Nothing* is withheld from a worker's paycheck under the RPUT.
* ***"Charity" Manipulation Precluded.*** One group of citizens cannot donate money to a charity and then have their taxes reduced, and thus shift the net cost of government to others. One group of citizens should not be forced to cover the cost of other people's share of government service because of private contributions to third parties. On the other hand, citizens should have the full right to donate their money to the charitable causes and organizations of their choice without having to select a government-sanctioned charity to lessen their tax bill.
* ***Freedom of Religion Enhanced.*** Citizens are not forced to support, through a tax code, religions they may or may not believe in. People should be allowed to support only the religious organizations they truly value.
* ***Religious Integrity Maintained.*** Religions should not be dependent on government approval and classification in a tax code to preclude increased tax assessment. "Unapproved" religions should not be forced to indirectly subsidize state "approved" ones. Religious

organizational independence and freedom are unimpeded under the RPUT.

* ***Foreign Influence in the Tax Code Stopped.*** Foreign companies cannot obtain special conditions or benefits through the RPUT. Instead of hiring private U.S. public relations firms to lobby for special tax preferences, foreign businesses will have to provide valued products or services in the American economy to accrue economic benefits here.
* ***Spouses Are Protected.*** A spouse is not liable for any RPUT unless he or she chooses to be by acquiring joint property ownership or jointly signing a rental contract. All tax remittance records are public and can be freely verified. All non-payment notices from the government must be acknowledged by all signatories in tax obligations. It would be much more difficult for a man, for instance, to divorce his wife and leave her with unexpected tax debt.
* ***Workers Don't Subsidize the Rich.*** Workers who pay taxes don't have to subsidize powered economic interests that would otherwise, through legal tax avoidance mechanisms, pay no taxes.
* ***Senior Dignity Preserved.*** Senior citizens will have the dignity of being able to keep what they've earned in a lifetime of work through pensions and investments without wanton expropriation by the government. They will no longer have the fear of the government taxing their income while they work, and then, ironically, having to go hat in hand later to the government for aid. Senior citizens will be able to work as long as they want, benefiting both themselves and society at large.
* ***Children Are Not Subjugated.*** Currently, children can be investigated by the IRS and their monies expropriated. With the RPUT—from lemonade stand to corporate empire—children can learn to become productive in America without penalty to themselves or their parents.
* ***Economic Liberty Maintained.*** Tax code construction to manipulate and control private economic activity does not exist under the RPUT. Citizens are free to make their own choices with what they've earned, unobstructed by unwarranted mechanizations of state bureaucracies.
* ***Care for Hair and Enjoyment of Spring.*** A sound tax system will help prevent taxpayer fits where hair is torn from the scalp while completing tax returns, as well as taking April 15th from a period of depression to just another nice Spring day.

3. Objective and Certain.

The tax is not hidden, but a specifically assessed amount separate from other economic transactions. Every single taxpayer can know before the assessment period exactly what he or she will owe and under what conditions payment is due. Tax rates are standard and uniformly applicable. Objective and Certain attributes are:

* ***Tax Base Identity.*** The total tax base is related to land—easily identified. Tax administrators do not have to wade through a miasma of financial minutiae in personal and business transactions to try and determine tax liability.
* ***Based on Rational Economic Exchange.*** The financial aspect of RPUT is based on simple assessment for value given.
* ***Universal Applicability.*** The tax applies to everyone at the same rates under the same conditions.
* ***Objective Category Rates.*** Tax rates are based on the level of implied government service and are stable over time. The Basic Rates are designed to be stable even over many appropriations and budgets.
* ***One Key Rate.*** One rate, the Master Rate, applies to all taxed property, whatever the status or size, and is an objective standard that can be used by all interests, public and private, to gauge federal tax liability across the country.
* ***Stable Rates.*** The Master Rate and Basic Rates are designed so they can be set once and remain constant for the related budget period.
* ***Supports Personal Economic Planning.*** Individuals, organizations, and businesses can engage in sound financial planning without fear of arbitrary and illogical changes in the tax code.
* ***Supports Budget Planning Participation.*** Citizens can calculate immediately any *proposed* tax increase through a proposed Master Rate, determine the relative value of those appropriations and their individual and business costs, and give immediate, valuable feedback to legislators in budget planning—*prior* to enactment of tax law.
* ***Tax Visibility.*** The RPUT is not a "hidden" tax. Taxpayers know exactly what they're paying when they pay it. They can thus directly relate their support cost to government service and efficiency.
* ***Foreign Country Privilege Removed.*** Individuals earning money overseas are *not* given tax exemption status while local citizens are expected to pick up the tab. World travelers don't travel on a ticket paid for by other taxpayers.
* ***American Exports Supported.*** The huge number of "hidden" taxes on income that are buried in the sale of domestic components no longer

exist with the RPUT. Inflated costs that would reduce overseas sales growth under the income tax would be eliminated.

* ***Black Market and Tax Evasion Reduced or Eliminated.*** People who have previously paid no taxes, and have thus effectively forced other taxpayers to indirectly subsidize them, will find it more difficult to avoid assessment for legal tax liability under the RPUT. Clear, objective assessment criteria that can be easily audited will help ensure appropriate compliance.
* ***Land Use Choice Insulated.*** Economic pressure to develop or sell land because of an increased and problematic market-value-based assessment does not exist. Nebulous and irrelevant market value is *not* a factor in assessment with the RPUT.
* ***Politically Impervious (Virtually).*** Once the basic RPUT law goes into effect, it may be extremely difficult politically to attempt to alter it for special, parochial interests without very valid reasons, public comment, and proper consensus.
* ***Tax Shelters Eliminated.*** Think what businesses can build with billions freed under an objective, stable tax system—certainly not tax shelters.
* ***Welfare Separated from Tax System.*** RPUT is *not* a tax system that is twisted and used for social-welfare purposes, but a mechanism for proper tax assessment and collection of appropriate government revenue. Service and social welfare programs of the government are left to operations and appropriations separate from tax-system functioning.
* ***No One Is a Dependent.*** The RPUT makes all men free. Especially parents of college students. Parents don't have to scratch their heads trying to determine if it's best to keep Junior at home as a dependent for tax purposes or shuffle him off to a college dorm. And Junior doesn't have to worry if claiming himself as a dependent on his own tax return for a part-time job is going to foul up Ma and Pa with the IRS.

4. Economical to Operate.

All taxpaying individuals and businesses have a standard, easily understandable assessment criteria that can be met with a minimum of private accounting resources. For many people calculating taxes will not be much more than a minute of work with a hand-held computer or calculator and then writing a check. For the government it means a definitive and easily audited tax base. Operational characteristics:

* ***Functionally Responsive.*** Mid-budget spending increases can be accounted for, either directly with an Adjusted Master Rate or by deferred liability to the next regular budget.
* ***Tax Regulations Understandable.*** The tax code is succinct and understandable. Tax regulations are designed to be stable in time, which means a more prosperous and reliable economy.
* ***American Jobs and Capital Enhanced.*** One of the first things modern businesses consider today are domestic costs—and whether business operations can be sustained under domestic tax conditions. Businesses have had to worry about the high cost of operations in the United States under the present income tax system. A stable tax system, on the other hand, means both workers and investors prosper.
* ***Increased Research & Development.*** More free capital means more investment for new products, inventions, and medical cures.
* ***Tax Avoidance Reduced or Eliminated.*** No complicated rules, no huge number of deductions or exemptions, and a sound audit mechanism means proper assessment and accountability—and appropriate tax compliance. People will know their fair share and pay it.
* ***End to Regular Lobbying.*** Regular tax lobbying will come to an end. The RPUT is not based on an arbitrary and capricious deduction/exemption schema, so tax lobbyists will be able to employ their talents in more socially productive venues.
* ***Environmental Land Use Protected.*** Users can continue to use their land for agricultural, park, or open space purposes, even deep within urban areas without suffering any federal tax penalty because of land value, thus providing a natural stopgap to unwarranted, accelerated development.
* ***Environmental Efficiency Supported.*** Areas of properties that are not developed, or minimally developed, such as outdoor recreational areas, landscaped areas of homes or businesses, farmland, grazing land, and timberland are taxed at a much lower rate than developed areas on the same property. Thus, instead of mindlessly expanding

buildings and factories—and increasing net tax liability—there is a given incentive to wisely use any existing developed space.

* ***Easily Measured.*** Physical property can be physically measured; areas of property assessment can easily be demonstrated as correct or incorrect. Quick validation by both the taxpayer and/or government auditor is possible with modern technology.
* ***Easily Calculated.*** For many people, after an initial property survey (which they may never have to do again in their lives), calculation of their period taxes may take . . . five seconds! The Master Rate is the only regular yearly variant, and that is created automatically by Congress based on the budget amount and total Tax Base.
* ***Large, Complex Properties Easily Worked.*** Modern computers make tracking RPUT on large, complex rental properties relatively simple.
* ***Tracking and Auditing Efficient.*** The complete tax base is readily identified by the RPUT administrative agency. It can be determined immediately who is behind in tax remittance by computer checking of property records against payments. No more complicated, undercover investigations of people's private lives, spending habits, and bank accounts to validate tax filings.
* ***Tax Filing for Many Reduced.*** The huge amount of time and resources required by businesses and individuals to track every single income, expense, investment, and employee is eliminated. Only the amount of and type of real property and its use-availability need to be reported.
* ***Tax Filing for Many Eliminated.*** Property renters don't file except for adjustments. Property owners who do *not* rent out their property, such as resident homeowners, and even people who *do* rent out their property but choose not to declare RPUT Rental Units, are not usually required to file any tax forms or returns unless they file a survey or claim a Vacation Status (vacate their property and put it up for sale or rent). Normally, a taxpayer can merely send in a check with his Property ID annotated on it at tax time—and for perhaps ninety percent of the population ninety percent of the time, no separate tax remittance form is needed!
* ***Tax Forms Simplified.*** Unlike the 280 forms currently used under the income tax code, all submissions, surveys, government billings, and request for corrections are processed through just *one* key form, the RPUT Report Form, with linked subforms and addendums.
* ***Integration of Form Function.*** The RPUT Report Form provides a cover face for recording taxpayer, Property ID, and other basic information, and all other subforms or addendums in the electronic form version are related, linked, and displayed through a computer

"drill-down" function. Only the applicable pages are produced when the RPUT Report Form is printed. The full paper form version has easy reference tabs and cross-referencing.

* ***Technology Integrated but Not Mandated.*** The tax system takes advantage of all the latest technologies—but none of them is *required* for taxpayer reporting. Surveys can still be accomplished with transit and tape measure, and tax filings calculated and remitted on plain paper forms.
* ***Frees and Assists Legislators.*** Legislators no longer have to invest enormous amounts of time dealing with tax system lobbying, analysis, and adjustments. They can spend their time wisely, directly serving the people.
* ***Intellectual Resources Freed.*** Think what 200,000 professional tax preparers and perhaps millions of private business people currently involved in tax accounting operations could do if they were freed to produce regular goods and services in the economy. Perhaps a cure for cancer? A non-polluting automobile? Or perhaps just the incremental addition in general national productivity that would allow citizens more free time each month with their families, friends, and in community involvement.
* ***Senior Productivity Harnessed.*** Society today can lose an enormous amount of potential service from people who choose to retire rather than continue to work and have their lives examined and large portions of their incomes taken by the government. Seniors under the RPUT system, with their wealth of knowledge and experience, are allowed to continue to contribute in the workplace, as they desire, for themselves, their families, and their communities, and without penalty.
* ***Compliance Increased.*** People are more likely to comply, and to comply completely and correctly, with an objective tax system that people understand and believe is fair.
* ***Civil Servants Are Supported.*** Many dedicated professionals and staff have existed within the Internal Revenue Service, Congressional budgetary agencies, and federal justice system. Unfortunately, they've been given the worst possible tax system by Congress to administer—the income tax. It's about time federal tax system personnel be given the support and tax system both they and the country deserve. Increased private sector productivity should be correlated with increased efficiency in the public sector, and increased benefits should be awarded industrious and innovative public servants as well.

* ***Confidence in Government.*** A basis of trust in a people's government is sound government fiscal policy. A sound tax system is the basis for that.
* ***Citizen Support.*** The RPUT will work because people will see that it can work and will support it.
* ***Tax System Cost Reduced.*** The huge financial cost—$538 billion—to the American economy of operating under and complying with (or *trying* to comply with) income tax law is eliminated. Compliance cost of the RPUT will be, for many people, minuscule.
* ***Exponential Benefits.*** A base savings, such as compliance cost, can be substantial, but it may be just the tip of the iceberg. Capital that is freed may generate even more wealth and prosperity, leading to an even more secure economy and prosperous nation.

5. Protected in Law.

Peoples rights and property are protected, and due process must be followed in any adjudication. All regular enforcement and adjudication is accomplished under civil law; criminal law is only applicable in the misappropriation of third-party funds. Lawful court adjudication with the right of appeal must occur prior to any lien or seizure by the state. The Federal government, with the RPUT, will have returned to its appropriate role in administering a tax system that incorporates the basic tenet of government for the people. Conditions include:

* ***Ex Post Facto Seizures Prohibited.*** The government cannot tax citizens today for conditions that existed six months ago, as is done in the income tax. Citizens do not have to keep looking behind their back for unexpected government seizures based on passed activities.
* ***Federal Tax Agency Policies Public.*** All administration and audit policies of RPUT activities are open to public review. There are no "secret" audit analyses or techniques. The press and the public have full right and access to review tax system operations. Taxpayers can see how the tax system works and have confidence in it.
* ***Public Disclosure on Assessments and Collections.*** All tax assessments, filings, payments, late notices, liens, penalties, and court filings are public record, as well as under full Congressional and Executive Branch oversight. One group of taxpayers cannot secretly be given special privileges while others are assessed heavy penalties.
* ***Investigative Directorates Ended.*** Every aspect of a person's economic life is no longer subject to review and approval by the state. Big Brother is sent packing.

* ***Criminalization Precluded.*** The criminalization of the federal tax code in the income tax system as a mechanism of state power and intimidation does not exist in the RPUT. The only people subject to criminal prosecution are landlords or others who engage in fraud or embezzlement of third-party funds; taxpayers are *not* treated as criminals when they make filing errors or get behind in their tax payments. Taxpayers may have to pay interest or a penalty when conditions warrant, but they are not threatened with jail on tax-compliance issues. Rather, they are accorded the basic courtesies and protections that should be found in the application of sound tax law.
* ***Civil Rights Protected.*** The government has to go through normal legal channels before it can seize a citizen's resources for non-payment of taxes. Unlawful search and seizure is not permitted.
* ***Right to Privacy Secured.*** RPUT assessments and payments are public record, but they have nothing to do with the private activities of citizens. Complete devolution of personal and private business activity via income and expenses—as in the income tax system—is excluded from RPUT law. As again, our nation's founders specified, "The right of the people to be secure in their persons, houses, papers, and effects, against unreasonable searches and seizures, shall not be violated. . . . "[215]

IX. Transition in Tax Systems

The transition from the existing federal income tax system to the RPUT can be relatively smooth and efficient if it is done properly. First, though, the income tax system needs to be recognized for what it is—a completely arbitrary assignation of benefits and privileges, charges and penalties. The whole antiquated platform needs to be removed, and assessment periods for the income tax must end before any assessment becomes active under a new replacement system.

There are constituent benefits associated with the current income tax system in the form of exemptions, deductions, conditions, subsidies, programs, payments, or refunds that Congress may desire to continue—or are obligated to continue.

Special interests that believe they warrant government preferences, and had such under the income tax system and want to continue them, will have to apply for direct and honest subsidy through federal appropriations after the transition to a new, objective tax system.

Other programs such as Social Security that have been financed through the income tax system exist as obligations that the federal government must continue to honor. People who have paid into the system over many years and expect what is due in retirement have a right to their retirement payments from the government.

All future funding of existing benefits and programs, either current obligations or special subsidies desired by legislators, can be funded directly through the regular appropriation process and assessment made through the new federal RPUT. Social Security trust funds have been borrowed, or spent in this case, by the federal government, so the outstanding obligation exists from the general fund anyway. There is nothing complicated about this.

Social Security, Medicare, and Federal Unemployment taxes can be, but do not have to be, funded through the RPUT. The current collection system of assessment through employment taxes could continue for those items after implementation of the RPUT if absolutely required.

However, as long as a federal worker savings program for worker retirement remains mandatory, there is no reason it could not be improved along with implementation of the RPUT, while retaining funding capabilities for existing Social Security obligations. A private investment/Social Security combination program, where employer strictures were removed and employees had some discretion in optimizing their investments, might be a boon to both workers and the economy.

It is a reality, though, that in close scrutiny of direct appropriations under a new, objective federal tax system some previous but unwarranted expenditures and subsidies may be less likely to be approved. Consider that a benefit of the RPUT system!

Close-out of the federal income tax system does pose some hazards. Substantial pressures may exist in Congress prior to the final income tax legislation for legislators to carve out the biggest piece possible of "preference pie." Various interests may wax noxious on how their tax investment planning needs to be validated with the appropriate adjustment to ensure the "correct" return on this deferred capital gains income or that long-term depreciation. Sufficient counter measures should be implemented by responsible Americans to minimize any kind of rout or "pork chop riot" during the demise of the national fiscal embarrassment known as the federal income tax. The truth is, since the federal income tax system was never "fair," shutdown of the system is not going to be "fair," and the best that taxpayers can hope for in phasing out the income tax system is a final income tax law that is . . . well . . . less unfair than before. And the best answer may be a quick wrap-up of the messy business.

One policy for closing down the federal income tax system may be to freeze all rates, conditions, deductions and exemptions, only altering the tax code to plug up the most egregious incongruities. Another option, since tax liability under the income tax system was never objective in the first place, is to have past liabilities and preferences in great measure discounted and a flat-rate tax applied retroactively.

Review, analysis, and implementation of RPUT law can be accomplished on a separate track from close-out of the federal income tax system if necessary. Tax liability, or assessment, in both the income tax system and RPUT, is based on a set time period (i.e., tax year), so there can be an effective cutoff date between the two systems and the problem of mingling tax systems precluded.

There is another option that may be even more attractive. Because any new Constitutional law enacted might make remaining federal income tax law illegal, it might be opportune to have a very rapid phase-out of the existing income tax. An entire nullification of past income tax law could occur by statute prior to Constitutional change, and then application of a temporary national excise tax or temporary deficit financing could be implemented, with a phase-in of the RPUT as quickly as possible.

Creation of a new national tax system will require work and commitment by national leaders in government, business, and academia, as well as support from the electorate. A suggested outline for transition in tax systems appears in Figure 1. [216]

♦

The scope of activity in the transition to a new tax system is not small, but the country certainly possesses the technical expertise and physical resources to accomplish the task. The one critical element for success is the will to succeed. And for that the country has historical precedent.

Outline for Transition in Tax Systems

1. Tax Reform Dissemination *by*
    a) This Book
    b) Regular Media Correspondence
    c) Internet Information
    d) University Liaisons
2. Professional Analysis *by*
    a) Economists
    b) Political Scientists
    c) Local, State and National Policy Makers
3. Public Debate *in*
    a) Op/Ed Pages In Newspapers and Periodicals
    b) Radio Stations
    c) High Schools/Colleges
    d) Clubs, Bars and Other Miscellaneous Areas of Public Gathering
    e) Town Halls
    f) Television Stations
4. New National Tax System Implementation is Planned *when*
    a) Congress Appoints Blue Ribbon Panel of Top Economists
    b) Top Economists Assemble Support Team
    c) Team Develops RPUT-System Options
    d) Team Develops Design for New RPUT Administrative Agency
    e) Team Finalizes Income Tax Transition Program
    f) Top Economists Review and Formalize Options
    g) Top Economists Present Options to Congress
5. Constitutional Basis for National Tax Policy Changes *with*
    a) Congressional Passage of Necessary Constitutional Amendment(s)
    b) States Review and Vote on Amendment(s)
    c) Amendment(s) Implemented Into Constitutional Law
6. New National Tax Legislation is Implemented *when*
    a) Congress Debates Options
    b) Congress Brings Options to Committee for Resolution
    c) Congress Passes RPUT Management Tax Law
    d) Congress Passes New Budget Under RPUT
    e) President Signs National Tax Legislation Into Law
7. Transition to New National Tax System Proceeds *with*
    a) Congress Appointing Head of New Tax Agency
    b) Engineers/Accountants/Programmers Brought in for Construction
    c) RPUT Line Personnel Recruited and Trained
    d) American Public Advised on New Tax System Operations
    e) IRS (legacy agency) Administering Income Tax Phase-Out
    f) New Tax System, the RPUT, Starting Operation
    g) Income Tax (legacy system) Closing Down
    h) Remaining Income Tax Personnel Reorganized/Reassigned

Figure 1

Part B: Technical Prescription

X. The Real Property Use Tax—Theory

The **Real Property Use Tax,** or **RPUT,** is a tax system that incorporates an objective assessment ratio, universally applicable, to real property, where individual taxpayer liability is related to the level of government service and to the interests, or stake, of the taxpayer. The tax is designed for acquisition of general revenue and not meant to replace existing, properly designed excise taxes, tariffs, user fees, or other valid federal charges, but rather to complement those assessments in a constructive tax-policy implementation. The Real Property Use Tax *is* meant to replace any unsound national tax mechanisms currently operating for the collection of general revenue, most importantly, the retirement and replacement of the current federal income tax system.

The RPUT involves an array of principles and conditions that form a matrix through which Congress assigns basic rates to assess the real property of citizens and taxpaying residents. Benefit and welfare mechanisms are excluded from the design of the tax, and such functions are deliberately left to government operations and appropriations separate from tax system functioning. *The Real Property Use Tax is based on the theory of rational economic exchange and liability for service rendered.*

Tax assessment in the RPUT is based on both physical property area and related use factors. The factors of area size, level of development, and time in use are calculated using objective criteria to arrive at an assessment for each legal property unit. The greater the property resource, the greater the implied level of government service to that resource, and thus, a greater tax liability is attached to it. Those possessing or using a smaller property resource-base have a correspondingly lower tax liability. The tax rests on a property-ownership assessment plus a use-value assessment ascribed to both owners and renters, which ensures very wide tax representation in the serviced population.

A **taxpayer** is the legal entity liable for the tax. A taxpayer can be an individual, a legal partnership, or a legal organization or corporate entity that owns or rents a **property**. An RPUT property is the unique land-parcel and structures on it as defined in county or state property **ownership** (title) registration.

RPUT classification and measurement of the area on a property is accomplished through a physical **survey**. The **Property Types** and the size of each on a particular property are identified in the survey to determine the **Taxable Area**. This can often be accomplished in minutes with modern laser equipment. The survey need not be repeated in the life of the property unless the owner or tax auditor desires verification, or the real property status changes. Thus, the same property-survey information can very often be used in multiple tax years even when tax rates change.

The overall concepts of the RPUT are easy to understand and regular operation is simple and straightforward. Although a knowledge of elementary algebra is helpful in understanding the tax theory explained here, only very basic math skills are required to calculate individual taxes. Property-survey information can be recorded in a hand-held computer, for instance, and actual (or proposed) tax rates entered when Congress announces a rate change (or proposed rate change); the actual tax amount due from the taxpayer can then be calculated in seconds. (Refer to Figure 2 for a conceptual outline of the RPUT.)

A continued reading of RPUT theory in the text is suggested for a comprehensive understanding. The reader can also enter test data with the RPUT analysis software that came with this book to get an immediate "hands-on" sense of tax-system functioning. Unlimited "what-if" tax-scenario testing is possible with the program.

———— ♦ ————

The RPUT system is composed of two separate legal components, the **Real Property Use Tax Law (RPUTL)** and the appropriation or budget laws, known as **Funding Statutes.** The RPUTL is a single law that incorporates core regulations that direct main RPUT functioning. Funding Statutes, on the other hand, are merely appropriation bills that specify the program or budget to be funded, denote the amount to be taxed, identify the time period for assessment, *and assign the RPUTL as the funding mechanism.*

Congress does not have to specify the RPUT as the tax for an appropriation; it could, for instance, acquire funding through an excise tax or tariff. However, if Congress desires assessment through the RPUT then the RPUTL is specified in the appropriation bill (the RPUT Funding Statute) as the tax mechanism. (See Figure 3 for a diagrammed view of the relationship between the RPUTL and Funding Statutes.)

The assessment base in the RPUT is the property ownership-and-use condition found on real property. Real property under the RPUT is defined in the same manner as in state and local statutory and common law, and includes open land, farmland, parks, houses, apartments, factories, office buildings, stores, parking lots, stadiums, sidewalks, and

Conceptual Outline of the RPUT

Assessment Based on Property Ownership:

Base Land + Developed Space = Service-to-Ownership Fee

Assessment on Property Use:

Base Land + Developed Space = Service-to-Use Fee

Total Tax Liability for Property:

Service-to-Ownership Fee + Service-to-Use Fee = Total Tax Due

Figure 2

Legal Components of the RPUT System

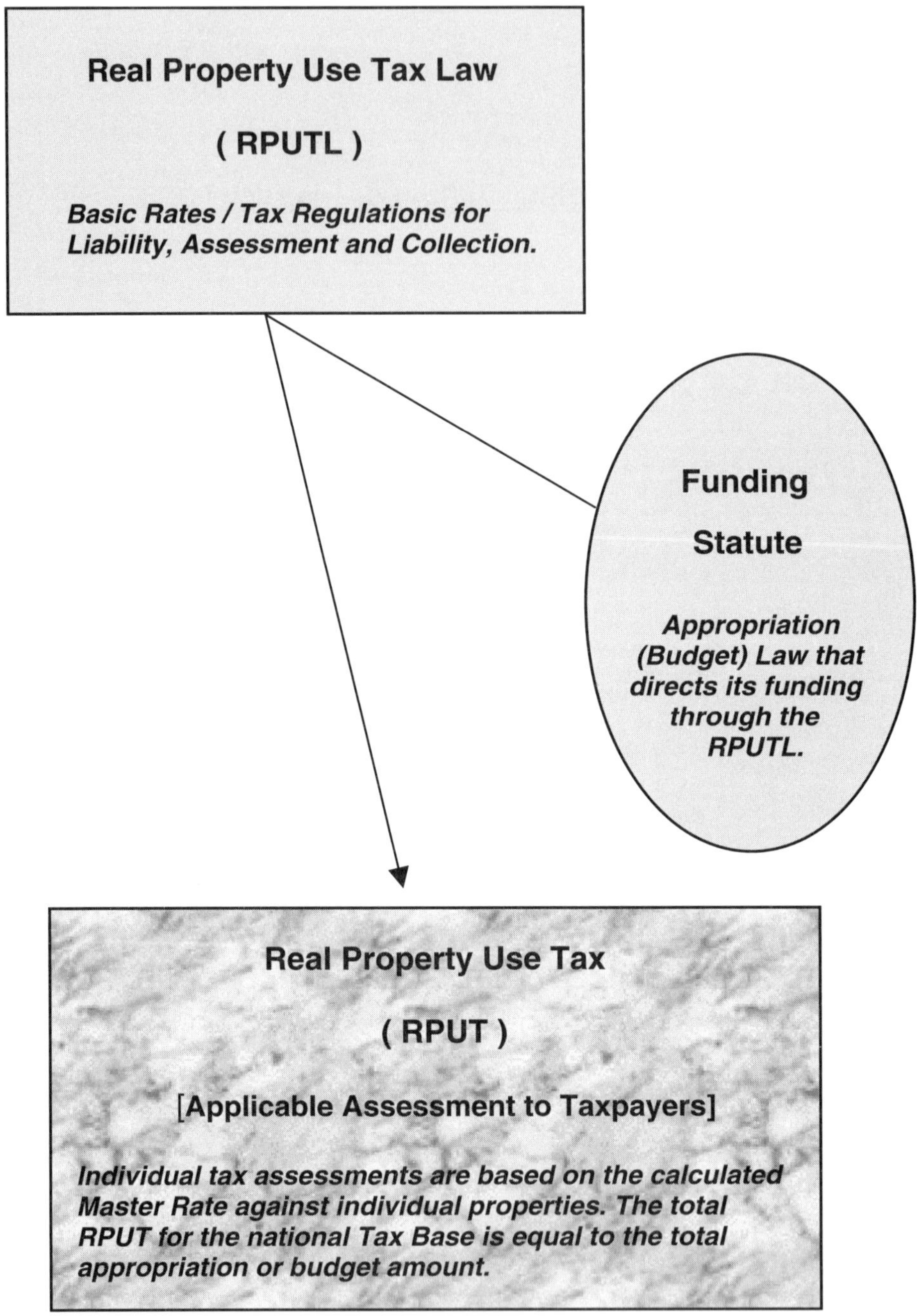

Figure 3

so on. But unlike assessment under the conventional property tax, the RPUT is *not* based on the estimated market value of real property.

The property and use conditions in the RPUT are defined by four primary **Tax Categories,** each of which represents a different property-ownership/use condition. Congress sets a **Basic Rate** for each of these four categories that is relative to the service liability for the ownership/use condition defined in each. The Basic Rates are set prior to any appropriation or tax assessment and are designed to be stable in time and remain constant over multiple budget periods.

The calculation of property area, level of development, and time in ownership/use—the calculation before the current-year tax rate is applied—determines the **Tax Base**. The Tax Base is that which is assessed (*not* the assessment). When applied to an individual *property,* the Tax Base is the assessment-base calculation for just that property. When applied to a *taxpayer,* the Tax Base is the total assessment-base calculation for the taxpayer for all his relevant properties, and when applied to the *nation* it is the total for all properties for all taxpayers.

The period that is specified in the Funding Statute for RPUT assessment of the Tax Base is the **Tax Period**. A Tax Period would normally be a dedicated fiscal, or calendar, year. The total budgetary amount that is to be financed through the RPUT for a Tax Period (the amount to be spent) is the **Revenue Requirement.**

Congress decides in appropriation budget law what tax mechanism(s) will be used and the portion that is to be financed through the RPUT. The Revenue Requirement (the RPUT portion of the budget) is then calculated with the Tax Base and the four Basic Rates to determine the **Master Rate.** (The mathematical formula for Master Rate calculation is shown in Figures 5–6, on pages 176–177, but the related RPUT terms and variables in that formula must first be defined. Review the paragraphs that follow, prior to Figures 5–6, for relevant definitions.)

The Master Rate is universally applicable to all taxpayers that are assessed under the RPUT *irrespective of their individual property-ownership/use conditions* and is the basis for calculation of individual taxpayer assessment in a given Tax Period. A flow chart of the Master Rate calculation is shown in Figure 4.

Individual assessment amounts (the tax each taxpayer pays) are determined by applying the Master Rate against each taxpayer's individual property-ownership/use conditions as defined under the four Tax Categories and the related Basic Rates.

Master Rate Calculation

The Master Rate is determined from a calculation of the Basic Rates, Tax Base and Revenue Requirement. *1

Revenue Requirement

(Budget, or spending amount, set by Congress for the Tax Period to be funded through RPUT assessment.)

Basic Rates

(Property rates set for each of the four Tax Categories.)

Tax Base

(Calculation of property area, level of development, and time in use for all properties in the country.) *2

↓

Master Rate

(Univerally applicable rate for all Property Types and condtions and the basis of calculation for individual taxpayer assessment.)

The Master Rate also serves as an ecomomic barometer for the cost of government.

***1 The actual formula for Master Rate calculation is shown in Figures 5–6. However, it is recommended that the reader review the chapter-portion before that for a definition of terms and formula variables.**

***2 Property use is dynamic and Tax Base computation includes an adjustment for this variance. Surveys and variance are explained in Chapter XI. Note that a survey does not have to be accomplished every year—survey information for a property is applicable indefinitely unless construction or demolition occurs.**

Figure 4

The Tax Categories have two **Divisions**, **Service to Ownership** and **Service to Use**, and two **Subdivisions**, **Base Land** and **Developed Space**. All four Tax Categories, each representing a different Basic Rate, are shown below:

1) **Service to Ownership / Base Land**
2) **Service to Ownership / Developed Space**
3) **Service to Use / Base Land**
4) **Service to Use / Developed Space**

Developed and undeveloped properties can be owned, owned and used, or owned and rented, and these conditions are accounted for through the separate Service-to-Ownership and Service-to-Use conditions.

Each Tax Category assessment charge is called a fee. The **owner** (or **landowner**), the holder of legal title to a property, is always liable for the Service-to-Ownership Fee. The owner is also liable for the Service-to-Use Fee if the property is **in use** (or available for use) by the owner. A **renter** or **leaseholder**, a legal entity that legally contracts for the use of a property from the owner, can be directly liable to the government for the Service-to-Use Fee but *not* the Service-to-Ownership Fee.

Calculation of tax liability under both the Service-to-Ownership and Service-to-Use Divisions is linked to the two Subdivisions, Base Land and Developed Space. The first Subdivision, Base Land, is the legal base land area (the measured land-surface area on a property)—whether or not something is built on, under, or over it, or not.

Base Land that does not have permanent structures on it, such as meadows, swamps, forests, annual croplands, orchards, unpaved storage lots, grazing lands, campgrounds, undeveloped areas on commercial or residential lots, and commercial or residential landscaping is classified as **Open Space**. The amount of Open Space can never exceed the area of Base Land on a given property.

The second RPUT Subdivision, Developed Space, is the gross habitable surface area (gross floor space) of developed portions of property. Examples of Developed Space are base surface areas within exterior floor dimensions of a house, apartment, factory, or office building, including the habitable basements and upper stories of those properties. Parking lots, sidewalks, roadways, stadiums, theaters, amusement parks, and any other permanent structures—except for incidentals found on Open Space like fences, signs, drinking fountains, and so on—are also Developed Space.

Developed Space can be increased (built up) or decreased (demolished) on top of Base Land; the Developed Space on a given unit of property can change over time. The amount of Developed Space on a property can *exceed* the Base-Land area. For example, a one-acre, ten-story office building on an acre of land with each office story spanning one acre would have ten times as much Developed Space as Base Land. By contrast, an undeveloped one-acre farm lot would have no Developed Space. The level of property development and the implied level of government service associated with it provide a basis for assessment under the RPUT; increased levels of human and industrial activity (Developed Space) are taxed more, areas of decreased development (Open Space), less.

◆

Calculation of the Real Property Use Tax is based on a unique relationship between tax-assessment criteria: The Master Rate and Basic Rates in the RPUT are in a deliberately designed, *consanguineous* relationship to each other (the rates are specially interrelated) so that one Master Rate can be applied against a taxpayer's property along with the applicable Basic Rates to yield the RPUT due, regardless of the taxpayer's property status. An explanation of how the rates interrelate and function follows.

The four Basic Rates, each representing a different Tax Category, are used first in a calculation with the Tax Base *to obtain* the Master Rate and then in a calculation *with* the Master Rate itself to determine individual assessments. (Table A shows the Master Rate and Tax Category Basic Rates.)

The Basic Rates are established by Congress prior to appropriations, remain in effect indefinitely until deliberately changed in RPUT Law, and can, as directed by Congress, apply without change to multiple appropriations or budgets (providing stability over time). Basic Rates are the fixed elements in the RPUT rate schema and are designed to reflect the relative service-to-cost ratio for the four Tax Categories. For instance, the implied increased level of government service to Developed Space would mean a higher assessment (higher Basic Rate) for Developed Space compared to Base Land.

A five-acre piece of farmland used for grazing goats, for example, receives much less direct and indirect service and protection by the state than does a five-acre piece of land with an active ten-story office building on it. Implicitly, government service and protection is going to be higher with the office-building complex because of the greater level of

RPUT Rate Descriptions

The Master Rate and Basic Rate schema is the basis from which actual assessment amounts are calculated for individual, taxable properties.

#	Tax Category Name	Rate Name / Type
	————	* 1 Master Rate
1	Service to Ownership / Base Land	* 2 Basic Rate #1
2	Service to Ownership / Developed Space	Basic Rate #2
3	Service to Use / Base Land	Basic Rate #3
4	Service to Use / Developed Space	Basic Rate #4

***1 The Master Rate is not set subjectively by Congress but calculated from the Appropriation (spending amount), Total Tax Base, and Basic Rate ratios. The Master Rate formula is shown in Figures 5–6.**

***2 Each Basic Rate is set by Congress as a percentage of the *total* of the four Basic Rates, where the total of the four Basic Rates equals 1. In other words, all four Basic Rates added together must equal 1 (100%).**

Table A

development; dozens of businesses and hundreds of people may work and function there, and tax assessment should be, commensurately, more. But that does not affect the *rates* of payment for the same Tax Categories on the two properties; Basic Rates are universally applicable and remain the same.

The Master Rate—in contrast to the Basic Rates—is *not* set through direct legislation. The Master Rate is recalculated or adjusted with each approved spending bill and can vary, depending on the size of the budget and the size of the Tax Base. A greater spending amount combined with a smaller Tax Base requires a higher Master Rate and vice versa. Thus, while the Basic Rates remain stable, the Master Rate can change each time there is a new budget; the Master Rate serves as both a universal assessment factor and as a public and highly visible gauge for the cost of government.

Note that the taxpayer is not required to compute the Master Rate. Rather, Congress calculates the Master Rate after determining the appropriation (spending) amount in the budget and provides the result to the public. The current Master Rate is used by all taxpayers to calculate their individual taxes; it is calculated with the applicable Basic Rates for the Property Types a taxpayer holds with the associated property size, status, ownership, and use conditions to determine the actual tax due.

The Basic-Rate part of this assessment schema and its relationship with the Master Rate will now be explained in more detail. Under RPUT theory the total of all four Basic Rates is designed to equal 100 percent, so that at a macroeconomic-planning or individual-taxpayer-assessment level Tax Category charges (the Basic Rates) can be easily demonstrated by percentage, reflecting the relative, implied level of government service for each Tax-Category property condition.

This 100-percent rule is not mathematically incumbent; tax legislators could arbitrarily assign any Basic Rate schema they wanted. However, since the primary element in actual tax assessment (the basic tax charge) is the Master Rate, and *gross* revenue receipts are not affected by manipulation of the Basic Rates [see the formula in Figure 6], it would seem unwise to depart from the 100-percent rule. A sample of rates is shown in Table B.

Notice, in Table B, the lower rates for Service to Ownership compared to Service to Use. Basic Rates established by Congress (#1 and #2) under the Service-to-Ownership Division are less than the Basic Rates (#3 and #4) under the Service-to-Use Division, because mere ownership demands a relatively small assignation of government service as compared to areas where people live, work, or recreate. For instance, an

Sample RPUT Basic Rates

Congress sets the Basic Rates for the Tax Categories under RPUT Law. The Basic Rates reflect the relative liability ratio in property development, ownership and use conditions, irrespective of current budget and assessment amounts, and are designed to remain stable over multiple budgets (multiple tax years). The sample rates shown here represent a greater liability for property use than for mere property ownership and a greater liability for developed space on land than for undeveloped areas.

#	Tax Category Name	Rate Name	Rate
1	Service to Ownership / Base Land	Basic Rate #1	5 %
2	Service to Ownership / Developed Space	Basic Rate #2	15%
3	Service to Use / Base Land	Basic Rate #3	20%
4	Service to Use / Developed Space	Basic Rate #4	60%
	————	Total	100%

Table B

owner receives a basic, implied level of government service to the aforementioned ten-story office building if it is vacant, but the level of service will be much higher if the building is in use by hundreds of people.

So in operational theory, the Base-Land rates (#1 and #3) established by Congress (in both the Service-to-Ownership and Service-to-Use Divisions) should be lower than the Developed-Space rates (#2 and #4) because undeveloped land normally would have a lower service requirement (implied government service to the locale) than developed areas where human or industrial activity is more prevalent. Examples of lower-assessed undeveloped Base Land would be farm, grazing, park, or open-landscaped areas of residential and commercial properties; higher-assessed Developed Space would be houses, apartments, office buildings, barns, factories, swimming pools, and so on.

One or more of the four Tax Categories may apply to a given piece of property depending on both the level of development and use. Base Land is always assessed under Service to Ownership. Developed Space, if it exists on the property, is also always assessed under Service to Ownership. Base Land and Developed Space, however, are only assessed under Service to Use for the period the property was actually in use or legally available for use (not **vacated** and posted for sale or rent).

The Basic Rates for the Tax Categories would be initialized by Congress after review with economists and the electorate. But unlike the income tax, where thousands upon thousands of specialized tax conditions are lobbied for by various special interests, the RPUT only has the four Basic Rates for regular review and adjustment; this facilitates policy-planning when legislators are creating or revising RPUT Law. As mentioned before, the other key rate, the Master Rate, is not set *directly* by Congress but is derived from a calculation of the budget, the four Basic Rates, and the current Tax Base.

The Basic Rates are designed to remain stable in time for at least a three- to five-year period. Basic Rates that are constantly changed by Congressional whim could contribute to economic destabilization, which is precluded by keeping rates under strict statutory control. As the public should have at least a year and a half's notice prior to Basic Rate changes going into effect, an eighteen-month delay would be required between the date of legislative passage of new Basic Rates and their effective date for assessment purposes.

Manipulation of Basic Rates can affect the individual tax liability of property owners, depending on the ownership/use status, but does not increase or decrease gross tax revenue (as demonstrated in the following pages). There should rarely be a need to change Basic Rates once a consensus has been reached and Basic Rates have been established; regular tax increases or decreases are predicated on the Master Rate, which is determined directly from budget appropriation (spending) amounts.

The unique character of the RPUT has gross funding tied directly to the gross tax assessment and precludes taxation not linked to actual appropriations. The relative link between taxation and spending is maintained at the budget level, but is also carried down and applied in assessments to individual taxpayers; relative cost and liability for expenditures is maintained at all levels.

While the Basic Rates are designed to be stable, the Master Rate can change as often as Funding Statutes are passed. Therefore, it would be prudent for Congress to integrate expenditures in an annual budget plan to preclude a mid-year Master-Rate variance.

Once appropriations are passed and funding is dedicated through RPUT Law, the Master Rate is calculated. The Master Rate will normally not change during the Tax Period unless additional appropriations or spending-adjustment decreases occur within the given budget period and Congress directs a special mid-year rate adjustment. The Master Rate, original or adjusted, is still universally applicable; the rate is the same for all taxpayers in all Tax Categories. (Refer to Table C, the Formula Key, for the identification of variables used in the following example and in the rest of the text.) The Master Rate is multiplied by each Basic Rate in the RPUT assessment calculation to give an **Effective Rate** for each Tax Category as shown in these equations:

$$MR * BR1 = ER1$$
$$MR * BR2 = ER2$$
$$MR * BR3 = ER3$$
$$MR * BR4 = ER4$$

The following equation results from the consanguineous relationship between the Basic Rates (which add up to one) and the Master Rate:

$$MR = (ER1 + ER2 + ER3 + ER4)$$

Whereas Basic Rates are designed to be stable, Effective Rates will change whenever the Master Rate changes. Basic Rates reflect *general tax-assessment policy* regarding Tax-Category Property Types, while Effective Rates (reflecting the current budget and Master Rate) are used by taxpayers to calculate their actual Tax Category *assessments* for the current

Tax Period. Figures 5 and 6 show the Master Rate Formula and its mathematical relationship to the Basic Rates.

The physical area pertaining to each Tax Category is the **Category Area**. One or more of the Effective Rates may be applicable to the Category Areas on a property depending on whether there is only Base Land, or also Developed Space, and whether the land is only owned, or owned and in use. Category Areas are identified through property survey to determine their size and tax-area assessment base.

Area surveys are required whenever, one, land is initially identified for tax assessment; two, new development or demolition occurs; three, an audit is desired by the owner or renter; or four, an audit is requested by a government auditor. Developed Space is determined by measurement of habitable floor areas (shelves in a home or pallet racks in a warehouse, for instance, would not be considered additional taxable space, nor would a low-ceiling, uninhabitable attic). Survey measurements for Developed Space are based on *exterior* building elements; space occupied by walls is counted as Developed Space even though that area is not, obviously, physically habitable. (This definition facilitates ease of survey because structures can then be "shot" from outdoor locations by lasers keyed on exterior structural corners to measure immediately the Developed-Space areas.)

The calculation of ownership and use liability includes two time factors: **Days In Ownership** and **Days In Use**. An owner for a given Tax Period (assumed in these examples to be a calendar year) is liable for the Service-to-Ownership Fee for that portion of the year that legal ownership exists (Days In Ownership/365), and is liable for the Service-to-Use Fee for that portion of the year the property in use (Days In Use/365). The land, though, does not have to be physically occupied or physically utilized to be considered legally in use. Property that is owned is considered available for, or at the pleasure of, the owner and thus is considered in use by the owner unless he vacates the land and legally posts it for sale or rent, or he actually rents or leases the land to someone else.

In summary, the tax calculation for each Tax Category involves multiplying the Master Rate by the Basic Rate to give the Effective Rate; multiplying the Effective Rate by the property area; the property area is then multiplied by the Days In Ownership or the Days In Use and divided by 365 to give the tax amount due. The formulas shown below are for Tax Category #1, where *a* = the tax assessment (the net tax due for Service-to-Ownership/Base-Land):

$$(MR * BR1 = ER1) \qquad a = ER1 * OBL * DIO/365$$

Formula Key

Primary Solutions		
Code	**Value**	**Comments**
a	Tax Category #1 Tax Amount	
b	Tax Category #2 Tax Amount	
c	Tax Category #3 Tax Amount	
d	Tax Category #4 Tax Amount	
w	Developed-Space Rental-Unit Ratio	For relative DS liability
x	Master Rate	
z	Total Tax Due	Total of Tax Categories
Other Variables		
Code	**Value**	**Comments**
BLA	Base-Land Area/Open Land	In acres for all Base Land
BLB	Base-Land Area/Annual Cropland	
BLC	Base-Land Area/Storage Management	
BLD	Base-Land Area/Developed LS	(Developed Landscape)
BLE	Base-Land Area/Base Land Below DS	(Below Developed Space)
BR1	Basic Rate #1	% set by Congress—All four Basic Rates totaled equal 1 (100%).
BR2	Basic Rate #2	
BR3	Basic Rate #3	
BR4	Basic Rate #4	
DIU	Days In Use	
DIO	Days In Ownership	
DSC	Developed-Space Common-Use Area	Total DS Common Areas
ER1	Tax Category #1 Effective Rate	(MR X BR1)
ER2	Tax Category #2 Effective Rate	(MR X BR2)
ER3	Tax Category #3 Effective Rate	(MR X BR3)
ER4	Tax Category #4 Effective Rate	(MR X BR4)
MR	Master Rate	
RR	Revenue Requirement	Appropriation (Spending)
RU	Rental Unit [ID is added]	i.e., apartment number
RUD	Rental-Unit Developed Space	(area of Developed Space)
OBL	Land in Ownership / Base Land	In Acres or Fraction Of
ODS	Land in Ownership / Developed Space	In Acres or Fraction Of
UBL	Land in Use / Base Land	In Acres or Fraction Of
UDS	Land in Use / Developed Space	In Acres or Fraction Of

Table C

Formula for Determining the Master Rate

The Real Property Use Tax system provides one universally applicable assessment value—the Master Rate—that is linked to all other assessment elements. The Master Rate is determined from a calculation of the Revenue Requirement, the four Basic Rates, and the national Tax Base.

Where x = Master Rate.

The Revenue Requirement (RR) is the appropriation or budget amount that Congress chooses to fund through the RPUT. The four Basic Rates (BR1, BR2, BR3, and BR4), representing four primary Tax Categories, are set by Congress in statutory law.

The Tax Base is the total areas for the four Tax Categories (the Property Types OBL, ODS, UBL, and UBS), and the total time in ownership and use (which is shown here based on a one-year Tax Period [365 days]). This is the total figure for all properties in the country that are assessed. (The Tax Base is based on initial physical surveys of individual properties. These surveys—as opposed to the *assessments* based on them—can be valid for the life of individual properties as long as their physical-area status does not change.)

Note that the property status and the time-in-use factors for *individual* properties (an individual 's portion of the total Tax Base) may change during the tax year *after* the Master Rate has been set for the year and this can affect the total budget. This is variance, and average variance is accounted for (for the budget) *prior* to the Master Rate calculation shown here (see Chapter XI for further explanation of variance).

Figure 5

Formula for Determining the Master Rate—Cont.

Basic Formula:

$$RR = [(BR1 * x) * OBL(DIO/365)] + [(BR2 * x) * ODS(DIO/365)] + [(BR3 * x) * UBL(DIU/365)] + [(BR4 * x) * UBS(DIU/365)]$$

Using the Distributive Law:

$$RR = ([BR1 * OBL(DIO/365)] + [BR2 * ODS(DIO/365)] + [BR3 * UBL(DIU/365)] + [BR4 * UBS(DIU/365]) * x$$

Then the Master Rate is:

$$x = RR / ([BR1 * OBL(DIO/365)] + [BR2 * ODS(DIO/365)] + [BR3 * UBL(DIU/365)] + [BR4 * UBS(DIU/365])$$

The computed Master Rate, "*x*," is then used in calculations on individual properties to determine individual assessment liability for taxpayers. The total individual assessments in the country will equal the Revenue Requirement (RR), with a plus or minus variance due to land status or use changes that transpire during the tax period and were not accounted for in the original variance-adjustment calculation (though unaccounted-for variance may be statistically insignificant).

Figure 6

Basic Formula for Computing an RPUT

The basic formula for computing the RPUT due from a taxpayer is shown below. The *Effective Rates* are first calculated from the current *Master Rate* by multiplying it by the *Basic Rate* in each Tax Category. The Effective Rates are then calculated in each Tax Category with the property area and period in use to give the net tax due for each Tax Category. The sum of the net tax due for all four Tax Categories is the total tax due for the property (the variable "z" below).

Tax Category	Effective Rate		Taxable Area		Time (Days)		Tax Due
1)	ER1	X	OBL	X	DIO/365	=	*a*
2)	ER2	X	ODS	X	DIO/365	=	*b*
3)	ER3	X	UBL	X	DIU/365	=	*c*
4)	ER4	X	UDS	X	DIU/365	=	*d*
					Total Tax:		*z*

Table D

A similar calculation is accomplished for each Tax Category that applies to a property; the total for all the applicable Tax Categories is then added together for the total RPUT property assessment. A complete calculation is shown in Table D.

The RPUT is designed so that any time there is a new appropriation or budget, or a *proposed* appropriation or budget, a new or adjusted Master Rate can be computed against a taxpayer's Tax Base to easily determine the new tax. *The Master-Rate-and-Basic-Rate design provides for the largest macroeconomic or smallest microeconomic planning, review, and assessment purposes.* Table E has a schematic demonstrating a sample calculation assessment.

———— ♦ ————

The two RPUT Division assessment-charges, as previously noted, are the Service to Ownership Fee for property ownership, and the Service to Use Fee for property use. Each of these assessments operate under unique conditions.

The property owner is always liable for the Service-to-Ownership Fee, but he is *not* assessed the Service-to-Use Fee if his entire property is vacated and formally offered for sale or rent, or he actually rents or leases the property. However, a landlord with *multiple* rental units on a single property is also not liable for the Service-to-Use Fee even if parts of the single property are being used, as long as the rented areas meet **RPUT Rental Unit** criteria.

RPUT Rental Units are physical divisions on an individual property that have been designated as Rental Units by the owner on the RPUT property survey, and otherwise meet RPUT Rental Unit criteria. In that case, the owner is not liable for the Service-to-Use Fee for an individual Rental Unit that is vacated, and the **RPUT Renter** is liable for the Service-to-Use Fee when the Unit is rented. Thus, owners would not be liable (as they are currently with the conventional property tax) for a property tax associated with the use of their land by others. The RPUT-Rental-Unit condition, however, does not alter owner liability for the *Service-to-Ownership* Fee under the RPUT. The landlord is still directly liable for that.

Once a landlord or a regular property owner vacates an entire property and legally offers it for sale or rent, liability for the Service-to-Use Fee ends and the owner is then only liable for the Service-to-Ownership Fee. A property in this condition is in **Vacation Status.** The difference between a landlord (that has physical rental units that meet

Schematic Sample—Calculation of Individual RPUT

Master Rate: (MR) Rate linked to appropriation and Tax Base. *1								
Service-to-Ownership Fee *2								
(Tax Category)		(Eff Rate)						
1	Base Land	5 % MR	X	Area	X	Days Owned/365	=	Net Tax
2	Developed Space	15 % MR	X	Area	X	Days Owned/365	=	Net Tax
		20 % MR						Subtotal
Service-to-Use Fee *3								
(Tax Category)		(Eff Rate)						
3	Base Land	20 % MR	X	Area	X	Days Used/365	=	Net Tax
4	Developed Space	60 % MR	X	Area	X	Days Used/365	=	Net Tax
		80 % MR						Subtotal
Total for Four Rate Sections								
Total		100 % MR						Total Tax

Table E

Notes – Table E

The schematic, or basic formula it represents, is applicable for all RPUT property calculations, including multiple Rental Units and rural land types. Rental units and rural land types, however, may have sub-unit calculations accomplished first, prior to total property-tax computation.

*** 1 The Master Rate (MR) can be calculated by applying the Revenue Requirement against the total Tax Base (see Figures 5–6 for formula). Congress sets the four Basic Rates (BR), which must total 100%. The Basic-Rate percentages are multiplied by the Master Rate to give four Effective Rates. *The Effective Rate percentages shown in chart are samples.* The tax due for a property is the total of the four (Tax Category) tax-assessment amounts.**

*** 2 Service-to-Ownership Fee—Always applicable and always assessed owner.**

*** 3 Service-to-Use Fee—Not applicable if property is *not* in use by owner *and* property is for sale or rent. Tax is applicable to owner if in use by owner, or may be applicable to renter (or leaseholder) if the land is rented out.**

RPUT rental criteria) and a regular property owner is that the landlord can claim Vacation Status for *individual portions* of his property (the RPUT Rental Units) if they are not rented. A landlord that chooses *not* to designate RPUT Rental Units can still rent portions of his property, but he cannot claim Vacation Status unless his entire property (like the single-unit property of a regular owner) is vacated and posted for sale or rent. Landlords are responsible for advising renters of applicable Service-to-Use taxes as well as informing the renter of the appropriate Rental-Unit survey and assessment information. Renters can validate their own Tax Base if desired.

A renter remits his RPUT Service-to-Use Fee to his landlord. The tax amount can be included in the rental check that is paid to the landlord as long as the rental contract and rental receipt properly denote the amount that is applied to the RPUT. The landlord then forwards all renters' tax payments (the collected Service-to-Use Fees) along with the appropriate Service-to-Ownership remittance (paid by the landlord) to the government by the RPUT due date. This process is similar to merchants remitting sales-and-use-tax receipts, only the number of remittance transactions would be far fewer. Non-payment by the renter of the Service-to-Use Fee would be noted by the owner on his RPUT-remittance form; subsequent notification to delinquent renters would be made directly by the federal RPUT tax agency, and resolution of past-due Service-to-Use assessments would be resolved directly between the federal tax agency and the renter.

———— ♦ ————

Rental property that is subdivided into RPUT Rental Units can include **Common Areas** that are jointly utilized by renters. These areas are accounted for in the RPUT assessment calculation through Common-Area averaging. Examples of Common Areas in an apartment building where Common-Area averaging would apply would be shared parking lots, landscaped areas, laundry rooms, walkways, and swimming pools.

The Base Land underneath Rental Units is also considered a Common Area since multiple-story apartments can exist over Base Land, and averaging can properly account for that condition. Common-Area assessment calculations are accomplished by computing the relative liability of gross Common Areas for each Rental Unit.

As an example, consider a one-acre apartment complex where there is a half-acre of Base Land underneath the apartment structure and a half-acre of outside Common Areas, and where the apartment building is divided into four rented apartments (four RPUT Rental Units). The entire RPUT *Service-to-Ownership* liability—both Base Land and Developed Space portions—would apply to the owner. But the owner, because he is not directly utilizing the property and has the Rental Units rented or vacated, is not liable for the *Service-to-Use* Fee. That liability is either assumed by the renters or does not apply if the Units are vacated. (Acre is the unit of measurement used in this example, but in practice measurements for small- to medium-sized properties would most likely be accomplished in square feet, with calculations performed using per-square-foot rates converted from the RPUT per-acre baseline rates.)

The *Service-to-Use* liability for the apartment complex (for both Service-to-Use Base Land and Developed Space) would apply to the renters. The Service-to-Use/*Base-Land* Fee is divided up proportionately among the renters according to the size of each Rental Unit: Three of four apartments in the example each takes up 1/10 of the one-acre property (for a total of 3/10 of an acre), and the last apartment is a luxury unit that takes up 2/10 of an acre (The total of all apartments, including the luxury unit, takes up 5/10 of an acre—which is one half of the total one-acre property; the other half of the land—grass and walkways—are Common Areas). These ratios are then divided by the *total Rental-Unit* Developed Space to provide the liability percentage for each renter: 20 percent for each of the three regular Units (60 percent for all three) and 40 percent for the luxury Unit. The individual liability percentages are then applied to the entire Base-Land area (the whole acre, including Common Areas) to compute the Base-Land liability for each renter.

The Service-to-Use/*Developed-Space* liability for *individual* apartments is easy to compute; liability is based on the actual Developed Space in each Unit, with each renter paying for his own Unit's assessment. The area liabilities in the apartment example would be 1/10 of an acre each for the first three Units and 2/10 of an acre for the luxury Unit.

Renters are also liable for the Service-to-Use/*Developed-Space Common Areas*. Here the chargeable area per renter would be based on the same liability percentages that were used for Base-Land computation, but multiplied against the total Common Areas on the property instead of the Base-Land area. Figure 7 shows the property areas for the sample apartment complex, and Table F displays the total liability (including Common Areas) for each Rental Unit.

Another example of an RPUT Rental-Unit complex is a shared office building, one acre square, three stories high on an acre of land, with the first two stories leased to separate businesses and the top story divided

Residential Rental Units With Common Areas—Part A

1 Acre Apartment Complex—Map

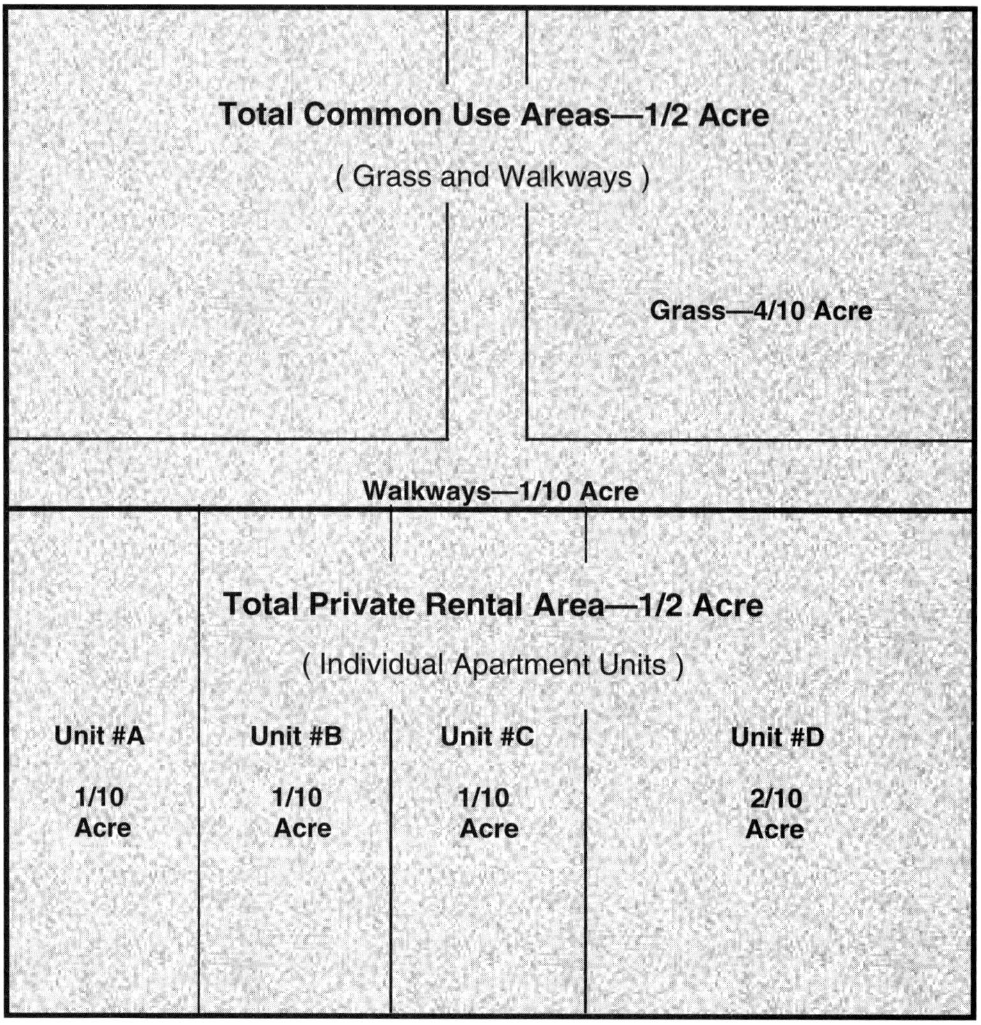

This sample property shows the physical size of both individual units on a rental property and the Common Areas on the property shared by the units. RPUT liability for Service to Use for the renters would be in proportion to the size of their units—Apartment #D having twice the liability of any of the other units because the property is twice the size.

Figure 7

Residential Rental Units With Common Areas—Part B

1 Acre Apartment Complex—Area Totals

Service-to-Use Liability for Apartment Renters				
Unit	Direct *1 Liability	Portion of Common Use Area Liability *2		
	Developed Space (acres)	Base Land (Total Area) (acres)	Landscaped Grounds (Grass / Planted Areas) (acres)	Developed Space (Walkways) (acres)
Apt. #A	.1	.2	.08	.02
Apt. #B	.1	.2	.08	.02
Apt. #C	.1	.2	.08	.02
Apt. #D	.2	.4	.16	.04
Total	.5	1.0	.40	.10

The RPUT liability Service-to-Use Fee for renters for the Developed-Space area of their units is based on the size of their units. Apartment #D is twice the size of each of the other units, and so has twice the Developed-Space liability (2/10 Acre).

The Base-Land area of a property is shared by all Rental Units, even in a multi-floor dwelling, and Base-Land liability is also proportional. The liability for the total Base-Land area for each renter is based on the ratio of Developed Space of his Rental Unit to the total Developed-Space area of all Rental Units (*not* including Common Areas). Thus, Base-Land liability for Apartment #D, being twice the size of each of the other apartments, is twice as large as that for the other apartments (4/10 Acre).

The liability for the Developed-Space Common Areas (walkways) on the property is likewise proportional, with Apartment #D having a Service-to-Use liability of .4/10 Acre. There is no separate, proportional tax for the Landscaped-Grounds (non-Developed-Space) Common Areas, as this is Open Space and is assessed only under the Base-Land criteria described above.

***1 Direct-Liability Developed Space is the total for all individual, rented apartment spaces exclusive of any Common Areas.**

***2 Base Land and Developed Space are the only two RPUT Common Area assessments. Landscaped Grounds is shown here for area comparison with Developed Space, but it is part of the total Base-Land area and is not charged twice.**

Table F

into four offices and leased to four other businesses (a total of six businesses in the building). A Common Area on each floor of the building exists consisting of a foyer and rest rooms that would be shared (Adjustments for stairways and elevators are not included in this example for simplicity). See the office building complex in Figure 8 and apportioned costs in Table G.

There is no Open Space on the office-building property, but renters would still be liable for the Service-to-Use/Base-Land area under the structure in proportion to the size of the Developed Space of their Rental Units. That means that for the Service-to-Use Fee for the acre of Base Land on the property the first-floor business would be liable for 1/3 (or 4/12), the second-floor business would also be liable for 1/3 (or 4/12), and the four businesses on the top floor, being of a smaller size, would each be liable for 1/12. The Base-Land and Developed-Space Common Area liabilities for the renters are added to their individual Developed-Space assessment (for their Rental-Unit office spaces) for the total Service-to-Use Fee due.

———— ♦ ————

There is no RPUT Service-to-Use liability for designated Rental Units that are vacant. The Base-Land assessment for Common Areas for remaining renters remains the same (it is not increased) when other Rental Units on a property become vacant; for the government, the gross Service-to-Use Fee due (the amount due for the total property) is reduced when Rental Units become unoccupied.

Open-Space areas, like Developed-Space areas, can—instead of serving as a Common Area for all renters—be rented *directly* to an *individual* renter. In that case, the privately rented Base-Land portion of the property would not be included in the liability weighted averaging for Common Areas but would be a direct liability of the renter. An example is an apartment that has a private backyard that is not shared with other tenants. (This type of situation could easily be accounted for in a regular RPUT accounting-system or computer-application program used by landlords, but the variable is not included in the formulas that follow for simplicity.)

In summary, for RPUT Rental Unit Service-to-Use liability:

- The *Developed-Space liability for the Rental Unit* is based on the actual Developed Space in the rented unit area.
- The *Base-Land liability* for shared land use is calculated from the ratio of a renter's Developed Space to the total Rental-Unit Developed

Space, where that ratio is applied against the total Base Land on the property to determine the assessment.

- The *Developed-Space Common-Area liability* for a renter is the total Common Areas on a property multiplied by the *same* renter Developed-Space-to-Rental-Unit ratio that is used for Base-Land liability.

The formula for computing the RPUT for a rental property is shown in Figures 9 and 10.

One can see that the concept of liability and the necessary mathematical relationships are easy to grasp, but the complexity of area types on some rental properties along with the Days In Use factored in to account for changing renters might make an actual calculation appear daunting at first. Proper record keeping and calculation when changes occur, however, should make tax processing fairly straightforward. Modern computer systems, though, make RPUT processing even easier.

From a computer-programming, -operating, and tax-management standpoint, tracking RPUT conditions and calculating assessments is very simple, and commercial as well as residential participants in the RPUT system would be encouraged to utilize the computer as an administrative tool. Once an initial survey is accomplished on a property to determine Tax Category, Common, and RPUT Rental-Unit Areas, all that is required is the entry of current time-in-ownership/use information into an RPUT application program; the assessment calculations can then be done automatically. Additionally, RPUT accounts can be linked to a regular accounts-receivable or computer-billing program to eliminate duplicate data-records and increase overall efficiency, such as utilizing a single renter address listing for RPUT, billing, correspondence, and other purposes.

◆

Developed Space property consists of units such as houses, apartments, factories, office space, and so on, and the level of Service to Use on those Developed Space areas can be easily determined by the owner and is relatively simple for the government to audit. But Open-Space property areas are different, and the relevant use-conditions on many of them need to be recognized in a different manner for proper assessment.

Open Space is Base Land without any Developed Space on it such as farmland, timberland, grazing land, or undeveloped recreational land. The property-use areas on these types of Open Space can go in and out of

Office Rental Unit with Common Areas—Part A

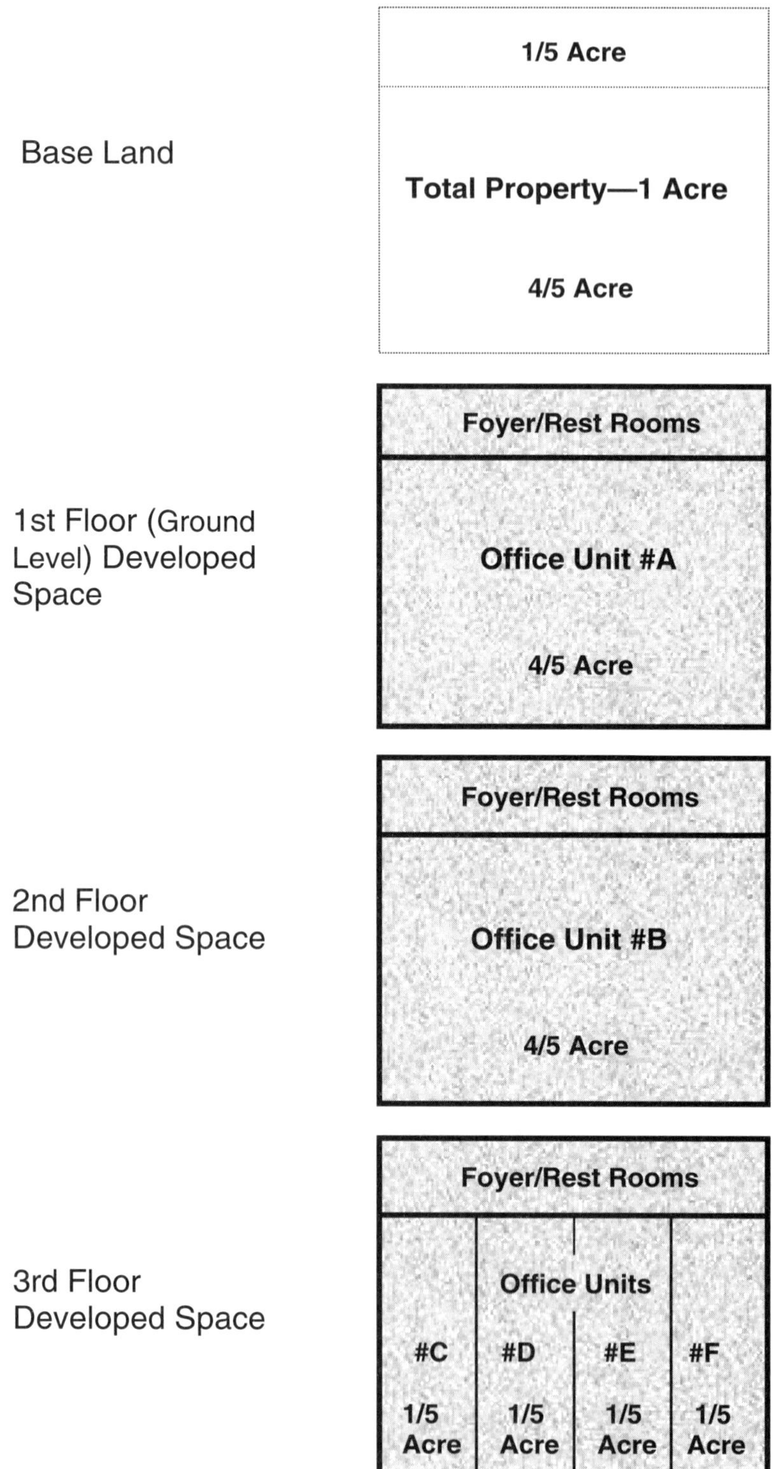

Figure 8

Office Rental Unit With Common Areas—Part B

Service-to-Use Liability for Office Renters *1				
Business Office	Direct Liability	Portion of Common Use Area Liability		
	Developed Space *2 (acres)	Base Land (Total Area) *3 (acres)	Landscaped Grounds (Grass / Planted Areas) (acres)	Developed Space (Foyer / Rest Rooms) *4 (acres)
Unit #A	4/5	4/12	None	4/20 .2
Unit #B	4/5	4/12	None	4/20 .2
Unit #C	1/5	1/12	None	1/20 .05
Unit #D	1/5	1/12	None	1/20 .05
Unit #E	1/5	1/12	None	1/20 .05
Unit #F	1/5	1/12	None	1/20 .05
Total	2.4	1.0	—	12/20 .6 *5

RPUT Service-to-Use area liability to renters for Developed Space in their units is the actual area (size) of the individual units. The Service-to-Use liability for Base-Land and Developed-Space Common Areas, on the other hand, is based on the size of the individual rented unit relative to the total size of all individual rented units (the larger the rented unit, the greater the liability for Common Areas). The total Service-to-Use Fee due from an individual renter under the RPUT is the individual unit assessment plus the proportional assessment for the Common Areas.

***1 Areas are shown in ratios with the lowest common denominator for comparison purposes. RPUT stairway/elevator calculation adjustment is excluded here for simplicity.**

***2 Direct-Liability Developed Space is the total for all individual, rented office space exclusive of any Common Areas.**

***3 The total Base Land is 1, or 12/12, acre. Each Office Unit shares a proportional liability for the Base-Land area that corresponds to their share of the total Rental-Unit Developed Space on the property (the areas exclusive of Common Areas).**

***4 The same relative liability ratio that applies to the 1 acre of Base Land also applies to the 3/5 (or 12/20) acre of Developed-Space Common Areas.**

***5 The total Developed-Space Common Areas is shown here in ratio *and* decimal format.**

Table G

Calculation for RPUT Rental Property

Service to Ownership

The calculation for Service to Ownership exists as an owner liability regardless of owner or renter occupancy or utilization of the property itself. Service-to-Ownership liability is assumed the day of property purchase and ends at midnight the day prior to sale.

$$a = ER1 * OBL * DIO/365$$

$$b = ER2 * ODS * DIO/365$$

Total Service-to-Ownership Fee = a + b

Service to Use

The total Service-to-Use Fee for a given piece of property that is fully occupied is the same amount for an owner, a single renter—or if the property is physically apportioned into Rental Units—for multiple renters (Each of multiple renters pays their apportioned share of the total Fee relative to their Rental Unit). Calculation of Base-Land and Common-Area assessment for multiple renters, however, includes additional variables to account for the property elements that are shared.

Calculation of Rental Unit Size Ratio:

This calculation must be done for each Rental Unit based on the Rental Unit Developed Space, or RUD (i.e., RUD1, RUD2, RUD3, . . .), prior to performing any other calculation.

RUD1 / (RUD1 + RUD2 + RUD3 . . .) = RUD1w

Service to Use continued in Figure 10.

Figure 9

Calculation for RPUT Rental Property—Cont.

Calculation for One Rental Unit on a Multi-Unit Property:

The entire Base Land on a rental property is considered as a Common Area, and the Service-to-Use liability for that Base Land is assigned to Rental Units proportionately, based on the size of their individual Developed-Space areas (i.e. the size of their individual apartments). Developed-Space Common Areas, on the other hand, such as parking lot, pool, or walkway areas, require a separate physical measurement, but relative liability to renters for this area is *also* based on the Developed-Space size of their individual Units. Note that "DSC" is the *Total* Developed-Space Common Areas; OBL, or owner's Base-Land area, is the total Base-Land property area and is the value also used in the calculation for the renter's Base-Land Service-to-Use liability.

RU1 *c* = ER3 * [RUD1w * OBL * (DIU1/365)]

RU1 *d* = ER4 * [(RUD1+ [RUD1w * DSC]) * (DIU1/365)]

Calculation for Total Property (All Rental Units) Liability:

c = ER3 * ([RUD1w * OBL * (DIU1/365)] +
[RUD2w * OBL * (DIU2/365)] +
[RUD3w * OBL * (DIU3/365)] . . .)

d = ER4 * ([(RUD1+ [RUD1w * DSC]) * (DIU1/365)] +
[(RUD2 + [RUD2w * DSC]) * (DIU2/365)] +
[(RUD3 + [RUD3w * DSC]) * (DIU3/365)] . . .)

Total Service-to-Use Fee = c + d.

Total RPUT for Property

Total tax due for the property (both Service to Ownership and Service to Use) is "z":

$$z = (a + b + c + d)$$

Figure 10

service often, and the property-use period can be difficult to determine—even by the owner.

Farmers, for example, need to be able to plant when and where it's appropriate and not have to worry about repeated Days-In-Use reporting and re-assessment of their Tax Base. Ranchers need to be able to utilize their land or rent it out based on the number of stock or other relevant use factors. It would be difficult to determine, for instance, the number of acres "in use" when a hundred head of cattle were let out on five hundred acres of range land and actually congregated in the northeastern fifty. The Days-In-Use determination for timber or outdoor-recreational lands would be similarly difficult.

Also, if actual Days In Use for agricultural or outdoor lands applied, there would be an economic incentive for landowners to continually take various segments out of use (vacate the land and put it up for temporary sale) in order to minimize their tax liability. Resources could thus be wasted in the economy through tax-avoidance activity of taxpayers frequently claiming temporary Vacation Status. There could also be additional paperwork, audits, and enforcement problems for the government.

Thus, calculating the *actual* Days-In-Use calculation is not practical for many Open-Space lands. So for certain types of Open-Space property a Base-Land **Standard Rate** based on **average relative use** is used in the RPUT assessment calculation. The Standard Rate is a fraction of the total number of days in the Tax Period and applies *irrespective* of the actual number of days the property was in use, or available for use.

Owners with Base Land where an RPUT Standard Rate applies do not have to track the actual period of land use; they may use their property more than the average-relative-use days for the specific Standard-Rate Property Type and not be liable for any increase in the Service-to-Use Fee. This is an effective discount. But once agricultural or outdoor lands have been so classified the landowner cannot claim Vacation Status even if the Open-Space land is physically vacated (not in use) and posted for sale or rent. (The exception is Base-Land portions of a property where the Standard Rate does not apply—farmhouses, warehouses, barns, and so on—where Vacation Status can still be claimed.)

There are two possible conditions, then, for factoring Days-In-Use in the RPUT assessment calculation—the actual Days In Use or the Standard Rate (average relative use). The Days-In-Use factor for Service to Use/*Developed Space* is always the actual Days In Use—the number of days the Developed Space was in use by an owner or renter during the

Tax Period, divided by the Tax Period itself (i.e., For 72 days use, the factor would be 72/365 for a one-year Tax Period). But the whether the Days-In-Use factor for Service to Use/*Base Land* is the actual Days In Use, *or* a Standard Rate, depends on a property's **Base Land Status**. Base-Land-Status types, including those with Standard Rates, are defined below:

A) **Open Land**. This type of Open Space includes commercial timberland, planted orchards not yet in production, range (grazing) land, fallow farmland (farmland out of production for the entire tax period), undeveloped recreational land (land used for hiking, skiing, boating, fishing, hunting, and so on), and general undeveloped land. Open Land, considered the least intensive land use, is taxed under a Standard Rate and has the lowest Base-Land tax charge under Service to Use.

B) **Annual Cropland**. Annual Cropland is farmland currently producing, or capable of production, including row crops and orchards in production. Annual Cropland is taxed at a higher Standard Rate than Open Land but still discounted off the Days-In-Use maximum.

C) **Storage Management**. Storage Management is a term applied to undeveloped land used more intensively, for agriculture or otherwise. Examples include active livestock yards (animals corralled with more than twenty-five per acre, for instance), temporary vehicle storage lots, junkyards, and marshaling yards. The actual Days-In-Use charge for Base Land applies to Storage Management.

D) **Landscaped Grounds**. This Property Type includes commercial and residential landscape, private parks (but not, for instance, developed amusement parks, which would come under Developed Space), and private stadium fields (i.e., baseball or football fields, but *not* the parking lots, concession stands, or spectator bleachers). The actual Days-In-Use charge applies.

E) **Base Land Under Developed Space**. Includes the land area under houses, roads, factories, and so on. Note that this category denotes *all* Base Land with Develop Space above it. The actual Days-In-Use charge applies for Base Land Under Developed Space.

A table showing Base-Land-Status types and those with Standard Rates is shown in Table H.

For Base-Land-Status types that have a Standard Rate, calculation of the average-relative-use time is simple. The Standard Rate is merely multiplied against the Tax Period in the Days-In-Use ratio, and then that value is used in the full RPUT assessment calculation. For instance, if the Standard Rate is 25 percent, then the number of days to be used in calculation of the Service-to-Use Fee would be 0.25 * 365, or 90 days (three months).

Let us take another Standard Rate example of a 100-acre farm. The Base-Land area of the farm is a 100 acres with 95 acres as standard farm land (Annual Cropland) and the remaining 5 acres as Developed Space (the Developed Space being a house, barn, outbuildings, and so on). If average Days In Use for Annual Cropland was set by Congress at four months, the Standard Rate would be 33.3 percent (120/365 Days). The RPUT Service-to-Use Fee for the Annual Cropland would thus be the Effective Rate for Service-to-Use/Base-Land times 95 (the Annual Cropland area) times 33.3%. The charge would apply for the Tax Period irrespective of the amount of time the land was actually in use even if the land was being farmed at twice the average use rate (240/365 Days) or more.

The farmer of this 100-acre plot cannot, however, claim Vacation Status for the Service-to-Use/Base-Land Fee if he happens to use his land less than four months (the Standard-Rate assessment). He could, though, claim Vacation Status for his house and barn (the Developed Space on his land) if he vacated them and put them up for sale or rent. (The *Service-to-Ownership Fee,* as opposed to the Service-to-Use Fee, still applies in its entirety to the owner and is not affected by Base-Land-Status type or Days In Use.)

Under the RPUT Standard Rate, farmers can manage the land any way they want, including leasing a portion or all of the land to other farmers—but the standard Service-to-Use/Base-Land Fee is always due. Land can be re-surveyed and reclassified if an owner does not want to continue using a Standard-Rate value in determining his RPUT and instead wants to use the actual Days-In-Use. But if the property status is changed the new Base Land Status does not become effective until the next tax year—and the Open Space areas would still not be eligible for subdivision into RPUT Rental Units for claiming Vacation Status. The formula for calculating Open-Space Base-Land-Status types (rural land calculations) is shown in Figures 11 and 12.

Base-Land-Status Types

#	Base Land Status	Formula Variable	Automatic Adjustment (Discount) Off Possible Maximum	Days-In-Use Calculation	Standard Use Rate Amount *1	Vacation Claim Possible
A	*Open Land*	BLA	Yes	Standard Rate	1 Month (1/12 Year)	No
B	*Annual Cropland*	BLB	Yes	Standard Rate	4 Months (4/12 Year)	No
C	*Storage Management*	BLC	No	Actual Days in Use	N/A	Yes
D	*Landscaped Grounds*	BLD	No	Actual Days in Use	N/A	Yes
E	*Base Land Under Developed Space*	BLE	No	Actual Days in Use	N/A	Yes

Base Land is the surface area, or legal-title area, on a piece of property—whether or not it has Developed Space (permanent real property structures) on it. Base Land that is totally undeveloped or under agricultural use (Open Land or Annual Cropland) has a lower implied level of service by the state, and thus a lower "Standard Rate" schema (see Rows A & B) applies. These rates, like the Basic Rates, are set by Congress.

***1 Sample rates are indicated.**

Table H

Calculation for Multiple Base-Land-Status Types

Base Land Status (the base-land area on a property under the RPUT) consists of five categories: Open Land, Annual Cropland, Storage Management, Landscaped Grounds, and Base Land Under Developed Space. The formula provided here accounts for these varied land conditions. It can be applied to a property that is being used directly by the owner or that is rented out as a single unit to compute the RPUT.

The formula here *cannot* be used directly for multiple renters on a given property, as Base-Land and Common-Area liability must be apportioned (see Figures 9–10). However, the concept displayed is ultimately applicable to all properties.

Service to Ownership

The calculation for Service to Ownership is the same (as previously discussed) for other RPUT conditions, and it is shown again below:

$$a = \text{ER1} * \text{OBL} * \text{DIO}/365$$

$$b = \text{ER2} * \text{ODS} * \text{DIO}/365$$

Total Service-to-Ownership Fee = a + b

Figure 11

Calculation for Multiple Base-Land-Status Types—Cont.

Service to Use

The physical areas for the five Base-Land-Status types are represented by BLA, BLB, BLC, BLD, and BLE; corresponding Days-In-Use values are represented by DIUA, DIUB, DIUC, DIUD, and DIUE. Note that for BLA (Open Land) a Standard Rate of .08 (30 Days) is applied here as a sample value; a Standard Rate of .33 (120 Days) for BLB (Annual Cropland) is entered. BLC, BLD, and BLE are all based on actual Days In Use.

$$c = \text{ER3} * ([\text{BLA} * (30/365)] + [\text{BLB} * (120/365)] + [\text{BLC} * (\text{DIUC}/365)] + [\text{BLD} * (\text{DIUD}/365)] + [\text{BLE} * (\text{DIUE}/365)])$$

$$d = \text{ER4} * (\text{UDS} * (\text{DIU}/365))$$

Total Service-to-Use Fee = c + d

Total RPUT for Property

Total tax due for the property (both Service to Ownership and Service to Use) is “z”:

$$z = (a + b + c + d)$$

Figure 12

XI. The RPUT—Practical Application

Government Organization

National fiscal activity under the RPUT begins with Congress establishing the Basic Rates. These are the rates that define the four Tax Categories for ownership and use of land. Congress then performs the appropriate collection of Tax Base information from area surveys. The government can accomplish this through site surveys, contractor certified building reports, or surveys provided directly by landowners. Once a property has been surveyed, that survey information can be used in subsequent tax years for the same property; re-survey is not required unless the physical status of the property changes.

Tax Base property area is based on survey and current-use information, but the actual figures later entered into the Master Rate formula for Master Rate calculation will normally have to be adjusted beforehand from a **Standard Variance**. Tax Base variance occurs during the active Tax Period after the initial budget has been passed when property-status and -use changes occur due to construction, demolition, or land-use change. For instance, if it is estimated that 9 percent of all properties will have some assessment change during the new Tax Period and a net 3 percent growth in the Tax Base is expected to occur, then the expected Standard Variance—the 3 percent increase—would be accounted for in a downward adjustment of the Master Rate at the beginning of the Tax Period. If the **Actual Variance** at the end of the Tax Period turned out to be 3.12 percent with a resulting revenue surplus, then the surplus amount could be rebated to taxpayers, or assigned to a **Secondary Dedication** previously identified in the Funding Statute.

Deficit spending may also occur, depending on the needs of the government, and in that case there would be a reduced *current* Revenue Requirement and thus a lower current tax. However, the principle (the total tax due over the long run) does not change in this case, and one additional element is added to the tax calculation and cost: the government interest that must be carried by taxpayers on the borrowed money. The deferred principle would mean lower-than-normal taxes in the current tax year but higher assessments in later years when the federal debt came due (when the bonds previously issued for financing the debt came due for the bondholders).

Once the Tax Base survey information is collected, deficit planning integrated into the budget, as needed, and variance is calculated, the budget process can then be initiated and the current Revenue Requirement for proposed government expenditures identified. A Master Rate is computed and published, and the taxpaying public can discern, *before appropriation measures are passed into law,* what their tax liability is going to be for the current Tax Period, as well as the projected liability in future Tax Periods for any deficit spending. Efficient economic analysis by professionals can occur, as well as individual citizen assessment and group feedback regarding the real-world economic feasibility and cost/value of the spending proposals.

The RPUT Funding Statute—the spending appropriation—is then passed after deliberation by Congress. A clause in the Funding Statute directs that assessment be made through the RPUT Law on the Tax Base to fund the government expenditures (government expenses, programs, and services) identified in the bill. The new Master Rate, the basis of assessment for the Tax Period, is calculated at this time (see Chapter X, Figures 5–6, for the formula for determining the Master Rate).

Individual taxpayers calculate their tax assessment for the new Tax Period based on the new Master Rate. This would take only seconds for taxpayers who have had their property-survey information previously recorded in a personal computer. Tax remittance is then mailed, or if preferred by the taxpayer, electronically transferred from the taxpayer's bank account. No tax remittance *form* is needed for taxpayers as long as they do not have any new or special filing conditions. The remittance check or funds-transfer is simply annotated or coded with the appropriate property-tax identification number and sent in.

The RPUT system also provides for effective audit controls. Statistical averaging and effective individual review can be accomplished quickly and efficiently because of an objective and relatively static tax base. Physical property-survey audits on many properties may be accomplished in minutes with modern technology. With all property area and assessment history information on computer, filing discrepancies should be immediately noted and easily, fairly, and expeditiously resolved for both taxpayers and the government.

The final element in RPUT management is democratic control, which already exists in our Constitutional system. Citizens concerned with the fiscal policies implemented by their representatives in Congress replace or reelect those officials, as appropriate, through the election process. The RPUT Fiscal process is charted in Figure 13.

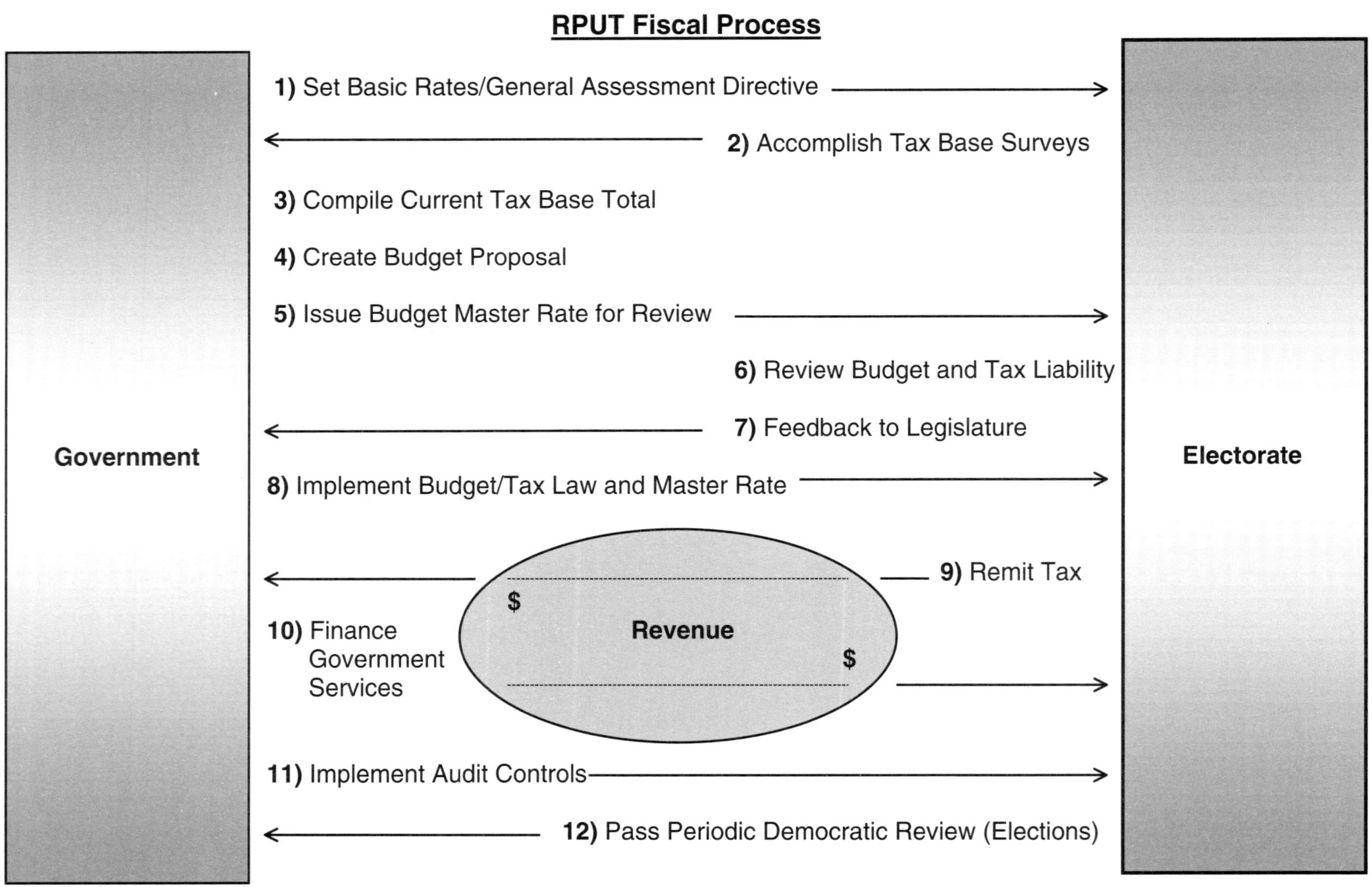
RPUT Fiscal Process
Government
Electorate
1) Set Basic Rates/General Assessment Directive
2) Accomplish Tax Base Surveys
3) Compile Current Tax Base Total
4) Create Budget Proposal
5) Issue Budget Master Rate for Review
6) Review Budget and Tax Liability
7) Feedback to Legislature
8) Implement Budget/Tax Law and Master Rate
9) Remit Tax
$
Revenue
$
10) Finance Government Services
11) Implement Audit Controls
12) Pass Periodic Democratic Review (Elections)

Figure 13

Government organization under the RPUT would remain as it is now at the legislative level; Congress and its budget committees and budget agencies would continue to plan spending and manage appropriations. The federal tax agency, though, charged with implementing the RPUT collection, enforcement, and audit controls would have significantly different responsibilities than under the current income tax system. The agency currently charged with income tax administration, the Internal Revenue Service, will have its hands full in phasing out that system, and a brand new agency should be created separate from the existing one to administer the new RPUT.

RPUT *assessment*, however, should *not* be implemented while income tax assessment is active—two tax systems should not be taxing citizens for the same tax period. Americans should not hold the punitive aspects of an old tax system, the income tax, and also bear the fiscal burden of a second system, no matter how good the second one is. There would have to be a cut-off period where assessment for the income tax ended and the RPUT began. Even after the final assessment period ended for the income tax and RPUT assessment began, however, income tax administration would have to continue in order to collect taxes and pay refunds for *past* income tax periods. For example, if income tax assessment ended and RPUT assessment started January 1, 2000, then the IRS might remain operational until 2003 to process paperwork for 1999 and prior income tax years, while the *new* RPUT administrative agency assumed *RPUT-related* functions and current-year assessment. As prior-year income tax processing was completed and the income tax system was closed down, remaining IRS civil servants could apply for transfer to the new RPUT agency.

As designed, the new RPUT administrative agency would have five divisions:

1) A management section for overall planning, coordination, and policy administration.
2) An accounting/engineering/data-processing section for operating the reporting system.
3) A customer service department for responding to customer queries and tracking assessments and payments.
4) An audit function for internal record and field review of the Tax Base, both on a statistical and specific problem basis.
5) A legal/enforcement section for legally addressing compliance questions.

The RPUT administrative agency may require far fewer individuals than currently required with the IRS, one reason being federal tax agencies would no longer be engrossed in complex analyses of other people's business income and expenses. *Most important of all, instead of being required to implement exceedingly complex, vague, and arbitrary income tax law, federal tax-agency civil servants would be in the business of objective administration of clear, concise tax code.*

All general policies, statistical audit examination of the Tax Base, and criteria for auditing suspect or problem conditions by the RPUT audit division—unlike the super-secret IRS auditing process—would be public. The survey, assessment and payment records would be a matter of public record and available to the public and the press. Americans could see their tax system working. Since the RPUT is based on an objective assessment of physical property and its use, citizens' financial privacy—the Constitutional right of citizens to be "secure in their persons, houses, *papers, and effects*" [italics inserted],[217] including their business and private financial activities—would be maintained.

The RPUT Law, with additional explanatory text, examples and figures, would be contained in easy-reference documentation—both in paper form and in "drill-down," search-capable computer format. The steps for tax reporting and audit processes would also be clearly identified for taxpayers for their tax preparations, and for federal tax agency representatives for their procedures and duties.

◆

As previously defined, there are two major legal elements in RPUT functioning. The first part is the central administrative element, the Real Property Use Tax Law (RPUTL); the second part is the appropriation or budget law, or Funding Statute. To effect financing of an appropriation (or full budget) through the RPUT a clause in the Funding Statute directs that the RPUTL be used as a funding base for the appropriation (instead of financing the expenditure through tariffs, excise taxes, user fees, or other means).

The original Master Rate for a particular Tax Period is then calculated from the Tax Base, the Basic Rates, and the Revenue Requirement (the spending appropriation). The Master Rate calculation is accomplished prior to the beginning of the Tax Period, and the Master Rate normally does not change for the duration of the applicable tax year. But a **Master Rate Adjustment**—an increase or decrease for the current Tax Period—can be implemented to reflect budget or spending changes that occur during the Tax Period when Congress directs an immediate assessment adjustment. The *new* adjusted rate (the original Master Rate plus the Master Rate Adjustment) is the **Adjusted Master Rate.**

Practically speaking, it might be rare that Congress would issue a mid-year assessment change after the main budget has passed, preferring to defer budget-adjustment rate changes until the next regular Tax Period. However, the concept and possibility is demonstrated. A chronological schematic of regular and Adjusted Master Rates and their relationship is shown in Figure 14.

Property Survey and Tax Base Determination

Individual property survey and Tax Base determination is straightforward for both the taxpayer and government tax administrator, and little tax preparation and audit time will be required by most. Initial RPUT implementation (when the law first comes into effect) would require all properties to be surveyed, but re-survey would normally be accomplished only if property status changed or there was a required audit.

Properties can be surveyed with traditional transit and tape measures, or with modern technologies such as infrared and laser measuring devices. Survey can be accomplished directly by landowners (or by renters wanting to validate their Tax Base). A small lot with one dwelling might be surveyed in minutes, whereas a larger property with Rental Units could take several hours or longer depending on the size and complexity of the property.

A property survey can also be accomplished through a contractor. A builder with a federal survey certification, for instance, could certify the land status on a building project based on the original architectural plans, provided this is done after both physical completion and physical review of the project. This would preclude a secondary survey for tax purposes after the initial building construction survey had already occurred, and would save time and money.

Citizens who secure an RPUT survey through a contractor can also obtain insurance on their property survey, either through the contractor in conjunction with his services or from a separate insurance company. The insurer then warrants the accuracy, and if the taxpayer is later audited and the survey deemed inaccurate by the government the insurer would pay for any additional tax assessment, interest, and penalty.

RPUT Laws and Assessment Relationship

Year | **RPUT Administrative Tax Law** | **Funding Statutes (Spending Bills)** | **Tax Assessment**

2005

RPUT Law (RPUTL) is the main part of the RPUT system, prescribing operations, regulations, administration, and the four Basic Rates. RPUT conditions become applicable in tax assessment for a given budget or appropriation when a budget or appropriation law is passed and specifies its funding base as the RPUT (Some appropriations, for instance, could be financed by tariffs or excise taxes.) The budget or appropriation amount is calculated against the Tax Base and Basic Rates to give the Master Rate (MR), which is used by individual taxpayers to compute their individual tax amounts due.

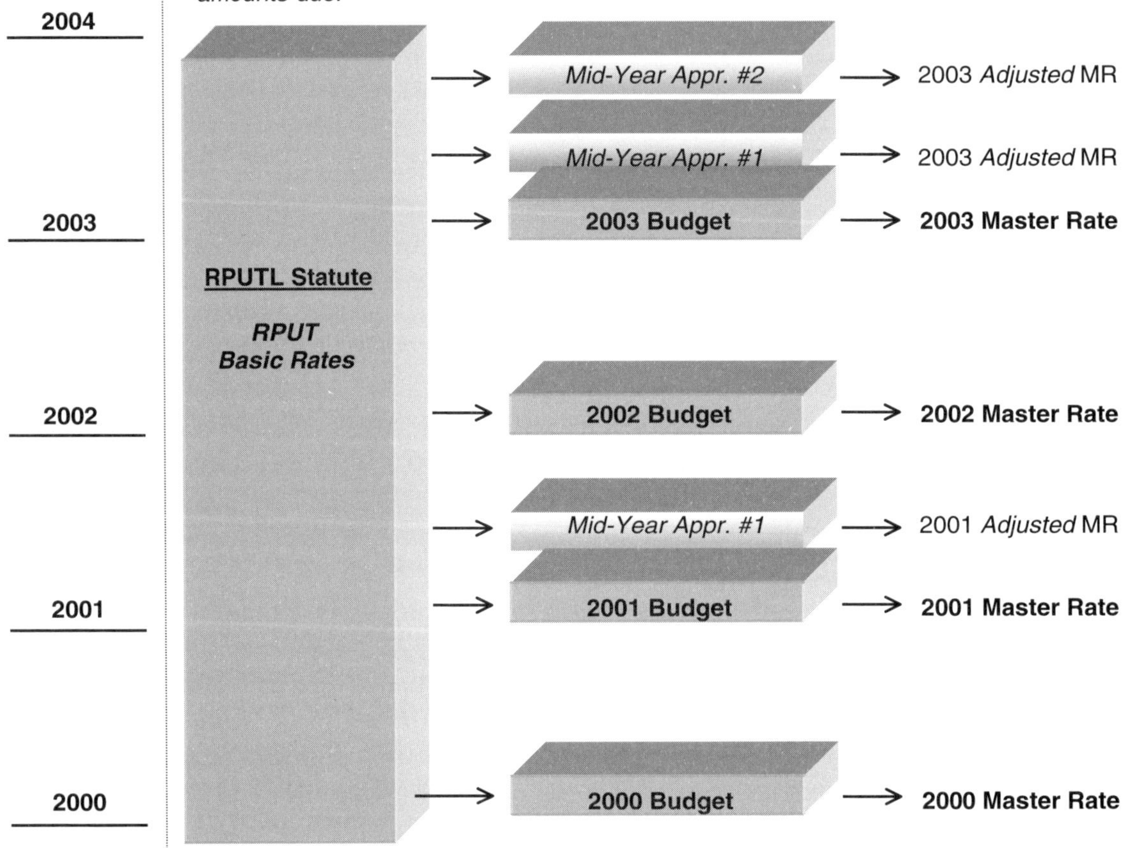

1999

A Federal Budget would normally be prepared prior to the effective tax year and the Master Rate would not be altered. Congress—if unforeseen, additional spending was required during the effective tax year—could defer assessment for that expense until the next tax year, finance the cost through other deficit spending, or if warranted, adjust the Master Rate during the current year. An example of the latter is shown in the Mid-Year Appropriation boxes.

Figure 14

Although computers are not required for RPUT compliance, owner tracking of land-use liability and taxes due under the RPUT is simplified using them, especially for complex rental properties. Property survey information can be entered into a computer application program designed specifically for RPUT accounting, or into a general-accounting system program modified to track RPUT information.

The same survey information for a property that is initially entered into a computer or manual ledger can later be used in subsequent tax years, even with new-year tax rates, until the property status changes (until there is new construction, structural remodeling, or demolition).

Each property is assigned a **Property ID** for tax identification purposes through the federal RPUT administration agency. The Property ID is not an arbitrary number. It is derived from an algorithm based on the geographical location of the particular RPUT property. The outer-point coordinates of the property area are marked by points in latitude and longitude (or surveys related to those points). These are then calculated to arrive at a figure representing the exact property location. An advantage of the RPUT system is that any property can be subdivided into smaller ones, or smaller properties conjoined into one large one, and always be identified by one unique Property ID.

A *single* property can be partitioned by the owner into RPUT Rental Units, provided the partitioned elements meet the RPUT criteria for Rental-Unit designation. Unlike the *government*-designated Property ID, a unique RPUT **Rental Unit ID** is assigned by the *owner* for each Rental Unit, who may use any coding technique he desires (such as apartment door numbers) as long as there are no two Rental Unit IDs on the same property. Rental Unit IDs are recorded during the property survey.

RPUT property identification for assessment purposes is validated by the federal tax administration agency against local (state or county) property title registrations for ownership currency. The Property ID and related Rental Unit IDs are the basis of identification in the federal system and are correlated with local records, and are stored and updated electronically. Thus a complete compendium of the Tax Base, ownership, and survey information, as well as current tax liability, is available from a few computer keystrokes.

Though a property-survey calculation must be established for all properties, landowners are not *required* to accomplish a survey. *The RPUT is not a tax system based on mandatory devolution of information, even socially benign information on property size, but rather a basic assessment, or charge, for services from the government by the government.* However, property that is not surveyed by the landowner, either directly or through a tax-surveying contractor, can be identified as unreported and then surveyed for assessment purposes directly by the government.

Government auditors accomplishing a survey may be able to take an accurate sight survey from the street (entirely possible with smaller, less-complex properties), request permission to enter a landowner's property and then take the survey, or file an assessment based on existing information and calculated estimates. The government might also obtain a Search Warrant to enter private property if that is the only way to complete or validate a property survey.

The advantage of a landowner accomplishing a survey, or having it done by a contractor who certifies the results, is that the owner receives an immediate qualification and an independent appraisal. Thus it is *in the interest of taxpayers* in the RPUT system to participate in and validate their own survey to preclude accidental over-payment, as well as to avoid interest and penalties by prompt remission of taxes due.

Tax Base Demographics

RPUT theory has only one policy direction with regards to privately owned properties, but two possible policy directions with regards to publicly owned properties.

◆

RPUTL policy for privately owned properties is universal applicability. The private entity that legally owns a property (owner), and the private entity that legally contracts with the owner to use the property (renter), are the prime benefactors of government service associated with a property and the legal entities liable for the apportioned RPUT. Special preferences or exclusions are not part of RPUT law.

An owner or renter may utilize private property directly or disburse benefits and costs associated with that property, including RPUT costs, in economic transactions with customers, vendors, or members. But in a rational economic exchange it is the *direct purchaser* who contracts and is liable for a benefit, irrespective of how he then redistributes that benefit.

For instance, suppose a young entrepreneur buys a dump truck on credit to go into the business of hauling gravel. If he receives compensation for hauling gravel from his new customers and he then uses part of that compensation to make payments on his truck, the truck costs are (effectively) paid from receipts from the gravel-hauling customers *through* the young businessman to the dealer who sold him the dump truck. But the *dealer* who sold the young entrepreneur the dump truck is *not* going to look to the *gravel customers* for payment. The person liable for the payments is the new *owner* of the truck, the young businessman.

RPUT liability is based on the same concept. The owners and immediate renters of real property are the direct purchasers of that resource and can choose to utilize it—commercially or otherwise—in whatever manner they desire. Property can be utilized directly, rented, subleased, or shared, and relevant tax costs, if desired, incorporated into charges or shared-costs with others. The owners or immediate renters, however, retain the *primary liability* for RPUT assessment as they retain the *primary right* to the property resource, and are the ones that are legally assessed the RPUT.

The legal entity that owns or directly rents real property is the entity that is charged the RPUT. This means any legal organization, partnership, or corporation that is reflected as a legal owner or renter of real property is directly liable, but not necessarily the *members* of those groups. In the case of a corporation, non-profit or otherwise, for instance, liability is limited to the organization and its assets and not the members or stockholders, whereas (as is normal in civil law) individual partners in a partnership can be liable for business tax debt, RPUT included.

Examples of other individuals (besides stockholders, et cetera) *not* directly liable under the RPUT are children, dependents, transients, and foreign visitors. This is not to say that these individuals do not benefit from any federal government services. It is just that the direct tax liability to the government for those services is assumed by someone else—as when parents provide a home for their child and assume that cost; or when a tourist pays for a hotel room and the proprietor has incorporated RPUT costs into the room charge.

The RPUT assessment, when applicable for a given property, applies to the legal owner or renter irrespective of their occupation, industry, or lifestyle. The owner or renter could be a homeowner, apartment dweller, service corporation, private college, manufacturing concern, educational cooperative, church, mosque or synagogue, charitable organization, agricultural corporation, law partnership, or production company. The same RPUT conditions and relative liability apply to all of them without exemption; government cannot arbitrarily exempt one group of taxpayers without transferring relative government costs somewhere else. The RPUT employs universal applicability to maintain its integrity as a tax system separate from the welfare and social-engineering functions in government administration. Government exemption, preference, or subsidy, if provided, does not come through the Real Property Use Tax.

If the national government chooses to authorize special funding for any individual, organization, or industry, it has to employ direct appropriation for the beneficiaries and finance it through a universal cost assignment to the taxpaying citizens and residents (through a tax increase and raise in the Master Rate) with the real cost of the appropriation commensurately apportioned across the Tax Base.

———— ♦ ————

Private properties are fully taxable under the RPUT, but the question of liability on government property is different.

The RPUT does not apply to any federal property, and agencies of the federal government do not pay the RPUT: A legal entity (the federal government) does not tax itself (the federal government). That means that the RPUT does not apply to areas like military bases, national parks, federal office buildings, Coast Guard stations, and national seashores.

The issue of whether or not local and state government properties should be taxed is more complicated. There are two policy options here. The first one is that since state and local governments are legal entities serving customers (the state and local electorates), they should be liable for the federal RPUT because of the equity in commerce principle.

The equity in commerce principle holds that services are services, whether provided through government agencies or not, and thus state and local government agencies that are exempt from federal taxes receive an effective economic subsidy and decided advantage in providing those services to the public over private sector enterprise, and thus should be subject to superior (higher) level government tax assessment at the same rate as related private activities.

An example is a city that, for discussion, will be called Alpha. Alpha has the normal city services such as administration, police, fire, street maintenance, garbage collection, dogcatcher, and public parks. It also has tennis courts, public arts-theater, polo field, gymnasium, and sailing marina. A second city, Beta, is the exact same size and has the exact same services, except that the tennis courts, public arts-theater, polo field, gymnasium, and sailing marina are all owned and operated privately. The decision to publicly finance the amenities in both cities has been the choice, either directly, or indirectly through their city councils, of the cities' voting citizens.

Alpha, however, may have a net economic advantage over Beta for those amenities it has publicly financed (the tennis courts, polo fields, and so on) if Alpha is not liable for federal taxes on them while Beta, which has the services privately owned, is. Beta, although paying a higher average federal tax, may still choose to maintain private level services as more efficient to the consumers in their city. But is it fair that Beta incur the average increase in tax liability?

The first RPUT policy theory, then, would be to apply the federal tax to all state and local government properties in an attempt to achieve equity in commerce. However, the taxation of state and local government properties could, in many cases, be not much more than an expensive mechanism for circulating tax receipts.

The reason is that assigning liability to state and local governments for a federal tax like the RPUT would mean that the Tax Base would be expanded and private-party (regular citizen taxpayer) property rates would go down under *federal* RPUT assessment. But state and local governments would have to raise *local* taxes to pay the federal assessment on their civic property holdings. Private-party taxpayers would thus pay more in *state and local* taxes and the tax remittance from citizens would be, effectively, just transferred back up to the federal level when the state and local governments remitted their federal tax payments.

State and local governments that were taxed might also attempt to implement state or local property taxes against federal land in their jurisdiction, which would just increase the operational complications. Whatever theoretical degree of equity might be thought in applying a tax like the RPUT to state and local governments might be more than offset by the cost of administering such a process. Regional disparity in government services that could affect state and local RPUT assessment may be insignificant compared to administrative costs in assessing state and local properties. Therefore, the suggested RPUT policy as it stands in this thesis is *not* to tax state and local government properties. The RPUT should only be universally applicable to *private* parties that own or directly utilize real property.

Property Definition

Following is a recap of the RPUT general property definitions:

- **Base Land**. The base-land area of a property with or without any Developed Space on it.
- **Developed Space**. Any habitable interior or exterior floor-space on developed property on, below, or above Base Land.
- **Open Space**. An area of Base Land without any Developed Space.

Specific definitions of these Property Types under various conditions follow.

———————— ♦ ————————

The primary criterion that determines Developed Space is the type of substrate. Ground that has been permanently developed (altered) is Developed Space. A concrete patio is considered Developed Space while a canvas tent floor is not. An asphalt driveway is considered Developed Space but a dirt or gravel driveway is not.

The measured area of Developed Space would be the floor space of houses, apartments, factories, stadiums, sidewalks, patios, and so on, but could also include, for instance, the space under industrial components in a factory or on an oil derrick. The base area extending from actual floor area into walls or other structural components is considered Developed Space (Developed Space is measured by the *outside* dimensions of exterior walls of habitable space, and not the interior, walkable area). Land underneath an enclosed structure—a roof and four walls—is considered Developed Space even if the floor is dirt.

Open Space is any natural surface area on Base Land not broken by permanent development; the measured area of Open Space can never exceed the measured area of Base Land. Developed Space, on the other hand, is measured by the gross floor area of any habitable, developed area, and includes the total area of all floors, including basements. The area of Developed Space, therefore, can exceed the area of Base Land, depending on the number of floors of Developed Space on a property and the habitable surface area of each floor.

Mobile homes and motor homes are not considered additional Developed Space unless they are parked on Open Space and connected to outside utilities (electricity and plumbing). A motor home on a concrete driveway is already on Developed Space; it would not charged twice if connected to utilities.

Incidental components such as fences, furniture, markers, signs, pumps, drinking fountains, park barbecues, or machinery that are on Open-Space Base Land are not considered Developed Space and therefore do not increase the tax liability. By contrast, a gazebo, guard shack, control tower, concrete landing pad, and metal walkway permanently affixed above the ground are all considered Developed Space. Architectural appendages, such as an exterior wooden arch or a platform for flower pots, are not. Floor space underneath machinery or equipment in a factory are. For a three-story building where half the interior is split from the floor to a vaulted ceiling, only the habitable surface area on the three floors—and not the vaulted area—is considered Developed Space.

Government measurement standards for estimating and calculating property areas, including areas under irregular structural conditions, would be incorporated into RPUT Law (after appropriate input from architects, engineers, builders, and land surveyors, as well as legal experts), and then published to provide a comprehensive standard and reference base for RPUT taxpayers.

———— ♦ ————

Areas under construction are not considered taxable Developed Space under Service to Ownership until substrate has been altered (developed) or added to (i.e., extra stories erected on a building). The day the altered space is initially walkable—a human can walk upright on it—is when the area is considered taxable Developed Space under Service to Ownership. For instance, the date a concrete floor has dried to the point workmen can walk on it is the first day it is taxable as Developed Space, even though other work such as laying floor tile or carpeting still has to be done. Additional floors, however, are not taxable until those platforms have been laid.

This definition of Developed-Space liability under Service to Ownership is important. Mere surveying of land or preparatory work should not create a Developed-Space liability. But once a significant base or additional portion of construction (Developed Space) is created, then it must be taxable; otherwise owners would forever keep at least a very small piece of their land "under construction" to avoid the RPUT Developed-Space liability.

Developed Space under the second Tax-Category Division, Service to Use, on the other hand, is never taxed while under construction—only when it is fully completed. The Service-to-Use/Developed-Space Fee is only applicable when Developed Space becomes fully available for use by the owner or renter. "Fully available for use" means the area has been certified by a contractor, even if only verbally, as ready for either occupation, or for the normal use the Developed Space was intended. Utilization by a contractor for storage of on-site construction materials, or a partial move-in of furniture, equipment and supplies by the owner or renter during construction, is *not* considered use under Service to Use.

Developed Space is measured for partial completion and full-use availability of the completed areas to determine the current Service-to-Use liability when projects have been partially completed. For instance, if a contractor finished the first two stories of a ten-story building and the owner or renter moved into those floors, those first two stories would be taxable Developed Space under Service to Use—but not the still-under-construction upper eight floors.

Property that is undergoing remodeling construction, from basic wall painting to elaborate structural alteration, is taxable under Service to Use unless such activity requires complete vacation by the residents for at least a day (or if the resident is doing the work, would require his vacation had he hired someone). Thus the Service-to-Use Fee would still be applied if minor repair and remodeling occurred, but not if residents were required to completely leave the property.

◆

A property owner is always liable for the Service-to-Ownership Fee, but he is only liable for the related Service-to-Use Fee if the property is not rented and is not under Vacation Status. Vacation Status is achieved when the landowner demonstrates that either his property or an RPUT Rental Unit on it is not currently in use, has been vacated, and is currently up for sale or rent. The owner then owes no Service-to-Use Fee for the time frame (days not in use) that the condition existed.

Vacation Status, though, is not automatic, and a property owner must demonstrate that condition through specific acts as well as maintain occupancy and advertising records. An owner that does *not* have RPUT Rental Units on a property and wishes to claim a Vacation Status for the site must first have a real domicile (primary legal home) elsewhere, have physically removed personal effects and inventory from the property, and have made some type of public rental or sale offering. The same conditions apply to properties with RPUT Rental Units, except that vacated Rental Units may contain furnishings and other items provided in the course of normal rent-service and still qualify for Vacation Status, as long as the Units are unoccupied when Vacation Status is claimed.

RPUT Service-to-Use liability can only be directly assigned to renters when property rental segments are designated valid RPUT Rental Units. Landowners that rent must submit RPUT Rental Unit definitions in their land survey *prior* to the budget tax period, including any Rental Unit expansions since their last assessment period.

Only formally surveyed Rental Unit spaces that are physically secure and separate (have walls and doors separating them from other activity) and meet the other conditions of vacation can be assigned as Rental Units. Landowners cannot arbitrarily designate property segments as rental space to avoid any Service-to-Use Fee when it would otherwise be due. Contiguous areas on a property—those areas not having physical controls such as walls and doors—are not eligible for RPUT Rental Unit designation for RPUT assessment purposes. The operator of a warehouse, for instance, cannot declare an empty area of warehouse floor space "vacated and not in use" for four weeks while waiting for another shipment of goods to arrive. Intimate areas are also not permitted for Rental Unit designation. A private homeowner, for instance, could not have bedrooms designated Rental Units, whereas a boarding house with a public entrance could.

Owners can still choose to rent whatever portion of their property they want. In the preceding examples, the warehouse operator could rent his empty floor space and the homeowner could rent his bedrooms, and, if they desired, incorporate the relative RPUT Service-to-Use cost into their rent charges. However, they cannot avoid the Service-to-Use assessment from the government by claiming it was a liability of the renter. They also cannot claim Vacation Status on those portions of the property if the warehouse space or bedrooms were empty, unless of course the *entire* property (warehouse or home) was not in use, vacated, and up for sale or rent.

Assessment and Reporting

RPUT liability is attached to the legal property. For an owner of a property, the length of liability is the period of legal property ownership; for the renter, it is the period of legal property use.

RPUT remittance is due within 15 days of the close of the Tax Period Quarter, unless RPUT Rental Units are being assessed and then the RPUT is due within 15 days of the close of the month. Initial paper assessments are not sent out. Tax Period assessment is based on the current Master Rate, disseminated in the general media and available through government information sources. The taxpayer calculates the tax due from a worksheet or in a computer program from the formulas previously described.

Taxpayers residing in owner-occupied property do not ordinarily have to file any paperwork with their remittance. If there are no Days In Use or other changes, they can merely annotate the Property ID and Tax Period they are paying for on their remittance check. Owners (that do not rent their property out) also have the option of filing only once a year, but must pay a basic interest rate for the first three fiscal quarters (but are *not* charged any penalties).

There is also the option, if a taxpayer so chooses, of setting up an automatic debit with the bank. The Master Rate is then applied at the end of the quarter to a property survey held in the bank's computer and the RPUT is automatically calculated against the current Master Rate. The bank advises its client, the taxpayer, of the amount, obtains transfer approval, and then sends the amount to the Treasury (or the bank may obtain prior debit approval from the taxpayer for automatic forwarding).

Automatic paycheck deductions can also be set up by private banks so the amounts for the estimated quarterly RPUT are deposited in a separate savings account for the taxpayer, ready for transmittal at the end of the quarter. Property owners with Rental Units or owners with property reporting adjustments should complete the appropriate RPUT documentation and send it by regular or electronic mail, along with any required remittance.

The unpaid RPUT of property owners is a normal encumbrance escrow officers would check during a land sale—just like an unpaid local property tax—and any unpaid federal tax amounts would be withheld from the seller's compensation during escrow (Payments from the buyer are taken by the government in the escrow process to pay the overdue taxes of the seller, before the tax liability of the seller is relieved). Relatively simple computer links can be established by RPUT administrators to county recorders to immediately identify sales and transfers of land and new property owners, and to properly recognize sellers as not liable for the RPUT on their former properties after the sale date.

RPUT-Rental-Unit processing starts with the landlord advising his renters in their rental contracts of the

- base rent (amount charged by the landlord).
- RPUT Property ID and Rental Unit ID.
- Tax Base (Base Land, Developed Space, and Common Areas size) for the Rental Unit.
- current Master Rate.
- current RPUT assessment amount chargeable to the Rental Unit (Service-to-Use Fee).
- current total for rent and RPUT, or current **Aggregate Rental Fee**.

The renter is obligated to pay the full Aggregate Rental Fee when rent is due the landlord. Any receipts issued the renter by the landlord must list the Service-to-Use Fee as a separate line item. The landlord, when preparing his RPUT filing, does not normally submit any information on tax collections for Rental Units other than the Rental Unit ID, Days In Use, and remittance amount.

The name and address of the renter is not submitted to the government by the landlord unless the renter is overdue in remitting his portion of the RPUT. In that case the landlord would report the arrears in the billing period following the current one. It is important for the landlord to report arrears to the RPUT administrative agency so that if later audited the landlord will not be held accountable for the Service-to-Use tax that was not paid on a Rental Unit that was not vacated. Collection responsibility for past-due Service-to-Use Fees that are thirty days overdue from renters is assumed directly by the government.

All RPUT survey, RPUT Rental Unit *and* remittance information is recorded on the **RPUT Report Form** and related subforms. The RPUT Report Form and linked subforms are made available to the taxpayer in paper format, and in a computer "drill down" software program where subforms on the entry-screens are linked for automatic calculation and update.

The RPUT Report Form software provides for direct computer-keyboard entry, for printing paper forms to a computer printer for field use or paper tax-filing submission, and for electronic transmission capabilities for both regular data and financial transactions (electronic bank transfers) for on-line filing and payment. Raw data from other software programs can be imported into the RPUT Report Form software, or existing commercial software customized for seamless RPUT accounting-system integration and reporting.

Submission options for the RPUT Report Form thus include a) completion by hand, with later entry into the federal RPUT data processing system by government data-entry personnel. b) preparation by hand in Optical Character Read (OCR) format for later paper scanning. c) preparation on computer, then paper or electronic transmission to the federal RPUT processing center. [218]

Landlords and individual resident owners can use the RPUT Report Form to submit RPUT amounts that are due, to report changes in land status and Days In Use, and to enter assessment correction requests. Renters will normally only need to remit an RPUT Report Form if they are in arrears of the Service-to-Use Fee and are sending past due remittance or other adjustment information.

Calculations are accomplished automatically by federal tax system computers on each RPUT Report Form to validate the taxpayer-entered data and compare it against the current Master Rate and recorded property survey information. The taxpayer would then be immediately notified of any errors or anomalies. For instance, if based on recorded survey information it appeared the taxpayer overpaid, he would be notified to re-file and correct his survey information or request a refund.

A formal paper assessment notice is sent out to all property owners at 10 days past due (i.e., 25 days past the end of a tax quarter) if no remittance or RPUT Report Form has been received by then. If payment or adjustment information is not forthcoming, a second notice is sent out at the end of the month, a third at the middle of the next month, a fourth at the end of the following month, and then two weeks after that a certified letter is sent out with a demand note.

Interest and penalties would accrue, as set by Congress. Taxpayers that do not address tax arrears eventually suffer a lien against their property if they are property owners, and a lien against their person if they are renters. No liens can be imposed or seizure of funds can occur, however, until formal legal action has been taken in a court of law.

The RPUT is an assessment-based tax and not an arbitrary demand for devolution of information and money. Regular compliance with RPUT law and regulations is in most instances entirely a civil matter, and criminal action cannot be taken against a taxpayer for errors, omissions, mistakes, or even nonpayment of taxes. Substantial interest and penalties, however, can accrue and result in liens and judgments against a property or person.

Taxpayers are not criminally or even civilly required to file the RPUT Report Form, even when RPUT assessment conditions otherwise warrant filing, but failure to file by the taxpayer may preclude an allowance of Vacation Status or other benefit, and may automatically flag a property for survey and audit. Appropriate civil collection actions by the federal tax-collection agency may then ensue to collect outstanding debt.

The government can only bring criminal prosecution under RPUT Law when collected taxes from a third party are deliberately misappropriated for personal gain (i.e., Service-to-Use Fees collected from renters by a landlord are not forwarded to the government but taken for personal use). But criminal law cannot be used under the RPUT as a means of unwarranted governmental intimidation. The conditions and protections in RPUT Law help ensure a rational and efficient tax system that also protects basic taxpayer rights.

The interest of the state in a democracy—the objective acquisition of needed revenue for government services—is also protected under RPUT operation. Immediate inability to pay an RPUT assessment that is due does not relieve a taxpayer of liability. The RPUT administrative agency cannot arbitrarily exempt one taxpayer yet harass another for severe penalties and interest, as can happen under the income tax system. However, given economic realities, some taxpayers—either through their own fault or from unforeseen circumstances—may be temporarily unable to meet immediate tax liabilities. This condition is provided for in RPUT operation.

A taxpayer unable to meet his immediate RPUT assessment can obtain a delayed or reduced payment schedule. But this can only occur in administrative (non-court) actions if the administrative requirements are met; a taxpayer is still liable for the full tax-amount due plus period interest charges, even if a delayed payment schedule is approved. Any extraordinary resolution or release for a taxpayer from standard assessment liability can only occur in regular civil-court proceedings overseen by a federal judge.

Legal Primaries

The RPUT has been examined in basic tax theory and in function but just as important—and primary to any new tax system operation—is the legal basis for enacting it. New taxation means repealing old statutes and passing new ones. But national tax system policy may encompass much more than changes in statutory tax law.

The first item that needs to be addressed is the Sixteenth Amendment. Americans should lobby Congress and state legislators for a repeal of that execrable legislation. However, mere repeal of the Sixteenth may not be enough. Repeal of the Sixteenth could certainly hinder the passage of any new federal income tax laws, at least initially, *but would not necessarily preclude them.* This is because great legal debate existed prior to enactment of the Sixteenth Amendment and probably would exist today on the general constitutionality of federal income tax laws, even under original (prior to the Sixteenth) Constitutional conditions.

The Supreme Court in the famous 1893 Pollock case only ruled on the existing income tax law in a lengthy and complicated proceeding, and the case law thus created may not be held valid against some or even all modern income tax law, depending on the interpretations of modern courts. A Constitutional Amendment may be necessary, then, to specifically prohibit direct federal taxation on personal and corporate income.

Constitutional prohibition of federal income taxation may still not be enough, however, as it makes no difference to lock the front door if you leave the back one wide open. The flip side of a national income tax is a national consumption (or sales) tax. Hence, as well as penalizing citizens just because they earn something, federal seizure of citizens' money *just because they spend it* should also be precluded. Any amendment should address protections against arbitrary federal consumption taxes as well as federal income tax seizures.

Constitutional change may also be required to permit the positive as well as prohibit the negative. The Constitution originally precluded forms of direct federal taxation but allowed federal taxation on the basis of population. Population-based assessment for federal expenditures at the beginning of this nation may have made sense with the minuscule size of the federal government at that time, but today's government is huge by comparison. Thus, legal provision for application of rate taxes that are based on other-than-population factors, like the RPUT, may have to be included in Constitutional change as well.

Timing is critical in the transition to a new federal tax system because assessment and collection activity may have to be finished on the existing tax system, the federal income tax, before Constitutional Amendments go into effect. Otherwise application of original law for uncollected receipts, for instance, may be unconstitutional. Implementation of a sound, new national tax system may require not only the coordination and talents of policymakers, economists, and management experts, but of dedicated Constitutional legal experts as well.

Sample Scenarios

A sample Tax Period budget and RPUT calculation are shown in the following nine plates (Figures 15–23). The displays are related. The budget and tax information shown in Figures 15 and 16 is the basis for calculations on those two pages as well as the calculations for all of the specific Property Types that follow in Figures 17 to 23. Thus, a data comparison can be made between Property Types under uniform tax conditions.

The Revenue Requirement in the sample is the 1996 federal budget amount of $1.56 trillion rounded to $1.5 trillion (The 1996 budget amount was the taxpayer liability under all forms of tax assessment—from the income tax to excise taxes and tariffs). The total geographical area of the United States of 3,615,278 square miles[219] has been converted in the sample to acres and rounded to 2.3 billion. The U.S. population figures shown in Figure 23 are from the U.S. Bureau of the Census. The population amounts, however, are *not* a part of the RPUT calculation. Population figures are shown for per-capita comparison purposes only.

The other values shown were chosen to facilitate understanding and do *not* represent actual, real-world amounts. THE INFORMATION DISPLAYED IS SAMPLE, HYPOTHETICAL DATA ONLY. Calculations for actual assessments under RPUT law can only occur after appropriate Tax Base surveys, budget preparation, Congressional review, and setting of RPUT conditions in law.

Note again that the demonstration here is provided to facilitate understanding and that the reporting-screen layout is not meant to represent a regular RPUT tax-filing system with all possible parameters. That would entail a more comprehensive but perhaps less demonstrative tax-filing program. However, a CD-ROM with test files is provided with this book and the test files can be copied and modified. Readers are encouraged to review the page samples here and then utilize the software links provided on the CD-ROM to better understand RPUT functioning and to test their own independent hypotheses with their own hypothetical or real-world data.

RPUT Calculation
1. Revenue and Tax Base

1	Tax Scenario Title	Sample Budget and Tax Base #1
2	**Revenue Requirement**	$ 1,500,000,000,000

Total Properties

	Property Ownership Status	Base Land (Area in Acres)	Developed Space (Area in Acres)
3	Total	2,300,000,000	375,000,000
4	Government	700,000,000	100,000,000
5	Taxable Private Land	1,600,000,000	275,000,000

Total Tax Base

	— Base Land — Base Land Status	Land Area (Area in Acres)	Service to Use — Standard Rate	Service to Use — Average Days In Use	% Yearly Liability *
6	Open Land	750,000,000	0.08	—	4%
7	Annual Cropland	350,000,000	0.33	—	7%
8	Storage Management	100,000,000	—	300	5%
9	Landscaped Grounds	250,000,000	—	325	14%
10	Base Land Under Developed Space	150,000,000	—	300	8%
11	Base Land Total	1,600,000,000			38%
12	— Developed Space —	275,000,000	—	310	85%

* Base Land areas are adjusted against Base Land Total.

Figure 15

NOTES – Figure 15

General	The Revenue and Tax Base Screen records budget and Tax Base totals. [Note: This and other sample calculation screens correspond to the computer worksheet pages in test files that are provided on the CD-ROM that came with this book.]
1	The title of the budget and tax sample. The same title *and* base information (revenue and rates) entered by a Spreadsheet user are linked to all Worksheets in an individual file.
2	The Revenue Requirement is the total appropriation or budget amount to be financed through RPUT taxation.
3–5	The total area in acres (taxable and non-taxable) of the Tax Base being computed. This would normally be the geographical area for the nation, but if this were a computation for a smaller taxing entity, such as a city, the area of that could be entered here.
6–7	Open Land and Annual Cropland are taxed at a "discounted" Standard Rate for the Service-to-Use liability, irrespective of the actual days the land is in use (unless it is completely vacated and declared as such for the entire tax period—then no Use Fee is due). The Standard Rate shown here for Open Land is .08, or 1/12, of the year, and for Annual Cropland is .33, or 4/12, of the year.
6–11	"% Yearly Liability" for Base-Land types shown here is the value of the area times the % of use for the year divided by the Base Land Total (the area value on Line 11).
12	Developed-Space "% Yearly Liability" is merely the Days-In-Use % for the year (there's no ratio subdivision).

RPUT Calculation

2. Tax Rates and Total Tax

Row	Tax Scenario Title	Sample Budget and Tax Base #1			
2				Master Rate	$ 3,925.64

Tax by Subdivision

Row	Property Tax Division	Property Area (Area in Acres)	% Days of Year Service to Ownership	% Days of Year Service to Use	Tax Assessment
3	Base Land	1,600,000,000	100%	38%	787,940,222,740
4	Developed Space	275,000,000	100%	85%	712,059,777,260
5		Total	~	~	$ 1,500,000,000,000

Tax by Division and Category

Row	Tax Category		Basic Rate	Effective Rate $ per Acre	Tax Assessment
	Service-to-Ownership Fee				
6	Tax Category #1	Base Land	5%	196.282	314,051,097,834
7	Tax Category #2	Developed Space	15%	588.846	161,932,597,321
8		Subtotal	20%	785.128	475,983,695,155
	Service-to-Use Fee				
9	Tax Category #3	Base Land	20%	785.128	473,889,124,905
10	Tax Category #4	Developed Space	60%	2,355.383	550,127,179,939
11		Subtotal	80%	3,140.511	1,024,016,304,845
12			~	~	~
13		Total	100%	3,925.640	$ 1,500,000,000,000

Figure 16

NOTES – Figure 16

General	The screen in Figure 15 (1. Revenue and Tax Base) displayed the Revenue Requirement and the area amounts for Property Types. The Basic Rates are entered into this screen to calculate against the Revenue Requirement and Tax Base information (from the Revenue and Tax Base screen). The calculated Master Rate and the Effective Rates for the four Tax Categories are then displayed here. The actual gross tax assessments are also calculated.
2	The Master Rate is applicable to all Tax Categories and is adjusted, as applicable, by the Basic Rate to provide an Effective Rate for each Tax Category.
3–5	This is a summary of the Tax Subdivisions from each Tax Division (Service to Ownership and Service to Use). Note that there is always 100% Ownership throughout the year (though not necessarily by the same owner).
6–13	Just one, or all four Tax Categories can apply to a property, depending on its level of development and use.
13	Note that the Total Tax Assessment, calculated against the Tax Base, equals exactly the Revenue Requirement.

RPUT Calculation

<u>3. Single Unit Property</u>

(Residential House)

Line	Tax Category	Subdivision	Property Area (in Square Feet)	Rate (per Square Foot)	Days In Ownership/Use	Property Tax Assessment
1	**Tax Scenario Title**	Sample Budget and Tax Base #1				
2	**SINGLE UNIT PARCEL**	J. Smith / Suburban Homeowner				
3				**Unit of Measure:**	SF	(Enter "A" for Acre or "SF" for Square Feet)
	Service to Ownership					
4	#1	Base Land	15,000	0.004506013	365	67.59
5	#2	Developed Space	4,500	0.01351804	365	60.83
6					**Subtotal**	128.42
	Service to Use					
7	#3	Base Land	15,000	0.018024053	365	270.36
8	#4	Developed Space	4,500	0.054072159	365	243.32
9					**Subtotal**	513.69
10					**Total**	$ 642.11

Figure 17

NOTES – Figure 17

General	This screen shows a sample private homeowner parcel, about 1/3 of an acre, with Developed Space (home, driveway, patio, and so on) of 4,500 SF.
2	Identifies the Single Unit Parcel described.
3	An entry of "SF" automatically displays the Areas and Rates on the Screen in Square Feet. The Area and Rate totals, though, are the same as if the computations were done in comparable Acre amounts. Whether the computation is done in Square Feet or Acres the calculated tax is going to be the same.
4 and 7	Lawn and shrubbery or other Open Space areas are taxed as part of the Base Land and no additional liability exists.
5 and 8	The Developed-Space areas include all habitable base surface areas. So if the house was 900 Square Feet and three equal stories, the taxable Developed Space would be 2,700 SF, plus any exterior Developed-Space areas like garage, sidewalks, pool, and patio.
4–8	A taxpayer enters the property areas and Days In Ownership and Days In Use to calculate the property tax assessment.
10	The total due from the taxpayer for this property.

RPUT Calculation

4A. Multi-Unit Property

(Apartment Complex)

1	**Tax Scenario Title**		Sample Budget and Tax Base #1			
2	**MULTI-UNIT PARCEL**		Oakridge Apartment Complex			
	PART A					
3		**Service to Ownership**		**Unit of Measure:**	SF	(Enter "A" for Acre or "SF" for Square Feet)
	Tax Category	**Subdivision**	**Property Area** (in Square Feet)	**Rate** (per Square Foot)	**Days In Ownership/Use**	**Property Tax Assessment**
4	#1	Base Land	43,560	0.004506013	365	196.28
5	#2	Developed Space	25,000	0.01351804	365	337.95
6					**Subtotal**	$ 534.23
7		**Common Area Developed Space:**	15,000 (in Square Feet)			

(See the top of this page for PART A, and the next page for PART B detail.)

8	**Total Tax Assessment—PART A and PART B**	$ 2,360.64

Figure 18

NOTES – Figure 18

General	Taxpayers are not required under the RPUT to declare any segments of their property as RPUT Rental Units. However, if an owner's rental units meet RPUT requirements, and an owner has them registered as RPUT Rental Units, then the owner is *not* ultimately liable for the Service-to-Use Fee when the Units are rented, or vacated (even if the rest of his property is in use). The sample multi-unit property shows on the above page the Service-to-Ownership liability, which exists regardless of the Use status of the property. The Service-to-Use Fee for the same property (which may or may not be due, depending on property use) is described on the following two pages.
2	Multi-unit property identification.
3	The owner has chosen to display his property area in Square Feet.
4–6	Area and Days In Ownership are entered to calculate the Service-to-Ownership Fee.
6	The total Service-to-Ownership tax liability.
7	A portion of the total Developed Space that is used as Common Areas (areas used by all renters) is displayed. These areas could be a parking lot, stairwells, mailroom, laundry room, walkways, and pool—but not landscaped or other Open Space areas.
8	This is the total Service-to-Ownership Fee AND Service-to-Use Fee (from the next page).

RPUT Calculation

4B. Multi-Unit Property

(Apartment Complex)

1	**Tax Scenario Title**	Sample Budget and Tax Base #1			
2	**MULTI-UNIT PARCEL**	Oakridge Apartment Complex			
3	**PART B** **Service to Use**	**Unit of Measure:**		SF	
		Property Area (In Square Feet)			**Rate** (Per Square Foot)
4	**Base Land**	43,560	~		0.018024053
5	**Common Area D.S.**	15,000	~		0.054072159
	RPUT Rental Unit	**Direct Liability Developed Space** (In Square Feet)	**Days In Use**	**Base Land Common Area Liability**	**Property Tax Assessment**
6	A	800	365	8%	170.95
7	B	800	200	8%	93.67
8	C	1,200	33	12%	23.18
9	D	1,200	365	12%	256.43
10	E	1,200	365	12%	256.43
11	F	2,400	365	24%	512.86
12	G	2,400	365	24%	512.86
13	H				
14	**Total**	10,000	~	100%	$ 1,826.40

Figure 19

NOTES – Figure 19

General	This is the portion of RPUT for Service-to-Use liability, which can apply to the owner (if he is using all or part of the property) and/or his renters. The relative individual liability is dependent on the amount of RPUT Rental Unit Developed Space that is being used (by the owner or renters).
2	The same unit as on the previous page—this page is for Service-to-Use liability.
3	Same Unit of Measurement as for Service to Ownership.
4–5	Identification of Base-Land and Common-Area Developed Space and applicable rates.
6–13	Rental Units and days rented or used (Days In Use) are entered here. There is a direct liability calculated for the size of the Rental Unit, and a relative liability (based on the size of the Rental Unit) calculated for liability of the property Common Areas.
14	Total for Service-to-Use Fee for the property.

RPUT Calculation

5. Single Unit Property

(Farm)

1	Tax Scenario Title		Sample Budget and Tax Base #1			
2	SINGLE UNIT PARCEL		Vermont Apple Farms, Inc.			
3				Unit of Measure:	A	(Enter "A" for Acre or "SF" for Square Feet)
	Tax Category	Subdivision	Property Area (Per Acre)	Rate (Per Acre)	Days In Ownership/Use	Property Tax Assessment
		Service to Ownership				
4	#1	Base Land	55	196.2819361	365	10,795.51
5	#2	Developed Space	2	588.8458084	365	1,177.69
6					Subtotal	11,973.20
		Service to Use				
7	#3	Base Land	55	785.1277446	120	14,196.83
8	#4	Developed Space	2	2355.383234	365	4,710.77
9					Subtotal	18,907.60
10					Total	$ 30,880.80

Figure 20

NOTES – Figure 20

General	A property that is not subdivided by RPUT Rental Units is considered a single-unit property, whether it is a single family house or a corporate headquarters. This example is a farm.
2	Name of farming enterprise.
3	The owner has chosen to identify his property in acres. This does not affect the net tax due.
4–8	Area and Day-In-Use are entered just like Residential House.
7	Open Land and Annual Cropland *cannot* be subdivided for RPUT Rental Unit purposes. A Standard Rate is applied instead that is based on average land use. In this particular case the land is designated as Annual Cropland and the Standard Rate is .33, or 4/12, of a year's worth of use—120 Days. Normally there would be a separate field for Standard Rate computations, but in this example "120" has been entered manually for the Service-to-Use / Base-Land liability. Even so, this is not totally accurate, as a real computation would be for 153 acres at the Standard Rate and 2 Acres (Base Land Under Developed Space) at actual Days In Use. An actual operational tax program would account for this condition, but it is not integrated into this example program for simplicity's sake. The layout here is made brief for an easier, conceptual understanding.
10	Total tax due for the farm.

RPUT Calculation

6A. Multi-Unit Property

(Office Building)

1	**Tax Scenario Title**	Sample Budget and Tax Base #1				
2	**MULTI-UNIT PARCEL**	Northern Industries Office Towers				
3	**PART A** **Service to Ownership**		**Unit of Measure:**	SF	(Enter "A" for Acre or "SF" for Square Feet)	
	Tax Category / **Subdivision**	**Property Area** (in Square Feet)	**Rate** (per Square Foot)	**Days In Ownership/Use**	**Property Tax Assessment**	
4	**#1** **Base Land**	125,000	0.004506013	365	563.25	
5	**#2** **Developed Space**	950,000	0.01351804	365	12,842.14	
6				**Subtotal**	$ 13,405.39	
7	**Common Area** **Developed Space:**	(in Square Feet) 50,000				
		(See the top of this page for PART A, and the next page for PART B detail.)				
8		**Total Tax Assessment—PART A and PART B**			$ 67,026.95	

Figure 21

NOTES – Figure 21

General	This parcel represents a ten-story office building on about three acres of land.
2	Multi-unit property identification.
3	The owner has chosen to display his property area in Square Feet.
4–6	Area and Days In Ownership are entered to calculate the Service-to-Ownership Fee.
6	The total Service-to-Ownership tax liability.
7	A portion of the total Developed Space that is used as Common Areas (areas used by all renters) is displayed. These areas could be parking lots, foyers, stairwells, shared rest rooms, elevators, and so on. Ground-level landscaped areas would not be included (those areas area taxed only under Base Land).
8	This is the total Service-to-Ownership Fee AND Service-to-Use Fee (from the next page) for the owner.

RPUT Calculation

6B. Multi-Unit Property

(Office Building)

#					
1	**Tax Scenario Title**	Sample Budget and Tax Base #1			
2	**MULTI-UNIT PARCEL**	Northern Industries Office Towers			
3	**PART B** **Service to Use**	**Unit of Measure:**		SF	
		Property Area (In Square Feet)			**Rate** (Per Square Foot)
4	**Base Land**	125,000	~		0.018024053
5	**Common Area D.S.**	50,000	~		0.054072159
	RPUT Rental Unit	**Direct Liability Developed Space** (In Square Feet)	**Days In Use**	**Base Land Common Area Liability**	**Property Tax Assessment**
6	Owner Occupied	500,000	365	56%	29,789.75
7	Lease - Widgets Ltd.	250,000	365	28%	14,894.88
8	Lease - Nofire Ins. Co.	135,000	365	15%	8,043.23
9	Lease - Minn. Catering	15,000	365	2%	893.69
10					
11					
12					
13					
14	**Total**	900,000	~	100%	$ 53,621.56

Figure 22

NOTES — Figure 22

General	There are four declared RPUT Rental Units in the Office Building, including one occupied by owner.
2	Multi-unit property identification flows from the previous page.
3	Square Foot Unit of Measurement flows from the previous page.
4–5	Identification of Base-Land and Common-Area Developed Space, and applicable rates.
6–13	Area and Days In Ownership are entered to calculate the Service-to-Use liability. The owner occupies the largest part of the building and leases three other parts to other businesses.
14	The total Service-to-Use tax liability.

RPUT Calculation

7. Macroeconomic Averaging

#	Tax Scenario Title	Sample Budget and Tax Base #1			
	Base Land Status	Taxable Properties Area (In Acres)	Use Liability Rate	Tax Due Ownership and Use	% of Total RPUT
2	Open Land	750,000,000	8%	194,319,116,785	13%
3	Annual Cropland	350,000,000	33%	159,380,932,151	11%
4	Storage Management	100,000,000	82%	84,159,241,115	6%
5	Landscaped Grounds	250,000,000	89%	223,842,071,016	15%
6	Base Land Under Dev. Space	150,000,000	82%	126,238,861,672	8%
7	Base Land Total	1,600,000,000	~	787,940,222,740	53%
8	Developed Space	275,000,000	85%	712,059,777,260	47%
9			Total	$ 1,500,000,000,000	100%

Comparison of RPUT and Average Population Tax Liability

RPUT liability is NOT based on population. Population info here is provided for comparison purposes only. Compare the figures in the single or multi-unit property worksheets to determine the possible relative savings under RPUT for an individual property liability.

#		Population		Average Per Person Cost $
10	Total Population	265,000,000	~	5,660
11	Adult Population (20 and over)	189,000,000	~	7,937
12	Working Population (20—64)	155,000,000	~	9,677

Figure 23

NOTES – Figure 23

General	This is a listing of Base-Land-Status types and their liability assessment and calculated percentage of the total RPUT, and some per capita estimates for comparison purposes.
2–6	The "Use Liability Rate" is the total percentage of the year for Days In Use; for instance, Landscaped Grounds are in use an average of 89%, or 325 days, of the year. The "% of Total RPUT" is the percentage of the total RPUT assessment ($1.5 trillion) the particular Base-Land-Status type is assessed; for instance, 13% of the total tax amount due will be from Open Land.
8	Developed Space totals.
10–12	Per capita tax averages for comparison purposes. Population figures are for the year 1996 (rounded), (Source: U.S. Bureau of the Census, *Current Population Reports*, P25-1095; and Population Paper Listings 57).

XII. The Real Property Use Tax Law

A legal text of the RPUT Law (RPUTL) appears on the following pages. RPUT theory and principles are important, but a fully vetted legal text is just as critical in the effective implementation of any new tax reform measure. The knowledge and expertise of qualified economists, legal experts, legislators, and the electorate themselves need to be tapped in preparing a final version of the RPUTL. The legal text that follows, therefore, is not meant to be a final prescription. Rather, it is provided as a basis for review, assessment, and further development, as warranted. See the RPUT Internet site at http://www.rput.com for current information on RPUT legal revisions.

RPUT law is shown here, but related change in Constitutional law is not. Change in Constitutional law—which may be necessary or at least desirable prior to passage of RPUT Law—is a totally separate piece of legislative action and is addressed at a different level than statutory tax law. The details of any Constitutional revision are best left to other examinations. The rationale as to why Constitutional revision may be necessary, though, has already been identified in this work (see the "Legal Primaries" section of Chapter XI).

The details of appropriation or budget law (Funding Statutes), or specifically, the clauses in spending bills that direct their financing through RPUT assessment, are also not discussed here, as that function is merely a legal directive at the end of an appropriation (nothing complicated about that).

The RPUT statutory law (RPUTL)—the *concepts* of which have been previously described in detail in this text—contains neither Constitutional authorization to tax nor provides any *independent* statutory tax assessment of citizens. Rather, the RPUTL contains the *conditions and regulations for assessment* when RPUT Law is dedicated as the funding mechanism. The rules or "heart" then, of RPUT functioning, is specified here in legal terms.

The Real Property Use Tax Law

RPUT—Tax Law Version: #RPUT001c

106th CONGRESS
xx Session

H. R. #XXXX

IN THE HOUSE OF REPRESENTATIVES

[Month] [Day], [Year]

Mr./Ms. xxxxxxxxxxxx [Representative] introduces the following bill; which will be referred to Committee on the Ways and Means, and in addition to the Committees on Government Reform and Oversight, the Budget, and Rules, for a period to be subsequently determined by the Speaker, in each case for consideration of such provisions as fall within the jurisdiction of the committee concerned.

A BILL

To provide a clear, sound, and objective tax mechanism to finance the Federal Government of the United States of America.

Be it enacted by the Senate and House of Representatives of the United States of America in Congress assembled,

SHORT TITLE

Short Title. This Act may be cited as the "Real Property Use Tax Act of 1999."

TABLE OF CONTENTS

Title I

TITLE I—The Real Property Use Tax

Title II—Supermajority Required

TITLE I—The Real Property Use Tax

SEC. 101 Scope of Application.
(a) The conditions that exist in this statute become operable and apply only when so designated in separate appropriation statutes where the required revenue is to be obtained by the processes identified here.[A]

SEC. 102 Terms Definition. The terms that are applicable within this statute are defined as following.
(a) Adjusted Master Rate: the current Master Rate after an adjustment during the budget period.
(b) Aggregate Rental Fee: the total of current rent and RPUT Service-to-Use Fee for an RPUT Rental Unit.
(c) Annual Cropland: farmland currently producing, or available for producing, annual crops.
(d) Base Land: the measured surface area of a Property exclusive of any Developed Space, and as identified in legal title.
(e) Base Land Under Developed Space: area under Developed Space that is taxable as Base Land, in addition to the Developed Space above it being taxed.
(f) Base Land Status: the classified condition of the measured surface area of property, including Open Land, Annual Cropland, Storage Management, Landscaped Grounds, and Base Land Under Developed Space.
(g) Basic Rate: one of four Tax Category rates that are set in this statute by Congress. The RPUT Basic Rate system is designed to provide a relative cost rate for Property Types.
(h) Category Area: the total area on a Property belonging to one of the four Tax Categories.
(i) Common Area: are used in common by renters on a RPUT Rental Property.
(j) Days In Ownership: the number of days a Property or Property Type is under particular ownership.
(k) Days In Use: the number of days a Property or Property Type is in use, or available for use.
(l) Developed Space: habitable, developed surface area on, under, or above Base Land, such as that found in

[A] In other words, the RPUT law is only applicable for the funding bills that designate it.

houses, patios, paved driveways, apartments, factories, office buildings, parking lots, et cetera.

(m) Domicile: a property that is the primary legal residence of an individual. A person can have many homes but only one domicile.

(n) Effective Rate: for each of the four Tax Categories, the Master Rate times the Basic Rate. The Taxpayer multiplies the Effective Rate times the Area, and then multiplies that by the Days In Use to obtain his tax due for the particular Tax Category.

(o) In Use: term to denote Property that is either physically in use or available for use (not in Vacation Status).

(p) Landscaped Grounds: commercial and residential maintained landscape, parks, and playing fields.

(q) Master Rate: a standard rate calculated from an appropriation, or budget, against the Basic Rates and total Tax Base. The Master Rate can be used by any Taxpayer in any situation against his personal Tax Base to give the tax due.

(r) Master Rate Adjustment: the increase or decrease in the Master Rate during a budget period caused by increased or repealed spending through the RPUT.

(s) Open Land: commercial timberland, planted orchards not yet producing, range (grazing) land, undeveloped recreational lands, and all other general undeveloped land.

(t) Open Space: all relatively undeveloped portions of Base Land including Open Land, Annual Cropland, Storage Management, and Developed Landscape.

(u) Owner: non-governmental legal owner of real property as recorded in official property title.

(v) Property: a legally defined ownership parcel as officially recorded in a county or state, such as in a County or State Recorders Office.

(w) Property ID: an identification number for a Property that is an algorithm based on the geographical points of land demarcation. A legal property then, no matter how much it is subdivided or conjoined with larger Properties, will always retain an accurate location definition.

(x) Property Types: Developed Space and various types of Open Space.

(y) Real Property Use Tax: the tax system codified in this statute, based on the implied liability for

government service related to the size of real property, its level of development, and amount of use.
(z) Real Property Use Tax Law: this law.
(aa) Rental Unit ID: a unique RPUT Rental Unit identification for each Rental Unit on a Property, assigned by the Owner and reported to the Federal Tax Service Agency (FTSA) in a Property Survey.
(bb) Renter: non-governmental legal entity that contracts for the use of real property from the legal owner.
(cc) Rent: the consideration given under legal contract, written or oral, for use of Property.
(dd) Revenue Requirement: the amount of money needed by Congress to fund government activities or purchases authorized in appropriation law.
(ee) RPUT: Real Property Use Tax.
(ff) RPUTL: Real Property Use Tax Law.
(gg) Service to Ownership: Property owner liability of the RPUT.
(hh) RPUT Rental Unit: a registered subdivision of Property as defined under this statute that is available for rental or vacation. A landlord that surveys and registers qualifying portions of his Property as Rental Units is not liable for Service-to-Use Fees if the Units are rented or in Vacation Status.
(ii) RPUT Renter: a renter that is directly liable to the government for Service to Use.
(jj) Service to Use: liability for Property use under the RPUT. Either the Owner or RPUT Renter can be directly liable.
(kk) Storage Management: undeveloped but controlled Base Land used for intensive purposes like livestock yards, unpaved vehicle storage lots, junk yards, and marshaling yards.
(ll) Survey: physical measurement of areas on a Property to determine the size of Property Types.
(mm) Taxable Area: physical surface area used in computing the RPUT.
(nn) Tax Base: the total Taxable Area, by Tax Category, multiplied against the Days In Use that is assessed by the government. "Tax Base" applies to total assessment for a property when applied to that property, to total individual liability when referring to a Taxpayer, and to total, national liability (the total of all

Taxpayers' liability) when referring to federal appropriations.

(oo) Tax Category: one of four classifications of RPUT property tax: (1) Service to Ownership/Base Land, (2) Service to Ownership/Developed Space, (3) Service to Use/Base Land, and (4) Service to Use/Developed Space.

(pp) Tax Division: one of two types of RPUT liability: Service to Ownership or Service to Use.

(qq) Tax Subdivision: one of the two major types of RPUT taxable land types, Base Land or Developed Space.

(rr) Taxpayer: the legal entity liable for the RPUT, either the Owner or legal RPUT Renter.

(ss) Vacation Status: the status of a full Property or RPUT Rental Unit when it is not in use, vacated, and up for sale or rent.

SEC. 103 When This Statute Is Operational.[B] All criteria in this Section must be met by any statute attempting to associate with and impose this Act or the Act is void with respect to the related statute.

(a) **Conditions Which <u>Preclude</u> Act Applicability.** No tax assessment shall be made through this statute against the Tax Base

(1) for a past time period, where past time period is defined as that period prior to the enactment of the appropriation or other statutes designating the assessment, or

(2) that is not linked to an approved appropriation enacted in statute, or

(3) does not have a finite cost, or

(4) extends an assessment period beyond three years, or

(5) any condition in an appropriation statute which attempts to invalidate or contradict this RPUT Statute, in whole or in part, or attempts to minimize or expand on it.

(b) **Conditions Required for Act to Be Applicable.**[C] The appropriation statute must specify four and only four criteria with respect to this statute, which are

---

[B] The RPUT Law is designed so that it cannot be easily altered by a second statute. If that is attempted the RPUT law is void with respect to the new act (unless the new statutory condition was passed with a Supermajority).

[C] This information is required for calculation of the Master Rate.

(1) direction that this Act be applicable for appropriation act funding, and
(2) the amount to be funded through this Act, and
(3) length of assessment period, and
(4) the start date of the assessment period.

SEC. 104 Legal Entities That Are Liable Under This Act.

(a) **Private Legal Entities.** All private legal entities including individuals, legal partnerships, and corporations. Foreign or international governments[D] or government organizations are considered Private Legal Entities under this Act and are not exempt from RPUT liability except as provided for in Section 104(b).

(b) **Governments and Government Organizations.**[E] All bona fide governments and government organizations, local, state and federal of or under the United States of America are NOT liable under this act, except where they are required to collect Service-to-Use Fees from Private Legal Entities as described in Section 104(d). Foreign governments are NOT liable only where other statutory law or treaty specifically provides for tax exemption, such as the ownership and use of embassy grounds.

(c) **Private Owners Renting to Governmental Entities.** Private Owners shall not assign Service-to-Use Fees to governmental entities renting properties from them but neither shall they be assessed or required to remit Service-to-Use Fees for those properties under that condition, and may claim non-payment status for Service to Use for the subject properties under Vacation Status.

(d) **Governmental Entities Renting to Private Parties.**[F] Governmental entities renting Property to private parties shall be required to survey the applicable properties and to charge Service-to-Use Fees to private parties and remit such funds to the Federal

---

[D] Foreign governments should not enjoy any more preference on American soil than American citizens.

[E] Special clarification may have to be made for semi-government agencies like Water Districts.

[F] It would be unfair to indirectly promote government rentals to private parties and have those private parties escape normal Service to Use Fees. This regulation negates that condition.

Treasury only for Developed-Space areas and related Open Space that is not Open Land or Annual Cropland.

SEC. 105 Legal Directive to Taxpayers. The legal entities identified in this statute are hereby charged to pay the Effective Rates for their respective Properties as prescribed from the conditions herein and the authorizing appropriation statute.[G]

SEC. 106 Creation of the Federal Tax Service Agency.[H] The Federal Tax Service Agency (FTSA) is created under this act to administer the functions of the RPUT as well as other revenue and fiscal management duties as assigned by Congress. FTSA is herein directed to perform the duties and responsibilities listed here under the guidelines, controls, and regulations listed in this Section and throughout the Act.

[*Specific Operational Directives of the FTSA*]

SEC. 107 Public Disclosure. All information related to the RPUT, including but not limited to assessments, collections, audits, penalties, policies, regulations, and FTSA operations on whatever person or interest, shall be available and open to inspection by all United States citizens, legal residents, or legal Property Owners or Renters, except for

(a) FTSA internal personnel files, or

(b) FTSA Taxpayer audits in the planning stage prior to completion, or

(c) FTSA fraud or criminal investigations prior to completion and appropriate legal action, or

(d) FTSA internal processing or reviews prior to completion, or

(e) Congressional reviews prior to completion.

SEC. 108 Property Identification.

(a) **Physical Land Identification.** The FTSA shall create and manage a database for efficient tracking of Property Area sizes and geographical location by both legal definition and global quadrant. Each Property

---

[G] Taxpayers are formally being charged with RPUT.

[H] Provisional name given to the Federal agency charged with administering the RPUT. Congress, ultimately, will have to decide on the final name.

shall be assigned a Property ID from an algorithm based on its geometric latitude and longitude definition.[I]

(b) **Land Ownership.** The FTSA shall coordinate with all appropriate local and state Property title recording offices for near real-time tracking and coordination of correct ownership information in order to validate RPUT assessment and audit actions by the FTSA.[J]

SEC. 109 Survey.

(a) General Requirements.

(1) **Physical Classification.** Property Types shall be identified and surveyed according to the technical specifications in Section 109(b).

(2) **Registration for Official Survey.** Private architects, builders, or other individuals may choose to contract for or certify Property Surveys under this statute and may choose to register with the FTSA as a Licensed RPUT Surveyor. The condition of license shall be a bond or active insurance policy were they warrant the correctness of the surveys they accomplish for clients.[K]

(3) **Responsibility for Private Survey.**[L] The Property Owner may choose to survey his own land or contract for an official private survey from a Licensed RPUT Surveyor, but is not required to do either. In the case of the owner accomplishing his own Survey or using an unlicensed survey contractor, the Owner is liable for any error, including Interest and Penalties as far back as three years. In the case of the owner using a Licensed RPUT Surveyor, liability is assumed by

[I] This in concept is simple, but with today's technology this should not be difficult to implement either, and it should give exact definition of land ownership no matter how much legal property is subdivided or conjoined.

[J] This can be linked to an excellent, automatic tracking and auditing system for identifying transferred properties and capturing past tax revenue due at time of sales.

[K] This allows the government to go directly to the Surveyor for revenue recovery instead of having to go to the Taxpayer who then sues the Surveyor.

[L] It may in almost all cases be prudent to accomplish a private survey, because Property Owners may want to validate a government survey anyway. If the private survey is done first and accepted by the government, the government survey is unnecessary.

that entity directly, and indirectly its bonding agent or insurance company.

(4) **Government Survey.** The FTSA is required to survey all Properties in which RPUT Report Forms have not been submitted by Owners. FTSA may use direct survey or estimate, or a combination of survey and estimate to establish the size of Property Types.

(5) **Rental Units.** Owners are permitted to designate subdivisions of Developed-Space and Communal-Use Property on their land as available for rent and thus be relieved of Service-to-Use Fee liability when that portion of their property is rented or in Vacation Status, so long as the designated areas meet the definable Rental Unit criteria in Section 112. FTSA will only survey Properties with Rental Units in an audit and the Owner is responsible for a Survey if he desires one with Rental Unit identifications.

(6) **Certification Survey.** A Survey review may base all or part of its information on previous physical measurements and actual re-measurement is not required, except that the Owner or Licensed RPUT Surveyor, as appropriate, is still liable for back taxes and Interest or Penalties resulting from any reporting error.

(7) **Physical Identification.** The FTSA shall assign a Property ID number based on a longitude and latitude algorithm for each Property. The original Property ID will be retired if the Property is subdivided or conjoined and a new Property ID(s) will be assigned. Owners of Property with designated RPUT Rental Units are required to assign unique RPUT Unit Numbers to them, which may correspond to existing physical unit descriptions on the Property, such as apartment or office suite numbers.

(b) Survey Technical Specifications

[*Technical specifications for identification and survey of all Property Types*]

SEC. 110 Conditions of Assessment Liability.

(a) **Service to Ownership—Ownership and Use.** Liability shall be solely to the legal entity holding legal ownership title in the property whether it be by individual, partnership or corporation. Joint owners shall be individually and severally liable for taxes, but a charge for taxes can never exceed the market value or sales price of property, whichever is greater, at any point in time.[M] Upon transfer of ownership of property before or after death, any unpaid RPUT ownership taxes shall be recovered from the sale or transfer of that property except that no such recovery shall exceed the appraised market value of the property or sales price, whichever is greater.

(b) **Service to Use for Renters.** Renters must rent a defined, surveyed and approved portion of property as described in this statute and property size, status, and full liability conditions must be contained in a written rental contract for a renter to be liable for RPUT taxes under this statute. Renters are jointly and severally liable in any communal contract, but RPUT liability is attached only to the Renter(s) specifically identified in the respective rental contract and shall not extend beyond the renter(s) or his(their) estates.

(c) **Length of Liability to Taxpayer.**[N] The government has up to four years from Due Date of any tax to audit Taxpayer paperwork or Property and file a Tax Correction and demand for back taxes, interest, or penalty, after which time the Taxpayer is not liable.

(d) **Length of Liability to Government.** Taxpayers have up to four years from Due Date to petition the government for correction of previous assessments and refund of erroneous payment amounts, after which the government is not liable.

SEC. 111 Tax Assessment Effective Dates. The government is specifically prohibited from ex post facto taxation, or assessment for time periods prior to the enactment of an appropriation statute.

[M] Practically, recovery of back taxes should occur long before the value of property is reached. The government has an obligation to mitigate damages and recover funds within a reasonable time.

[N] Taxpayers cannot be expected to retain historical financial information forever to challenge potential tax claims. The government has an obligation to validate Surveys, tax remittances, or assessments within a reasonable time.

Assessments can apply to the Tax Base for up to any three-year time period in the future but cannot start until the first day of the second calendar quarter following the quarter the applicable appropriation bill was passed.[o]

SEC. 112 RPUT Rental Units.

(a) **Designation of Rental Units.** A landlord is not required to designate rental units on his property as RPUT Rental Units but must assume direct liability for all Service-to-Use assessment if any portion of his Property is then in use. Renters can only be assigned direct Service-to-Use Liability by the Owner, or the Owner can only claim partial Vacation Status if the relevant rental units have been officially designated as RPUT Rental Units with the FTSA. The conditions of RPUT Rental Unit designation are that rental unit areas

(b) cannot be Open Land or Annual Cropland, and

(c) must be clearly definable areas with physical barriers such as walls, fences, and lockable doors, and

(d) cannot be intimate areas such as rooms in a private home but must have a public or separate access point, and

(e) be clearly defined and surveyed, and

(f) have had been identified and filed along with the total Property Survey with the FTSA at least one calendar quarter prior to operation as RPUT Rental Units.

(g) **Limits of Designation.** Only the Owner may designate appropriate RPUT Rental Unit status and transfer, pursuant to other criteria, Service-to-Use liability to a Renter. A renter, private contract permitting, may sublease all or part of a RPUT Rental Unit, but the original Renter retains direct liability to the government for the RPUT. Transfer of direct liabilities to renters that sublease is not recognized by the government.

(h) **Ownership Management of Service to Use.**

---

[o] In other words, the government has to give Taxpayers at least one calendar quarter's notice before implementing a new tax.

(1) **Contracts.** For an assignation of Service-to-Use Fee to the Renter to be effective, a landlord must include in his contract

(A) the Base Rent excluding any Service-to-Use Fee,

(B) the current Master Rate,

(C) the Property ID,

(D) the Rental Unit ID,

(E) the Rental Unit area and Communal Property Area,

(F) the current Base Rent plus Service-to-Use Fee total, and

(G) an advisory on RPUT policies.

(2) **Service-to-Use Fee Collections.** The Renter shall be required to remit the total for Base Rent and Service-to-Use Fee to the Owner and may include both amounts in the same check, but should annotate such on check or receipt. The landlord must submit all such Service-to-Use Fees to the government with a RPUT Report Form, identifying any Rental Units in arrears or Vacation Status. The landlord does not report a renter's name and address to the FTSA unless the renter is in arrears, in which case future billings for past-due Service to Use are assumed directly by the FTSA.

SEC. 113 Vacation Status.

(a) **Owners Renting RPUT Rental Units.** Owners may claim a Vacation Status for RPUT Rental Units if the applicable rental units

(1) meet other qualifications of RPUT Rental Units and are surveyed and registered with the FTSA,

(2) are not in regular use by the Owner or Renters (construction, repair and maintenance of vacated premises is permitted),

(3) the RPUT Rental Units are displayed or advertised as for rent, and

(4) are filed as Vacated Units on the RPUT Report Form when it is filed with the FTSA.

(b) **Owners Not Declaring RPUT Rental.** Owners may still declare Vacation Status if they do not rent (or do not rent through RPUT Rental Units), if

(1) the entire Property is Vacated (construction, repair and maintenance on vacated premises is permitted),
(2) the Property is advertised as for sale or rent,
(3) the Owner files an RPUT Report Form with a Notice of Vacation at least one working day prior to the effective date of vacation.

SEC. 114 Government Access to Private Property. Government representatives or agents shall not enter private property for the purposes of survey or audit under this statute without
(a) obtaining permission from the Owner, or Owner's on-site agent, representative, renter, or leaseholder, or
(b) first obtaining a Search Warrant from the appropriate legal authority.
Nothing, however, precludes government representatives or agents from performing visual or technological measurements off of, or in the air over, Taxpayer property, except no means, visual, technological, or otherwise shall be used to penetrate or analyze interior areas or inhabitants that are normally private, even if such areas are temporarily open, such as windows or shades, unless the permissions already described above are first acquired.

SEC. 115 Budget Period. Congress shall, whenever possible, issue one budget for the calendar year where one Master Rate will apply for the entire period, but may, funding requisites existing and within the other limits of this Act, issue a Master Rate Adjustment to reflect an increase or decrease in taxes.

SEC. 116 Publication of Master Rate. Congress must publicize a new Master Rate, its effective date and duration within ten calendar days of passage of an appropriation bill through the FTSA and other relevant public and private points of dissemination.

SEC. 117 Calculation of RPUT Rates.

[*Detailed Descriptions for Computation of RPUT Rates—See Chapter X for examples.*]

SEC. 118 Basic Rates. The Basic Rates are set for
(a) Service to Ownership/Base Land as 5% of the applicable Tax Base,
(b) Service to Ownership/Developed Space as 15% of the applicable Tax Base,
(c) Service to Use/Base Land as 20% of the applicable Tax Base, and
(d) Service to Use/Developed Space as 80% of the applicable Tax Base.

SEC. 119 Tax Remittance.
(a) **Due Date.** The Due Date for all taxes under this Act shall be the 15th day of the month following the calendar quarter the tax assessment is applicable, except that Property Owners that do not rent any portion of their Property may pay a yearly tax instead by the 15th day of the month following the fourth calendar quarter the yearly tax assessment is applicable, but in such case must pay Interest (but not Penalty) on the first three-quarter tax periods.
(b) **Delivery.** Taxes shall be due to the remission address(es) as publicly designated by the FTSA, and shall be considered overdue and subject to Interest and Penalty unless remittance is sent
 (1) by physical delivery by the end of the working day of the Due Date to one of the designated locales, or
 (2) by mail postmarked by United States Postal Service by the Due Date, or
 (3) by electronic transfer of funds to the appropriate Federal Treasury account by the Due Date.

SEC. 120 Interest and Penalties.
(a) **Interest Rate.** Interest Rate for outstanding tax debt shall accrue as described in this statute at the rate of 2% above Prime Rate for a Daily Periodic Rate (1/365 the Annual Percentage Rate).
(b) **Penalty Charge.** Penalties shall as described in this statute at the rate of 15% per annum.
(c) **Application Conditions.** All Interest and Penalties shall be calculated per annum and prorated

on a calendar day basis from the date they first accrue. Interest and Penalties shall not be compounded but all remittance shall be applied to Penalties first, then Interest, then to principle.

SEC. 121 Submission of Correction. Taxpayers have the full right to challenge any Survey or Assessment on their Property interests. Taxpayers may submit an RPUT Report Form requesting a Correction Hearing and the FTSA must respond within 30 days. Taxpayers may appeal a primary and secondary hearing with the FTSA and continue the appeal in Federal civil court. All collection action through liens or other legal instruments is suspended during the appeals process but Interest and Penalty continues to accrue until mitigated, waved, or otherwise resolved by competent legal authority.

SEC. 122 Financial Liability and Reporting Obligation.
(a) **User/Owners and Renters.** Renters and Owners who use their own Property and do not rent and do not claim Vacation Status are not required to submit any survey, tax form, or other information to the government, but if such documents or information are submitted Taxpayers are not liable for any error or omission, except that the government may pursue full recovery in lawful civil court for whatever taxes are later determined due (within the recovery time limits specified) plus applicable interest and penalty amounts herein defined. All remedies and penalties in the recovery of taxes due the government shall be limited to those stated in this statute and Taxpayers identified here shall not endure criminal investigations or prosecution in these conditions.[P]
(b) **Owners Renting or Claiming Vacation Status.** Owners that have RPUT Rental Units being rented and/or claim Vacation Status are immediately subject to all recovery actions and Interest and Penalties as described above. They can also be subject to criminal liability if

[P]A government should not treat its citizens as criminals merely because they make filing mistakes. However, Taxpayers are still accountable for their mistakes and should be subject to applicable Interest and Penalty.

(1) they deliberately retain Service-to-Use Fees from Renters and do not forward them to the government, or

(2) they, with or without collusion with renters, deliberately declare Vacation Status when RPUT Rental Units are rented.

(c) **Criminal Liability.** Violators of Section 122(b), in addition to liability for relevant Interest and Penalties, shall be subject upon conviction in criminal court of law to some or all of the following penalties as directed by the court:

(1) for theft or embezzlement under $5,000

(A) full repayment of investigative and court costs not to exceed $5,000,

(B) community service hours up to 480 Hours,

(C) fine up to $10,000, and

(D) up to 90 days in jail.

(2) for theft or embezzlement over $5,000

(A) full repayment of investigative and court costs not to exceed $20,000,

(B) community service hours up to 1000 hours,

(C) fine up to $25,000, and

(D) up to 1 year in jail.[Q]

SEC. 123 Assessment and Collection Actions.

(a) **Regular Assessment**: Publication of the Master Rate is formal assessment under the RPUT to the taxpaying public. No written assessment is sent to taxpayers for initial on-time charge. Taxpayer is obligated to remit the appropriate tax based on the Master Rate, the conditions in this statute, and a valid and correct survey of his Property Tax Base by the Due Date.

(b) **Assessment for Estimated, Unpaid RPUT.** Written notification is sent out if full Taxpayer remittance is not received at

(1) Days (30 days Past End of Quarter)

[Q] Any punishment should be designed to reimburse the government or society, either by fines or public service when possible. Jail time can be quite expensive to the government directly and then indirectly through loss of labor productivity. A person found guilty who is allowed to continue to produce income can be punished without punishing society.

(A) Notification of Taxpayer Assessment (TA) including Interest and Penalty sent out to the Taxpayer by standard U.S. mail or private carrier.

(2) Days (60 days Past End of Quarter)

(A) Notification of Taxpayer Assessment (TA) including Interest and Penalty sent out to the Taxpayer by standard U.S. mail or private carrier.

(3) Days (90 days Past End of Quarter)

(A) Notification of Taxpayer Assessment (TA) including Interest and Penalty sent out to the Taxpayer by standard U.S. mail or private carrier.

(4) Days (120 days Past End of Quarter)

(A) Demand Notice of Taxpayer Assessment (TA) including Interest and Penalty sent out to the Taxpayer by certified U.S. mail or private carrier, with warning on court action.

(5) Days (150 days Past End of Quarter)

(A) Demand Notice of Taxpayer Assessment (TA) including Interest and Penalty sent and court summons for Federal civil court sent out to the Taxpayer by certified U.S. Mail or private carrier. (If court rules in the government's favor, a lien on the property is requested from the court if action is against an owner).

(6) Days (180 Days Past End of Quarter) and continuing.

(A) Court and collection actions are pursued and recurring notices are updated and sent out each month until the matter is resolved.

SEC. 124 Administrative and Judicial Liability Adjustments.

(a) **Administrative Reprieve on Payment of Taxes.** Individual Taxpayers may petition FTSA for an Administrative Reprieve on Payment of Taxes (ARPT) if it can be demonstrated through appropriate financial documentation and sworn testimony that temporary, serious financial hardship exists which precludes full payment of the regular assessment at the current time.

FTSA may then delay current payment requirements up to 12 months, but regular assessments continue to accrue with Interest but without Penalty. Repayment shall begin at the end of the ARPT on a minimum of 10% per annum of unpaid outstanding principle plus Interest. An ARPT cannot be issued again until at least 50% of the principle has been paid back.

(b) **Temporary Release From Liability (TRFL).** A Temporary Release From Liability (TRFL) may be provided to any Taxpayer, or group of Taxpayers as defined by region, calamity, or other factor the court believes is relevant, for a period of up to 24 months by a Federal magistrate or judge in which time remittance for regular taxes shall not be required. Liability for past and future tax assessment amounts, however, shall continue to accrue during the TRLF period with Interest but without Penalty. Taxpayer shall be liable at a repayment rate of 10% per annum on the principle plus Interest at the end of the TRFL period, where such payments shall be made in addition to current tax assessments due at the regularly stated intervals, unless a Permanent Release From Liability (PRFL) is issued by Congress.

(c) **Permanent Release From Liability (PRFL).** Taxpayers may petition the court and the court may recommend Permanent Release From Liability by Congress. Federal courts shall recommend Permanent Release From Liability when they believe it is in the national interest to do so, but shall not use this clause as a substitute for release of normal economic obligations of Taxpayers nor as a replacement for personal or business bankruptcy in normal economic intercourse. All Federal courts issuing TRFLs shall submit copies of those with any such recommendations to Congress within 30 Days of the close of the calendar quarter in which the TRFL was issued. Congress shall disapprove or approve such recommendations under this law within 60 days and such release may be for whatever time period, past or future, up to 24 months.

(d) **Adjustment of Assessment Amount.** The FTSA must adjust the Assessment and all previous interest and penalty charges if

(1) the Primary Reviewing Officer is provided with Demonstration of Correct Assessment by FTSA survey, or
(2) the Primary Reviewing Officer is provided with Demonstration of Correct Assessment by the Taxpayer, or
(3) a federal magistrate or judge has discharged previous tax debt in bankruptcy hearings, or
(4) a Federal magistrate or judge has directed correction of Assessment Amount after reviewing and applying all applicable law and evidence, or
(5) a Federal magistrate or judge has directed a Temporary or Permanent Release From Liability because of
  (A) war
  (B) insurrection
  (C) major riot
  (D) natural disaster
  (E) regional plague or epidemic
  (F) major regional or national economic upheaval
  (G) unresolved cloud on ownership title and tax liability, or
  (H) extraordinary personal hardship such as kidnapping, prisoner of war status, abandonment of owner/child (but not personal financial difficulty, sickness, or death), or
  (I) any situation in which the court believes it is in the national interest to temporarily relieve Taxpayer of liability,

SEC. 125 Recovery of Funds.
(a) **Recovery From General Capital and Personal Property.** A court may order payment for non-real property and recovery may be exercised, at the discretion of the court, from monies, investments, sale of personal property, or other items of a Taxpayer in arrears, except that the court shall be precluded from taking those resources needed for basic living or for the performance of Taxpayer's trade or profession.
(b) **Recovery From Real Property.**

(1) **Voluntary Sale.** The government shall recover through a lien on real property if the property is sold or transferred, at which time the government's escrow claim will take precedence over the seller's or benefactor's claims.

(2) **Forced Sale.** The government may only force a sale to recover through a lien on real property if

(A) (for a non-domicile Property) the amount due the government is over $5,000.00, and the Taxpayer has been in continuous outstanding arrears for at least three years, or

(B) (for a Property that is the owner's domicile) the amount due the government is over $5,000.00, and the Taxpayer has been in continuous outstanding arrears for at least seven years.

SEC. 126 Discovery of Error.

(a) **Error in Taxpayer's Favor.** If government audit or survey indicates error in the Taxpayer's favor the FTSA shall notify Taxpayer by certified mail. Taxpayer may then submit evidence and a claim directly to FTSA for refund of overpaid taxes of up to three years. By discovery of the government or the Taxpayer, it is Taxpayer's responsibility to demonstrate beyond a mere preponderance of evidence that a refund is due.

(b) **Error in Government's Favor.** Government will bill, based on reasonable investigation, estimated back assessment amount to Taxpayer for estimated period of assessment error plus Interest and Penalty up to three years. Taxpayer may then appeal to FTSA back assessment administratively or in civil court. It is the government's responsibility to demonstrate beyond a mere preponderance of evidence that a back assessment is due.

SEC. 127 Sale or Transfer of Property.

(a) **RPUT Liability Begins and Ends With Ownership.** A buyer, inheritor, or benefactor of Property assumes RPUT liability for the Property starting with the day of sale or transfer, whatever hour of the day the change in legal title takes place, and continues to hold liability through the day before it is resold or transferred again. The former Owner retains liability for any taxes due during his ownership period. The buyer is then liable for the balance of RPUT through the current quarter and after.

(b) **Title Clearance at Time of Sale.** Any liens by the government on a Property must be satisfied through escrow before title is transferred. Current taxes through the day of sale or transfer must be paid (if by check deposited and cleared) on or before the day of sale or transfer by the seller.

SEC. 128 Audit Practices and Enforcement Controls.

(a) **General Directive.** The FTSA is charged with a quad-annual review of audit practices and enforcement controls. Data from operational history and the latest scientific and statistical techniques shall be analyzed for development or modification of assessment, audit, and recovery of revenue to both minimize labor and resource cost and maximize Taxpayer compliance and collection of accurate assessment amounts. Options shall be presented to Congress and, as appropriate, Section 128(b) shall be amended accordingly.

(b) **Audit and Enforcement Regulations.**

[Audit and Enforcement Regulations]

TITLE II - Supermajority Required

SEC. 129 Supermajority Required for RPUT Changes.

It shall not be in the order of the House of Representatives or the Senate to consider any bill, joint resolution, or amendment thereto to waive, suspend, repeal, modify, or add to this Act unless by affirmative vote of three-fifths of the Members of the Senate and House of Representatives.

Glossary

- **Actual Variance.** The *actual* net change that has occurred in Property Type, Ownership and Days In Use in the Tax Base during a Tax Period. (*see* Standard Variance).
- **Adjusted Master Rate.** A Master Rate that has been adjusted (increased or decreased) during the current Tax Period.
- **Aggregate Rental Fee.** The total of current rent and the applicable RPUT Service-to-Use Fee for an RPUT Rental Unit.
- **Annual Cropland.** Farmland currently producing, or available for producing, annual crops.
- **Average Relative Use.** The average or standard Days-In-Use that are legally denoted as the use-period for a specified Property Type during a Tax Period, irrespective of the *actual* Days-In-Use on individual properties (*see* Standard Rate).
- **Base Land.** The land surface area of a property. The Base-Land area of a property is the land area denoted on its legal title.
- **Base Land Under Developed Space.** The land area under Developed Space.
- **Base Land Status.** One of five basic land-surface-area conditions of property under the RPUT: Open Land, Annual Cropland, Storage Management, Landscaped Grounds, and Base Land Under Developed Space.
- **Basic Rate.** One of four Tax Category rates in the RPUT that is set by Congress.
- **Category Area.** The total area on a property belonging to one of the four Tax Categories.
- **Consanguineous.** Relational; as used in the RPUT, a set of tax rates and conditions that are interrelated and provide one universally applicable assessment reference: the Master Rate.
- **Common Area.** Area used in common by renters on an RPUT Rental Unit property, such as a parking lot, mailroom, walkway, swimming pool, and so on, or the total of all such areas on a property.
- **Days In Ownership.** The number of days in a Tax Period that a property is under a particular ownership.

- **Days In Use.** The number of days in a Tax Period that a property is in use, or available for use, by the legal owner or renter of the property (*see also* In-Use and Vacation Status).
- **Developed Space.** Habitable, developed floor space on, under, or above Base Land, such as that found in or on houses, patios, paved driveways, basements, apartments, factories, office buildings, parking lots, and so on.
- **Division.** One of two major tax divisions of RPUT liability, Service to Ownership or Service to Use. Both Divisions incorporate the Subdivisions of Base Land and Developed Space (*see* Tax Category).
- **Economical to Operate, principle of.** Application of taxation in a manner that is convenient and cost-effective for the taxpayer and the government.
- **Effective Rate.** For each of the four Tax Categories, the Master Rate times the Basic Rate. The taxpayer multiplies the Effective Rate times the Area, and then multiplies that by the Days In Use to obtain his tax due for the particular Tax Category.
- **Equitable to the Citizen, principle of.** Tax assessment of individuals based on their relative economic interest and benefit from government service (*see* Liability for Service Rendered).
- **Equity in Commerce, principle of.** Tax assessment of all relevant and like ownership conditions, whether in subsidiary government or private ownership [See Chapter XI on non-inclusion in RPUT theory].
- **Funding Statute.** Appropriation or budget law that specifies what is spent by the government and that denotes the RPUTL as the means of assessment and revenue acquisition.
- **In Use.** Term to denote property that is either physically in use or available for use (not in Vacation Status).
- **Landowner.** (*See* Owner).
- **Landscaped Grounds.** Commercially or residentially maintained landscape such as lawns, gardens, parks, playing fields, et cetera.
- **Leaseholder.** Long-term renter.
- **Liability for Service Rendered.** Tax liability based on the relative level of government service to the taxpayer.
- **Master Rate.** A standard, universally applicable rate in the RPUT calculated from an appropriation or budget, the Basic Rates and total Tax Base. The Master Rate can be used by any taxpayer in any situation against his personal Tax Base to calculate the RPUT due (*see* Effective Rate). The Master Rate also functions as an economic barometer for the cost of government.

- **Master Rate Adjustment.** The increase or decrease in the original Master Rate during a given budget period.
- **Objective and Certain, principle of.** The application of taxation in a stable, objective, and visible manner.
- **Open Land.** Commercial timberland, planted orchards not yet producing, range (grazing) land, undeveloped recreational lands, and all other general undeveloped land (but *not* Annual Cropland, Storage Management, or Landscaped Grounds**;** *see* Open Space).
- **Open Space.** All undeveloped, agricultural, or other open portions of Base Land including Open Land, Annual Cropland, Storage Management, and Landscaped Grounds. (Note that Open Land is a type of Open Space, but not vice versa.)
- **Owner.** The legal owner of real property as recorded in the official property title.
- **Ownership.** The holding of legal title to real property.
- **Primacy of the Citizen and Taxpayer.** Theory that holds that the objective application of tax assessment and taxpayer rights must be primary in the application of tax law; as opposed to Primacy of the State, where mere acquisition of revenue is primary.
- **Primary Liability.** The liability for a tax that is associated directly with a particular ownership or service right and not with third-party economic transactions (*see* Primary Right).
- **Primary Right.** A property, ownership, or service right that is directly associated with a related tax; as opposed to the interests of secondary contractors or beneficiaries that are not directly taxed, but that also do not hold the related ownership or service rights on which the tax is based (*see* Primary Liability).
- **Property.** A legally defined ownership parcel as officially recorded in a county or state, such as in a county or state Recorders Office, and used as the basis of assessment in the RPUT.
- **Property ID.** An identification number for a property based on an algorithm related to the geographical points of the property's land demarcation and assigned by the federal RPUT administration agency.
- **Property Type.** Base Land, Developed Space, or one of various types of Open-Space properties on Base Land.
- **Protected in Law, principle of.** Taxation that is concurrent with other contemporary law, human rights, and basic economic liberty.

- **Rational Economic Exchange.** An economic transaction where goods or services are transferred from the provider for a return of relative value (compensation) from the receiver in a manner that advances the economic interests of both parties.

- **Real Property Use Tax (RPUT).** A tax based on relative liability for government service to the assessed and billed against the size, status and use-conditions of real property that is owned and/or rented by the taxpayer.

- **Real Property Use Tax Law (RPUTL).** The federal statute that defines administrative and regulatory operation of the RPUT (*see also* Funding Statute).

- **Relative to Appropriations, principle of.** Tax assessment directly related to and commensurate with spending, both at the macroeconomic and individual taxpayer level.

- **Rental Unit ID.** A unique RPUT Rental Unit identification for each Rental Unit on a property, assigned by the owner and reported to the federal RPUT administration agency.

- **Renter.** Legal entity that contracts for the use of a property from the legal owner.

- **Revenue Requirement.** The spending or budget amount in statutory law that is funded through the RPUT.

- **RPUT.** Real Property Use Tax.

- **RPUTL.** Real Property Use Tax Law.

- **RPUT Rental Unit.** A registered RPUT subdivision of property that is available for rent and where Service-to-Use liability lies directly with the renter.

- **RPUT Renter.** A renter that is directly liable to the government for the Service-to-Use Fee (*see* RPUT Rental Unit).

- **RPUT Report Form.** The master document and its related subforms in which RPUT survey, Rental Unit, and tax remittance information is prepared and submitted to the government; in both paper and electronic (computer based) formats.

- **Secondary Dedication.** Additional appropriation item(s) specified in a Funding Statute that are to be funded with any surplus tax revenue that exists after the original (or primary) appropriations have been paid off (as opposed to the surplus going to an undedicated general fund).

- **Service to Ownership.** Liability and assessment for property *ownership* under the RPUT. The owner is always liable for the period of ownership, irrespective of use status.

- **Service to Use.** Liability and assessment for property *use* under the RPUT when property is not in Vacation Status. Either the owner or RPUT Renter is liable, depending on who is using the property.
- **Standard Rate.** A standard Days-In-Use number divided by the Tax Period. Standard Rates are used for RPUT calculation on Open Land and Annual Cropland and apply irrespective of the *actual* number of days a property is being used; used in the RPUT to account for the agricultural and similar land-use conditions.
- **Standard Variance.** The *estimated* net change that will occur in Property Type, Ownership and Days In Use in the Tax Base during a new Tax Period. The Standard Variance is used to adjust the Master Rate at the beginning of the Tax Period so as to account for the estimated Tax-Base change during the Tax Period (*see* Actual Variance).
- **Storage Management.** Undeveloped but controlled Base Land used for intensive purposes such as livestock yards, unpaved vehicle storage lots, junkyards, and marshaling yards.
- **Subdivision.** The Base Land or Developed Space subdivision under Service to Ownership and Service to Use (*see* Tax Category).
- **Survey.** Physical measurement of areas on a property to determine the size of Property Types.
- **Taxable Area.** Physical surface area used in computing the RPUT.
- **Tax Base.** The total assessment base under the RPUT for all Tax Categories for a) a property, b) an individual Taxpayer, or c) the country (depending on the context).
- **Tax Category.** One of four main property-assessment classifications of the RPUT—(1) Service to Ownership/Base Land, (2) Service to Ownership/Developed Space, (3) Service to Use/Base Land, and (4) Service to Use/Developed Space.
- **Tax Period.** The RPUT assessment period for a given appropriation or budget; typically the calendar tax year.
- **Taxpayer.** The legal entity liable for the RPUT, either the owner or RPUT Renter.
- **Vacate.** The act of leaving a property, or RPUT Rental Unit, so it is no longer in use or available for use, and usually demonstrated by physical departure as well as evacuation of personal assets and effects.
- **Vacation Status.** The status of a full property or RPUT Rental Unit when it is *not* in use *and* also vacated and up for sale or rent. The owner is not liable for the Service-to-Use Fee when a property is in Vacation Status.

Listing of Tables and Figures

Endnotes

Special advice on the Endnote postings in this work:

This is the first book to take advantage of the new Justinnote Coding method. Justinnote Coding supplants the traditional and well-servicing Ibidem (*Ibid.*) method of denoting repeat-entries in footnote and endnote listings. See "Addendum–Justinnote Coding" at the end of this section for an explanation of this system.

---

[1] From *The Debate on the Constitution: Federalist and Antifederalist Speeches, Articles, and Letters During the Struggle over Ratification, Part One: September 1787 to February 1788* (New York: The Library of America, 1993), p. 617. The *New York Journal* commentary was originally republished in *The Documentary History of the Ratification of the Constitution, Vol. XV* (Madison: The State Historical Society of Wisconsin, 1984), pp. 113–114, and is reprinted here with the Society's kind permission.

[2] See Bernard H. Siegan's *Economic Liberties and the Constitution* (Chicago: University of Chicago Press, 1980), pp. 32–33.

[3] Eighteenth-century writer Thomas Paine coined this term as the title of one of his Revolutionary War period pamphlets where he argued for American self-government.

[4] [S001] Webber, Carolyn, and Wildavsky, Aaron, *A History of Taxation and Expenditure in the Western World* (New York: Simon and Schuster, 1986), pp. 361–63.

[5] -S001- p. 361.

[6] -S001- p. 361.

[7] -S001- p. 361.

[8] -S001- p. 362.

[9] -S001- p. 362.

[10] -S001- p. 362.

[11] -S001- p. 364.

[12] -S001- p. 364.

[13] -S001- p. 364.

[14] -S001- p. 363.

[15] -S001- pp. 362–63.

[16] -S001- p. 362.

[17] -S001- pp. 364–66.

[18] -S001- p. 364.

[19] -S001- p. 364.

[20] -S001- pp. 364–66.

[21] -S001- p. 366.

[22] -S001- p. 371.

[23] McCarthy, Clarence F., . . . [et al], *The Fedeal Income Tax: Its Sources and Applications* (Englewood Cliffs, New Jersey: Prentice Hall, 1968), p. 2.

[24] [S018] Baldwin, Leland D., *Whiskey Rebels: The Story of a Frontier Uprising* (University of Pittsberg Press, 1968), p. 236–231.

[25] Neither bank notes nor hard money circulated in the interior parts of western Pennsylvania and whiskey was used as a medium of exchange. Distillation was sometimes the only feasible means of moving grain to market, so the heavy 25-percent whiskey excise tax was a substantial burden. [S002] Miller, John C., *The Federalist Era* (New York: Harper & Row, 1960), p. 156.

[26] President Washington called upon the states to furnish 12,900 men for the expedition—a very large deployment. But the President and Alexander Hamilton agreed that "the crisis was arrived when it must be determined whether the Government can maintain itself." [S002] Miller, John C., *The Federalist Era* (New York: Harper & Row, 1960), pp. 155–62; and [S018] Baldwin, Leland D., *Whiskey Rebels: The Story of a Frontier Uprising* (University of Pittsberg Press, 1968), pp. 257–64.

[27] An interesting anecdote of the Whiskey Rebellion, somehow resonant of modern income tax planning, is of remaining distillers who chose to continue operations by being more cautious, trading down river, and hiring better lawyers. -S018- p. 264.

[28] -S018- p. 264.

[29] Jeffersonian Republicans do not belong to the same group as the modern Republican Party, or "Grand Old Party" (GOP). The modern Democratic Party, at least in political lineage if not philosophy, is the party linked to the old Republicans.

[30] [S002] Miller, John C., *The Federalist Era: 1789–1801* (New York: Harper & Row, 1960), pp. 70–125.

[31] -S002- pp. 33–54.

[32] Part of the deal was movement of the national capital from New York to the area of the present capital, Washington, D.C. See -S002- pp. 48–49.

[33] [S001] Webber, Carolyn, and Wildavsky, Aaron, *A History of Taxation and Expenditure in the Western World* (New York: Simon and Schuster, 1986), pp. 371–72.

[34] -S001- p. 372.

[35] -S001- p. 372.

[36] -S001- p. 378.

[37] -S001- p. 378.

[38] -S001- p. 380.

[39] [S005] Internal Revenue Service, "Major Categories of Federal Income and Outlays for Fiscal Year 1996," *1997 1040 Instructions* [booklet] (Washington, D.C.: Department of the Treasury, Internal Revenue Service, 1997), p. 52.

[40] Federal expenditures were $10.8 million in 1800. [S001] Webber, Carolyn, and Wildavsky, Aaron, *A History of Taxation and Expenditure in the Western World* (New York: Simon and Schuster, 1986), p. 384.

[41] -S001- p. 373.

[42] -S001- p. 373.

[43] -S001- p. 379.

[44] -S001- p. 379.

[45] -S001- p. 379.

[46] -S001- p. 379.

[47] See Choades, John; Daskal, Steven E.; DiLorenzo, Thomas J. . . . [et al]. (Edited by Burton W. Folsom) *The Industrial Revolution and Free Trade* (Irving-on-Hudson, New York: Foundation for Economic Education, 1996).

[48] [S001] Webber, Carolyn, and Wildavsky, Aaron, *A History of Taxation and Expenditure in the Western World* (New York: Simon and Schuster, 1986), pp. 373–74.

[49] -S001- p. 374.

[50] -S001- p. 384.

[51] -S001- p. 374.

[52] -S001- p. 374.

[53] See the Laffer Curve in Laffer, Arthur B., and Seymour, Jan P., *The Economics of the Tax Revolt* (New York: Harcourt Brace Jovanovich, 1979), pp. 5–12.

[54] Walton, Gary M. and Robertson, Ross M., *History of the American Economy* (New York: Harcourt Brace Jovanovich, 1983), pp. 546–47.

[55] Steinberg, James, "Farmers in La Jolla? Checks are in the Mail," *The San Diego Union-Tribune*, June 4, 1995, p. A-1.

[56] Anderson, Curt; Associated Press, "Wide-Ranging Fraud Found in Nutrition Aid for Low-Income People," *The San Diego Union-Tribune*, April 26, 1998, p. A-17.

[57] Copley News Service, "So Far, Cuts in 'Corporate Welfare' Little More Than Superficial," *The San Diego Union-Tribune*, July 29, 1995, p. A-28.

[58] For some essays, examples, and analyses of government involvement in economic management see Laffer and Seymour, *The Economics of the Tax Revolt: A Reader* (New York: Harcourt Brace Jovanovich, 1979).

[59] Laissez-faire is a doctrine opposing governmental interference in economic affairs beyond the minimum necessary for the maintenance of peace and order.

[60] [S001] Webber, Carolyn, and Wildavsky, Aaron, *A History of Taxation and Expenditure in the Western World* (New York: Simon and Schuster, 1986), p. 373.

[61] -S001- p. 373.

[62] -S001- p. 418.

[63] -S001- pp. 418–19.

[64] -S001- p. 419.

[65] Davis, Shelley L., *Unbridled Power: Inside the Secret Culture of the IRS* (New York: Harper Collins, 1997), p. 190.

[66] [S001] Webber, Carolyn, and Wildavsky, Aaron, *A History of Taxation and Expenditure in the Western World* (New York: Simon and Schuster, 1986), p. 375.

[67] -S001- p. 387.

[68] -S001- p. 375.

[69] -S001- p. 385.

[70] -S001- p. 384.

[71] -S001- p. 385.

[72] -S001- pp. 375–86.

[73] It is ironic today that citizens, previously forced to forgo prevention of environmental damage to their land *for the public good* without compensation, can now be forced to preserve and manage their land under Multiple Species Conservation Act for environmental preservation *for the public good*—without compensation.

[74] Adams, James Ring, *The Tax Revolt Tradition in American Politics and Law.* (Ann Arbor, Michigan: University Microfilms International, 1985), pp. 33–34.

[75] [S001] Webber, Carolyn, and Wildavsky, Aaron, *A History of Taxation and Expenditure in the Western World* (New York: Simon and Schuster, 1986), pp. 417–18.

[76] -S001- p. 419.

[77] -S001- p. 420.

[78] McCarthy, Mann, Abbin, Gregory, Lindgren, *The Federal Income Tax: Its Sources and Applications* (Englewood Cliffs, New Jersey: Prentice-Hall, 1968), p. 3.

[79] [S003] Waltman, Jerold L., *Political Origins of the U.S. Income Tax* (Jackson, Mississippi: University Press of Mississippi, 1985), p. 4.

[80] -S003- p. 5.

[81] [S004] Coletta, Paolo E., *The Presidency of William Howard Taft* (Wichita, Kansas: University Press of Kansas, 1973), p. 63.

[82] -S004- p. 62.

[83] -S004- p. 63.

[84] -S004- p. 64.

[85] -S004- p. 65.

[86] [S001] Webber, Carolyn, and Wildavsky, Aaron, *A History of Taxation and Expenditure in the Western World* (New York: Simon and Schuster, 1986), p. 420.

[87] [S003] Waltman, Jerold L., *Political Origins of the U.S. Income Tax* (Jackson, Mississippi: University Press of Mississippi, 1985), p. 5.

[88] This income tax was an amendment to the tariff bill; (Introduced by Democratic Senator Joseph Bailey, of Texas, and supported by the Republican insurgents Albert B. Cummins, Iowa, and William E. Borah, Idaho) the levy was a 3 percent tax on individual and corporate incomes above $5,000. Bailey and Cummins negotiated the bill to 2 percent and convinced 19 Republicans to board ship before Aldrich won postponement and turned to Taft for help. [S004] Coletta, Paolo E., *The Presidency of William Howard Taft.* (Wichita, Kansas: University Press of Kansas, 1973), pp. 66–67.

[89] The meeting between Taft and Aldrich included Henry Cabot Lodge and, apparently, Senator Murray Crane of Massachusetts. Hechler, Kenneth W., *Insurgency: Personalities and Politics of the Taft Era* (New York: Russell & Russell, 1964), pp. 146–53.

[90] [S001] Webber, Carolyn, and Wildavsky, Aaron, *A History of Taxation and Expenditure in the Western World* (New York: Simon and Schuster, 1986), p. 420.

[91] -S001- pp. 420–21.

[92] Coletta, Paolo E., *The Presidency of William Howard Taft.* (Wichita, Kansas: University Press of Kansas, 1973), p. 67.

[93] Considerable question has actually been raised as to whether or not the Sixteenth Amendment was ever constitutionally, and thus legally, passed. See Bill Benson and M. J. "Red" Beckman's book, *The Law That Never Was* (Holland, Illinois: Constitution Research Association, 1985). The Sixteenth Amendment and the income tax are *de facto*

law, however, and currently embraced by the major political power bases and the courts in the country. Although some defendants in tax cases may have attempted to use Messrs. Benson and Beckman's arguments or evidence in court, whatever constitutional challenges that have been made to income tax law in the courts to-date have not been successful.

[94] [S003] Waltman, Jerold L., *Political Origins of the U.S. Income Tax* (Jackson, Mississippi: University Press of Mississippi, 1985), pp. 5–6.

[95] [S001] Webber, Carolyn, and Wildavsky, Aaron, *A History of Taxation and Expenditure in the Western World* (New York: Simon and Schuster, 1986), pp. 421–22.

[96] -S001- pp. 421–22.

[97] Conlan, Timothy J.; Wrightson, Margaret T.; and Beam, David R., *Taxing Choices: The Politics of Tax Reform* (Washington, D.C.: CQ Press, 1990), p. 17.

[98] Rand, Ayn, *Capitalism, The Unknown Ideal* (New York: The New American Library, Inc., 1966), p. 12.

[99] [S001] Webber, Carolyn, and Wildavsky, Aaron, *A History of Taxation and Expenditure in the Western World* (New York: Simon and Schuster, 1986) p. 441.

[100] -S001- p. 441.

[101] -S001- p. 442–3.

[102] -S001- p. 443.

[103] -S001- p. 452.

[104] -S001- p. 444.

[105] -S001- p. 444.

[106] -S001- pp. 454–55.

[107] -S001- p. 456.

[108] -S001- p. 473.

[109] -S001- p. 456.

[110] -S001- p. 455.

[111] -S001- p. 454.

[112] Some of the critiques of Roosevelt's economic policies include [Edited by Gregory P. Pavlik] *Forgotten Lessons: Selected Essays of John T. Flynn*, or Flynn's *The Roosevelt Myth*; John McKay, *The Welfare State: No Mercy for the Middle Class*; Paul Johnson, *A History of the American People*; Burton W. Folsom, Jr., *Empire Builders: How Michigan Helped Make America Great.* Additional Comments on the New Deal. Confounding variables are not exclusive to the hard sciences, and economics has its own variety of influencing factors that determine an outcome—or *options* for an outcome. The period-appeal of socialism, the then status of the science of economics, and the need for immediate action with the limited knowledge-at-hand may have pointed the Roosevelt Administration toward the direction that it went. But the big factor that influenced that direction of action may have been the *economic knowledge and political acceptance of the electorate*, which has to be considered in the implementation of any economic policy—or any tax system. If a hard-line laissez-faire policy had been implemented with the incoming Roosevelt Administration, would that have resulted in a large political expansion of the socialist and communist left at a time when no one was prepared philosophically nor empirically to deal with those consequences? What was the best

choice possible with the facts at hand? And what was *politically* possible? And is good leadership with a second-rate policy better than bad leadership with a "technically-sound" policy? . . . We who deal in the luxury of hindsight. For all the criticisms of politicians, it is they who must deal with limited knowledge in finite time in both the regular and crisis moments of government—and hope in history that the charts they followed had error-free cartography.

[113] [S005] Internal Revenue Service, "Major Categories of Federal Income and Outlays for Fiscal Year 1996," *1997 1040 Instructions* (booklet), (Washington, D.C.: Department of the Treasury, Internal Revenue Service, 1997), p. 52.

[114] Current national debt as of 3/10/98; *U.S. National Debt Clock* Internet Site, http://www.brillig.com/debt_clock/.

[115] [S005] Internal Revenue Service, "Major Categories of Federal Income and Outlays for Fiscal Year 1996," *1997 1040 Instructions* (booklet), (Washington, D.C.: Department of the Treasury, Internal Revenue Service, 1997), p. 52.

[116] -S005- p. 52.

[117] Aid to the Communist nation was apparently done in the name of humanitarian interests and to preclude further development of a graphite reactor program that might be used for plutonium bombs. However, it is questionable whether such U.S. aid and pay-outs, or perhaps payoffs, will mitigate—or extend—the Korean crisis. Caldwell, Robert J., "Korean Crisis: When Dealing With a Dictator, Prepare for the Worst," *The San Diego Union-Tribune*, March 27, 1994, p. G-4. / New York Times News Service; "South Korea Says It Needs Help Paying For Nuclear Power Plants In North," *The San Diego Union-Tribune,* February 5, 1998, p. A-19. / Associated Press, "North Korea Nuclear Plants Break Ground," *The San Diego Union-Tribune,* August 20, 1997, p. A-2. / Jensen, Holgar, "Look Again At Korean Weapons Sales," *The San Diego Union-Tribune,* August 29, 1997, p. B-7. / Myers, Laura, "Threats to U.S. Abound, Policy Makers Caution," *The San Diego Union-Tribune,* August 18, 1997, p. A-2.

[118] Kellman, Laura; Associated Press, "President Backs Higher Tobacco Tax," *The San Diego Union-Tribune*, March 13, 1998, p. A-13. / Sobieraj, Sandra; Associated Press, "Clinton Calls on Congress to Enact Anti-Cigarette Law," *The San Diego Union-Tribune*, March 8, 1998, p. A-1. / Will, George F.; Washington Post Writers Group, "Cashing In On the Tobacco Lottery," *The San Diego Union-Tribune*, February 15, 1998, p. G-2.

[119] Producer: Michael Raplutzky; Correspondent: Ed Bradley. "Painkiller," News Segment, *60 Minutes,* CBS News Television Magazine, December 8, 1996. / Freedberg, Martin, Chronicle Staff Writers, "U.S. Warns Pot Doctors; Attack on Medical Marijuana Aimed at Patients, Too.," *The San Francisco Chronicle*, December 31, 1996, p. 1.

[120] Kreisher, Otto; Copley News Service, "Joint-Chiefs Nominee Backs Military Role in Border Drug War," *The San Diego Union-Tribune*. September 10, 1997. p. A-8. / O'Connell, Jim; Scripps Howard News Service, "Pentagon Wants to End Armed Military Patrols on Border," *The San Diego Union-Tribune*, January 15, 1998, p. A-7. / Stern, Marcus; Copley News Service, "Military Wary of Bigger Role in Drug War," *The San Diego Union-Tribune*, p. A-13. / Green, Stephen; Copley News Service, "New House Judiciary Chairman Takes Aim at Asset-Seizure Abuses," The San Diego Union-Tribune, June 17, 1995, p. A-3.

[121] [S006] Fumento, Michael, "When Government Can Take Property," *The San Diego Union-Tribune*, December 29, 1995, p. B-13. / Greenhouse, Linda, "Court Mulls Double Jeopardy In Forfeitures," *The San Diego Union-Tribune*, April 18, 1996, p. A-2. / Will,

George F; Washington Post Writers Group, "Questioning Our Forfeiture Laws," *The San Diego Union-Tribune*, March 10, 1996, p. G-2.

[122] [S006] Fumento, Michael, "When Government Can Take Property," *The San Diego Union-Tribune*, December 29, 1995, p. B-13.

[123] -S006- p. B-13.

[124] Representative Henry Hyde (R-Illinois), *Forfeiting Our Property Rights: Is Your Property Safe from Seizure?* (Washington, D.C.: Cato Institute, 1995).

[125] La Rue, Steve; Rodgers, Terry; Weisberg, Lori; and Associated Press; "Ruling on Threatened Species May Boost Preservation Here," *San Diego Union-Tribune*, June 30, 1995, p. A-1. / La Rue, Steve; and Associated Press; "Court Says Gnatcatcher Must Have Safe Habitat," *San Diego Union-Tribune,* May 22, 1997, p. A-3. / Pierce, Emmet, "Many Fight To Preserve Land Rights," *San Diego Union-Tribune,* July 23, 1995, p. B-1.

[126] [S007] Moulton, Andrew; Knight-Ridder News Service, "Foes of 'Low-Flow' Toilet Law Send Gripes to Seat of Government," *The San Diego Union-Tribune*, December 13, 1997, p. A-21.

[127] -S007- p. A-21.

[128] Ainsworth, Bill, "Judge Again Strikes Down Proposition 187," *The San Diego Union-Tribune*, November 15, 1997, p. A-1. / Mendel, Ed, "Final Ruling; Prop. 187 is Struck Down," *The San Diego Union-Tribune*, March 19, 1998, p. A-1.

[129] Mendel, Ed, "Final Ruling: Proposition 187 is Struck Down; Appeal Due on Aid to Illegal Immigrants," *The San Diego Union-Tribune*, March 19, 1998, p. A-1.

[130] This figure is based on the total *regular* 1996 income tax collections ($828 billion) multiplied by a cost factor of 65.01% (The computation does not include Social Security collections). The cost factor is from economist James L. Payne's seminal work *Costly Returns: The Burdens of the U.S. Tax System* (San Francisco: Institute for Contemporary Studies, 1993. See Chapter 10). The percentage-of-revenue-collected breakdown is Business—15.68%, Individuals—8.75%, Enforcement Costs—1.97%, Economic Disincentive—35.04%, Evasion and Avoidance Costs—2.96%, and Government Costs—0.61%. If Social Security and other retirement fund collections for 1996 were included (a total of $509 billion), then the estimates given here *would increase by 61 percent, or over half again as much!* This actually may be more accurate since Social Security funds can be "spent" for current expenditures instead of remaining in trust funds—leaving Social Security, effectively, as just another tax-expenditure liability of government instead of a government savings plan. However, the conservative cost-assessment estimate *excluding* Social Security funds is used here. The source for the 1996 monetary collection indicated ($828 billion) is the Internal Revenue Service, [S005] "Major Categories of Federal Income and Outlays for Fiscal Year 1996," *1997 1040 Instructions* (booklet), (Washington, D.C.: Department of the Treasury, Internal Revenue Service, 1997), p. 52.

[131] The economic cost of tax avoidance and tax evasion is estimated at $26 billion for 1996. Note that this figure is *not* the amount of lost tax revenue resulting from such activities, but the *increased cost* to the economy (to both the government and taxpayers) from taxpayers engaging in such activities.

[132] The monetary estimate is a 1996 value based on a cost factor from Professor James L. Payne's *Costly Returns* (See above notes). The number of man-hours is based on a 1985 figure from Arthur D. Little, Inc., *Development of Methodology for Estimating the Taxpayer Paperwork Burden* (Washington, D.C.: Internal Revenue Service, June 1988.

p. I-7, table 1.7). The 1985 man-hours number has been extrapolated here to the 1996 condition based on the relative increase in monetary cost (68%).

[133] Income tax revenue receipts for 1996 were $656 billion for individuals and $172 billion for corporations, for a total of $828 billion. The additional $509 billion of Social Security and retirement collections is not included here. Source is [S005] Internal Revenue Service, "Major Categories of Federal Income and Outlays for Fiscal Year 1996," *1997 1040 Instructions* (booklet), (Washington, D.C.: Department of the Treasury, Internal Revenue Service, 1997), p. 52.

[134] The deficit figure is from the [S005] Internal Revenue Service, "Major Categories of Federal Income and Outlays for Fiscal Year 1996," *1997 1040 Instructions* (booklet), (Washington, D.C.: Department of the Treasury, Internal Revenue Service, 1997), p. 52.

[135] "Vietnam War," Section: The Aftermath of the War, *The Grolier's Multimedia Encyclopedia*, online edition, (Grolier Electronic Publishing, Danbury, CT, 1996).

[136] The total federal income for 1996 was $1.45 trillion, including $828 billion from personal income and corporate taxation. Internal Revenue Service, "1997 Tax Rate Schedules," *1997 1040 Instructions* (booklet), (Washington, D.C.: Department of the Treasury, Internal Revenue Service, 1997), p. 51.

[137] For an another view of the high economic cost of income tax systems, defined in "deadweight" costs, see *Losses of Nations: Deadweight Politics VS. Public Rent Dividends* (London: Othila Press, 1998) by Fred Harrison, Richard Noyes, Ronald Banks, . . . [et al].

[138] Lewis, Finley; Copley News Service, "Top Democrat, Republican Unveil Competing Tax-Cut Plans," The San Diego Union Tribune, January 21, 1998, p. A-10. / Wilkie, Dana; Copley News Service, "Tax-Reform Debate Likely to Grow in '98," *The San Diego Union-Tribune*, February 1, 1998, p. A-1.

[139] Writers Art Buchwald and Alain Berhneim wrote "King for A Day," later used as a basis for Paramount's "Coming to America." Medina, Hildy; Copley News Service, "Ugly Story Behind Some Film Stories," *The San Diego Union-Tribune*, January 26, 1997, p. A-1. / Reuters News Service, "Cast of Thousands Permitted to Sue Hollywood Studios Over Pay Method," *The San Diego Union-Tribune*, June 18, 1996, p. A-6.

[140] Jim Jones was an American cult leader that led 912 followers to suicide in Guyana in 1978 after U.S. Congressman Leo Ryan and four others (who had flown down to South America to investigate Jone's operations) were killed. Wilkie, Dana with Christine Berg, "Cult Suicide in Rancho Santa Fe: 2 Horrors Have Much in Common," *The San Diego Union-Tribune*, March 28, 1997, p. A-4. / Associated Press, "Guyana Pushes Timber Company to Halt Jonestown Destruction," *The San Diego Union-Tribune*, March 9, 1993, p. A-12.

[141] [S013] Pechman, Joseph A., . . . [et al]. (Introduction by Walter W. Heller.), *Tax Policy: New Directions and Possibilities* (Washington D.C.: The Center for National Policy, 1984), p. 6.

[142] [S008] Kilpatrick, William A., *The Big Tax Lie* (New York: Simon & Schuster, 1986), p. 55–60.

[143] -S008- p. 58.

[144] See Internal Revenue Service, "1997 Tax Rate Schedules," *1997 1040 Instructions* (booklet), (Washington, D.C.: Department of the Treasury, Internal Revenue Service, 1997), p. 51.

[145] Pyle, David J., *Tax Evasion and the Black Economy* (London: The MacMillan Press, 1989), p. 35.

[146] [S008] Kilpatrick, William A., *The Big Tax Lie* (New York: Simon & Schuster, 1986), p. 53.

[147] [S009] Armey, Dick, *The Flat Tax: A Citizens Guide to the Facts On What It Will Do for You, Your Country, and Your Pocketbook* (New York: Fawcett, Columbine, 1996), p. 2–3.

[148] A bill passed the Senate in July 1998 that shifted the burden of tax disputes that wind up in court from the taxpayer to the IRS. It also allows reimbursement of legal expenses incurred by taxpayers who take their cases to court and win. However, since most of the problems associated with income tax law compliance and enforcement are associated with conditions *prior* to court action, it remains to be seen if these new regulations will have any practical effect for most of the taxpayers who are audited. There are probably very few taxpayers wishing for a confrontation in court with the IRS, even if they *think* they complied with all possible tax requirements, and litigation can be very costly as well as risky.

[149] [S009] Armey, Dick, *The Flat Tax: A Citizens Guide to the Facts On What It Will Do for You, Your Country, and Your Pocketbook* (New York: Fawcett, Columbine, 1996), p. 45.

[150] September 1997 Congressional hearings on IRS abuses.

[151] [S014] Pace, David "IRS Targets Poor Southerners for Random Audits, Report Says" Associated Press for *The San Diego Union-Tribune*, Sunday, March 1, 1998, p. A-1.

[152] -S014- p. A-9.

[153] Davis, Shelley L., *Unbridled Power: Inside the Secret Culture of the IRS.* (New York: Harper Collins, 1997), p. 117–133.

[154] See September 1997 Congressional Hearings on IRS abuses.

[155] The actual level of public accessibility to property tax payments, arrears, and penalties for private citizens may vary between jurisdictions. The point is that public charges, payments and penalties *should* be public record and can easily be made so in a tax system like the property tax.

[156] To arrive at this figure, gross income tax revenues for 1996 of $828 billion are multiplied by 38% (35.04% for disincentives to production, and 2.96% for the increased economic cost to the economy from tax avoidance and evasion). [The cost ratios are taken from James L. Payne's *Costly Returns: The Burdens of the U.S. Tax System* (San Francisco: Institute for Contemporary Studies, 1993. p. 150, Table 15), and then multiplied by the 1996 revenue amount.]

[157] [S009] Armey, Dick, *The Flat Tax: A Citizens Guide to the Facts On What It Will Do for You, Your Country, and Your Pocketbook* (New York: Fawcett, Columbine, 1996), p. 34.

[158] Schulte, Brigid, *Knight-Ridder News Service,* "Legislate in Haste, Fix at Leisure: Tax Bill Full of Typos, Time Bombs," in the *The San Diego Union-Tribune*, Tuesday, August 5, 1997, p. A-6.

[159] [S009] Armey, Dick, *The Flat Tax: A Citizens Guide to the Facts On What It Will Do for You, Your Country, and Your Pocketbook* (New York: Fawcett, Columbine, 1996), p. 21–23.

[160] -S009- p. 46.

[161] Scripps Howard New Service and Cox New Service, "IRS Can Be Real Taxing, Analyst Says," *The San Diego Union-Tribune*, September 11, 1996. P. A-11.

[162] Davis, Shelley L., *Unbridled Power: Inside the Secret Culture of the IRS* (New York: HarperCollins Publishers, Inc., 1997), p. 263.

[163] Recent U.S. Budget history [in billions of dollars]: (Reagen and Bush) 1980—$681; 1983—$878; 1986—$1,073; 1988—$1,186; 1991, $1,323; (Clinton) 1993—1,408 billion; 1996—$1,612. Source: [Manager: Superintendent of Documents] Budget of the United States Government, [books published by fiscal year] (Washington, D.C.: U.S. Government Printing Office).

[164] The 14th Amendment to the United States Constitutions deals with protections against slavery, the 5th Amendment protects against unjust seizure of private property, and the 10th deals with the limit on powers of the federal government.

[165] Crocket, Joseph P., *The Federal Tax System of the United States* (New York: Columbia University Press, 1955), p. 112–127.

[166] Davis, Shelley L., *Unbridled Power: Inside the Secret Culture of the IRS* (New York: Harper Collins, 1997), p. 187.

[167] Simons, Henry C., *Personal Income Taxation*. Chicago: University of Chicago Press, 1938. pp. 39–40.

[168] Kellman, Laura; Associated Press, "President Backs Higher Tobacco Tax," *The San Diego Union-Tribune*, March 13, 1998, p. A-13. / Sobieraj, Sandra; Associated Press, "Clinton Calls on Congress to Enact Anti-Cigarette Law," *The San Diego Union-Tribune*, March 8, 1998, p. A-1. / Will, George F.; Washington Post Writers Group, "Cashing In On the Tobacco Lottery," *The San Diego Union-Tribune*, February 15, 1998, p. G-2.

[169] Schiller, Erin, "Cigarette Taxes May Not Save the Day," *The San Diego Union-Tribune*, February 18, 1998, p. B-7.

[170] Harper and Wessel, "Economy: A Primer: What Congress Will Face in Debate Over Taxes and Revenue" *The Wall Street Journal*, December 27, 1994.

[171] [S010] See Smith, Stephen, "Taxation and the Environment," *The Economics of Tax Policy* (Oxford University Press, 1996), pp. 215–58. (First published in *Fiscal Studies* (1992) vol. 13, no. 4, pp. 21–57.)

[172] -S010- p. 216. The Pigouvian tax is named after A.C. Pigou, professor of political economy at Cambridge, 1908–43, who discussed the assessment mechanism circa 1920.

[173] -S010- pp. 217–18. Smith in his U.K. work spells *mutualization* "mutualisation."

[174] State of California, Board of Equalization, *Regulation 1506, Miscellaneous Service Regulations*, Sections 6006, 6007, 6015, 6018.1, Revenue and Taxation Code, State Sales and Use Tax Regulations.

[175] State of California, Board of Equalization, *Instructions 97-3, State, Local, and District Sales and Use Tax Return*, p. 4.

[176] Ando, Albert; Blume, Marshal E.; and Friend, Irwin, *The Structure and Reform of the U.S. Tax System* (Cambridge, Massachusettes: The MIT Press, 1985), p. 174–176.

[177] The Tea Act passed by the British Parliament in May 1773 levied a threepence per pound charge on imported tea delivered to the American colonies that was strongly resisted by many American colonists. The colonial tax protest has some parallels to the current tax debate and it will be interesting—at least from an historian and sociologist's

view—to see how the circumstances play themselves out in modern times. *Will Americans of today accede to political conditioning and authoritarian propaganda—or discern the true nature of today's tax and fiscal problems and effect positive change?* For historical parallels, and the vacillation and ultimate commitment by the American colonists dealing with the British Tea Act see G. B. Warden's *Boston: 1689–1776* (Boston & Toronto: Little, Brown and Company, 1970), p. 274–276.

178 [S011] Internal Revenue Service, "Publication 15 (Rev. January 1997) Cat. No. 10000W," *Circular E, Employers Tax Guide* (Washington, D.C.: U.S. Department of the Treasury, Internal Revenue Service, 1997).

179 -S011- .

180 The former Union of Soviet Socialist Republics (Soviet Union) and the current economic condition of Russia is a prime example.

181 See Jarvis, Howard, with Robert Pack, *I'm Mad As Hell* (New York: Times Books, 1979).

182 [S012] Roybal, David, "Property Owners in Tax Shock After Receiving Bills," *Albuquerque Journal/ News*, November 8, 1988.

183 -S012- .

184 Bird, Kay, "Elderly Woman's Tears No Help in Property Tax Hike," *The New Mexican*, November 10, 1988.

185 [S013] Pechman, Joseph A., . . . [et al]. (Introduction by Walter W. Heller.), *Tax Policy: New Directions and Possibilities* (Washington D.C.: The Center for National Policy, 1984), p. 47.

186 Marino, Vivian, Associated Pres; "Too 'Rich' For Your Own Good?" *The San Diego Union-Tribune*, March 22, 1998, p. I-3.

187 [S013] Pechman, Joseph A., . . . [et al], (Introduction by Walter W. Heller.), *Tax Policy: New Directions and Possibilities* (Washington D.C.: The Center for National Policy, 1984), p. 28.

188 -S013- p. 19–24.

189 Americans for Fair Taxation, *National Retail Sales Tax.* from the organization's Internet information base http://www.fairfax.org.

190 [S009] Armey, Dick, *The Flat Tax: A Citizens Guide to the Facts On What It Will Do for You, Your Country, and Your Pocketbook* (New York: Fawcett, Columbine, 1996), pp. 69–71.

191 -S009- p. 51.

192 The speech was on February 6, 1978. Also see Howard Jarvis' *I'm Mad as Hell* (New York: Times Books, 1979, p. 104) for more information about the political environment surrounding Proposition 13.

193 [S015] Groves, Harold M., *Tax Philosophers: Two Hundred Years of Thought in Great Britain and the United States* (Madison, Wisconsin: University of Wisconsin Press), 1974. p. 150.

194 President Bill Clinton made the famous "feel your pain" comment during the 1992 Presidential election campaign in relating to voters' social and economic concerns.

[195] [S009] Armey, Dick, *The Flat Tax: A Citizens Guide to the Facts On What It Will Do for You, Your Country, and Your Pocketbook* (New York: Fawcett, Columbine, 1996), p. 107–108.

[196] Wells, Rob; and Associated Press; and The New York Times News Service; "IRS Reform Bill Backed by Clinton," *The San Diego Union-Tribune,* October 22, 199, p. A-1.

[197] Dionne, E.J., Jr., *The Washington Post*, "Running Away From Reality on Taxes," *The San Diego Union-Tribune*, June 26, 1998, p. B-7.

[198] Gay, Lance, *Scripps Howard News Service*, "Legislators Agree on IRS Reform; Clinton Says He'll Sign," *The San Diego Union-Tribune*, June 25, 1998, p. A-13.

[199] Stevenson, Richard W., *New York Times News Service*, "Senate Oks Major IRS Overhaul," *The San Diego Union-Tribune*, July 10, 1998, p. A-1.

[200] [S015] Groves, Harold M., *Tax Philosophers: Two Hundred Years of Thought in Great Britain and the United States* (Madison, Wisconsin: The University of Wisconsin Press, 1974) p. 18–19.

[201] [S016] Smith, Adam, *An Inquiry Into the Nature and Causes of the Wealth of Nations*, bk. 5, chap. 2, pt. 2. (Various reprints are available of Adam Smith's work; one is Oxford: Clarendon Press, 1976.).

[202] [S015] Groves, Harold M., *Tax Philosophers: Two Hundred Years of Thought in Great Britain and the United States* (Madison, Wisconsin: The University of Wisconsin Press, 1974), p. 19.

[203] -S015- p. 19.

[204] [S016] Smith, Adam, *An Inquiry Into the Nature and Causes of the Wealth of Nations* bk. 5, chap. 2, pt. 2.

[205] -S016- bk. 5, chap. 2, pt. 2.

[206] [S015] Groves, Harold M., *Tax Philosophers, Two Hundred Years of Thought in Great Britain and the United States* (Madison, Wisconsin: The University of Wisconsin Press, 1974), p. 18–19.

[207] [S016] Smith, Adam, *An Inquiry Into the Nature and Causes of the Wealth of Nations,* bk. 5, chap. 2, pt. 2.

[208] [S009] Armey, Dick, *The Flat Tax: A Citizens Guide to the Facts on What It Will Do for You, Your Country, and Your Pocketbook* (New York: Fawcett Columbine, 1996), p. 7.

[209] [S015] Groves, Harold M., *Tax Philosophers: Two Hundred Years of Thought in Great Britain and the United States* (Madison, Wisconsin: The University of Wisconsin Press, 1974), pp. 123–26.

[210] See George, Henry, *Progress and Poverty* (New York: Dalton, 1913).

[211] Bast, Joseph L. and Bast, Diane Carol, "How Fair? How Efficient?" *Heartland Policy Study #90* (Chicago: The Heartland Institute, forthcoming in 1999).

[212] There can actually be some variance because property conditions are not static. A percentage of property is always under construction or demolition. The variance, though, is accounted for in budget estimates and the process is explained in Chapter XI.

[213] A portion of property must be qualified and properly denoted under RPUT law by the property owner before the government will hold a renter directly liable. An owner may choose to forego such qualification and declaration if he chooses (and perhaps just charge

higher rent to cover his tax expense) but cannot then claim that portion of his property as exempt from the use fee if it is vacated.

[214] See Chapter X for a full explanation of theory and mathematical formulas.

[215] [S017] Amendment IV, Constitution of the United States of America.

[216] Call to action: Those who find the national tax system an important determiner of their own, their family's, and the nation's economic success should consider actively supporting positive federal tax reform. See upcoming strategies and opportunities associated with the Real Property Use Tax on the Internet at http://www.rput.com.

[217] -S017-.

[218] Both OCR and electronic filings have been tested and are currently used in the income tax system. The technologies are proven.

[219] Source for U.S. land area: (Lauren S. Bahr, Editorial Director), "United States of America," *Collier's Encyclopedia,* Volume 22 of 24 (New York: Collier's, 1995).

Addendum—Justinnote Coding. "Parent," or *supranote*, codes in the Justinnote Coding system provide reference information for other footnotes or endnotes that follow and that denote the same source. These codes are created by authors themselves in their works when they note other sources; the codes for particular sources can be unique for each publication.

Each supranote code is enclosed in *brackets* at the front of an entry (i.e., **[S024]** for "Supranote 24"). Note that a supranote may be repeated more than once in the footnotes or endnotes as a service to the reader (though still retaining the same identification code). The footnotes and endnotes, or *sub-notes*, that follow a supranote and that also denote the same work have the same supranote code referenced *between dashes* followed by page-number or other appropriate data (i.e., **-S024- pp. 217-24.**).

Justinnote Coding provides for concision in listings, and also allows text that is associated with notes to be moved around during editing without sub-notes losing their connections with parent-notes. Justinnotes are helpful in manual transcription, but especially so with modern word-processor computer-application programs where texts with linked notes are commonly moved electronically before being printed to paper. The Jusinnote Coding system also provides for a single reference base across chapters and volumes and, if desired, across multiple publications in a series. A complete explanation of the Justinnote Coding method can be obtained on the Internet at http://www.maxp.com/justinnote.

Bibliography

Books

Adams, Charles, *Fight, Flight, Fraud: The Story of Taxation.* Curacao: Euro-Dutch Publishers, 1982.

Adams, Charles, *For Good and Evil: The Impact of Taxes on the Course of Civilization.* London: Madison Books, 1993.

Adams, James Ring, *Secrets of the Tax Revolt.* New York: Harcourt Brace Jovanovich, 1984.

Adams, James Ring, *The Tax Revolt Tradition in American Politics and Law.* Ann Arbor, Michigan: University Microfilms International, 1985.

Americans, general (Debates in private correspondence, the press, and state ratifying conventions), *The Debate on the Constitution: Federalist and Antifederalist Speeches, Articles, and Letters During the Struggle over Ratification; Part One: September 1787 to February 1788.* New York: Library Classics of the United States, 1993.

Ando, Albert; Blume, Marshall E.; and Friend, Irwin, *The Structure and Reform of the U.S. Tax System.* Cambridge, Massachusetts: Massachusetts Institute of Technology, 1985.

Armey, Dick, *The Flat Tax: A Citizens Guide to the Facts on What It Will Do For You, Your Country, and Your Pocketbook.* New York: Fawcett Columbine, 1966.

(Edited by Henry J. Aaron and Michael J. Boskin.), *The Economics of Taxation.* Washington, D.C.: The Brookings Institution, 1980.

Arthur D. Little, Inc., *Development of Methodology for Estimating the Taxpayer Paperwork Burden.* Washington, D.C.: Internal Revenue Service, 1988.

Baldwin, Leland D., *Whiskey Rebels: The Story of a Frontier Uprising.* University of Pittsburgh Press, 1968.

Barlett, Donald L. and Steele, James B., *America: Who Really Pays the Taxes.* New York: Simon & Schuster, 1994.

Bawly, Dan, *The Subterranean Economy.* New York: McGraw-Hill Company, 1982.

Break, George F. and Pechman, Joseph A., *Federal Tax Reform: The Impossible Dream?* Washington, D.C.: The Brookings Institution, 1975.

Blum, Walter J. and Klaven, Harry, Jr., *The Uneasy Case for Progressive Taxation.* Chicago and London: University of Chicago Press, 1966.

Carson, Gerald, *The Golden Egg: The Personal Income Tax: Where It Came From, How It Grew.* Boston: Houghton Mifflin Company, 1977.

Coletta, Paolo E., *The Presidency of William Howard Taft.* Wichita, Kansas: University Press of Kansas, 1973.

Commission to Revise the Tax Structure, *Reforming the Federal Tax Structure.* Washington, D. C.: Fund for Public Policy Research, 1973.

Congress, United States of America, *Title 26, Internal Revenue Title.* Reprint: United States Government Tax Law.

Conlan, Timothy J.; Wrightson, Margaret T.; and Beam, David R., *Taxing Choices: The Politics of Tax Reform.* Washington, D. C.: CQ Press, 1990.

Constitutional Congress, United States of America; Congress, United States of America, *Your Rights* [*Constitution of the United States* Reprint]. Tucson, Arizona: KR Publishing Company, 1987.

Crockett, Joseph P., *The Federal Tax System of the United States: A Survey of Law and Administration.* New York: Columbia University Press, 1955.

Chodes, John; Daskal, Steven E.; DiLorenzo, Thomas J. . . . [et al]. (Edited by Burton W. Folsom.), *The Industrial Revolution and Free Trade.* Irving-on-Hudson, New York: Foundation for Economic Education, 1996.

Davis, Shelley L., *Unbridled Power: Inside the Secret Culture of the IRS*. New York: Harper Collins, 1997.

Eisenstein, Louis, *The Ideologies of Taxation.* New York: The Ronald Press Company, 1961.

Ferguson, James E., *The American Revolution: A General History, 1763–1790.* Homewood, Illinois: The Dorsey Press, 1974.

Goode, Richard; Gephardt, Richard . . . [et al]. (Edited by Joseph A. Pechman.), *Options for Tax Reform.* Washington, D. C.: The Brookings Institution, 1984.

Groves, Harold M., *Tax Philosophers: Two Hundred Years of Thought in Great Britain and the United States.* Madison, Wisconsin: University of Wisconsin Press, 1974.

Hall, Robert E. and Rabushka, Alvin, *Low Tax, Simple Tax, Flat Tax.* New York: McGraw-Hill Book Company, 1983.

Heady, Christopher; Keen, Michael; Smith, Stephen . . . [et al]. (Edited by Michael P. Devereux.), *The Economics of Tax Policy.* Oxford University Press, 1996.

Hechler, Kenneth W., *Insurgency: Personalities and Politics of the Taft Era.* New York: Russell & Russell, Inc., 1964.

Ilersic, A. R. . . . [et al]. *Tax Avoision: The Economic, Legal and Moral Inter-Relationships Between Avoidance and Evasion.* London: The Institute of Economic Affairs, 1979.

Internal Revenue Service, *1997 1040 Instructions* (booklet). U.S. Government Printing Office: Department of the Treasury, Internal Revenue Service, 1997, 419-561.

Internal Revenue Service, *Circular E, Employer's Tax Guide* (booklet). U.S. Government Printing Office: Department of the Treasury, Internal Revenue Service, 1996, 407-074.

Internal Revenue Service, *Tax Guide 1997 for Individuals* (booklet). U.S. Government Printing Office: Department of the Treasury, Internal Revenue Service, 1997, 419-505.

Hicko, Scott E., *Flat Tax: Why It Won't Work for America.* Omaha, Nebraska: Addicus Books, 1996.

Jarvis, Howard with Robert Pack, *I'm Mad As Hell.* New York: Times Books, 1979.

Kilpatrick, William A., *The Big Tax Lie.* New York: Simon and Schuster, 1986.

Laffer, Arthur B., and Seymour, Jan P., *The Economics of the Tax Revolt.* New York: Harcourt Brace Jovanovich, 1979.

(Edited by Henry G. Manne and Roger LeRoy Miller.), *Gold, Money, and the Law.* Chicago: Aldine Publishing Co., 1975.

McCarthey, Clarence F., . . . [et al]. *The Federal Income Tax: Its Sources and Applications.* London: Prentice Hall, 1968.

Miller, John C., *The Federalist Era.* New York: Harper & Row, 1960.

Paine, Thomas, *Collected Writings: Common Sense, The Crisis, and Other Pamphlets, Articles, and Letters; Rights of Man; The Age of Reason.* New York: The Library of America, 1995.

Payne, James L., *Costly Returns: The Burdens of the U.S. Tax System.* San Francisco: Institute for Contemporary Studies, 1993.

(Edited by Joseph A. Pechman), *World Tax Reform: A Progress Report.* Washington, D.C.: The Brookings Institution, 1988.

Pechman, Joseph A., . . . [et al]. (Introduction by Walter W. Heller.), *Tax Policy: New Directions and Possibilities.* Washington D.C.: The Center for National Policy, 1984.

Pyle, David J., *Tax Evasion and the Black Economy.* London: The Macmillan Press, 1989.

Reese, Thomas J., *The Politics of Taxation.* Westport, Connecticut: Quorum Books, 1980.

Siegan, Bernard H., *Economic Liberties and the Constitution.* Chicago: University of Chicago Press, 1980.

Simth, Adam, *An Inquiry Into the Nature and Causes of the Wealth of Nations.* Oxford: Clarendon Press, 1976.

Temin, Peter, *The Jacksonian Economy.* New York: W.W. Norton & Company, 1969.

OECD, *Revenue Statistics of OECD Member Countries, 1965–1995.* Paris: Organization for Economic Co-operation and Development, 1996.

Waltman, Jerold L., *Political Origins of the U.S. Income Tax.* Jackson, Mississippi: University of Southern Mississippi, 1985.

Walton, Gary M., and Robertson, Ross M., *History of the American Economy.* New York: Harcourt Brace Jovanovich, 1983.

Webber, Carolyn, and Wildavsky, Aaron, *A History of Taxation and Expenditure in the Western World.* New York: Simon and Schuster, 1986.

Westin, Richard A., and Neff, Alan H., *Tax, Attacks and Counterattacks: Your Indispensable Guide to Long Range Tax Strategy.* New York: Harcourt Brace Jovanovich, 1983.

(Edited by George W. Wilson), *Classics of Economic Theory.* Bloomington, Indiana: Indiana University Press, 1964.

Periodicals, News Services, and Other Sources

Associated Press
Copley News Service
Cox New Service
Knight-Ridder News Service
New York Times
San Francisco Chronicle
San Diego Union-Tribune
Scripps Howard New Service
Washington Post
60 Minutes News Magazine
Internet Information Sites
(As defined in Endnotes)

Index

Income *tax continued next page . . .*

RPUT *continued next column . . .*

Colophon

Research and Development, Information Sources: City of San Diego Public Library System; University of California, San Diego (University of California Library System); local and Internet booksellers; daily papers and periodical news sources; television news services; private and public Internet-based information sites.
Review Submissions Prior to Publication: Heartland Institute, Chicago; Cato Institute, Washington, D.C.; Claremont Institute, Claremont, California; Heritage Foundation, Washington, D.C.; additional private institutes and individuals.
Information Assembly, Figures Creation and Text Layout: Author. (PC) Microsoft® Word 97 and Excel 97 application programs (AP). Manuscript fonts: Arial 8, 9, 10, 11, 12; Book Antiqua 10, 11 (main text), 12, 14, 16, 18, 19, 20, 26, 46 pt.; Courier New 11, 12, 16, 20, 24 pt.; Times New Roman 9, 10, 11, 12 pt.
Cover Illustration Concept and Design: Author.
Cover Illustration: Artist *Greg High*, Escondido, California. Art elements assembled in final digital format with (MAC) Adobe® Photoshop 4.0.
Latin Translations: *Anthony T. Edwards*, University of California, San Diego.
Copy Edit Services: *Elaine Kleiss,* B E Editorial, Escondido, California; [Math and Theory] *Dr. Richard M. Neumann,* Florence, Massachusetts; [Latin] *Dr. Robert C. Knapp,* University of California, Berkeley.
Book-Jacket Layout: *Nectarios Tradas*, Artworks Type & Image, San Diego, California. AP: (MAC) Macromedia® Freehand 7.0 and Adobe Photoshop 4.0. Cover fonts: URW Palladio, Vivaldi, and Helvetica.
Book Printing: Liaison: *Phil Wagner,* Bang Printing, Brainerd, Minnesota. / Layout: *Chris Olesen*. AP: Adobe Distiller Version 5.0 for file preparation, Preps 3.1e imposition software. / Production Supervisor: *Jim Lorentz*. Book Trim Size: 7 X 10 in. Spine: 7/8 in. Text: black print, 1800 dpi. on Variquik press. Paper: 60# Artica Offset white, 454 ppi. Binding: adhesive case, Roxite B-grade black cloth, rounded back, head/footbands; 80# Union Camp standard white end sheets; foil stamped spine. Book Jacket: 80# 4-color gloss text w/silver-foil title stamp on front and spine, film laminated.
CD-ROM Reproduction: Liaison: *Ramon Alcantar*, Paramount Software Services, San Diego, California.
Publicity and Distribution: *Walter Hemmings*, Maximus Profectus (Publisher), San Diego, California.

Order Information

PUBLISHER: Maximus Profectus

DELIVER TO:

Name: ______________________

Address: ______________________

____

City: __________ State/Prov.: __________ Zip: __________

Phone: __________ Country: __________

Item	QTY	Price	**Total**
Book: *Taxation and National Destiny: A Tax Systems Analysis and Proposal* [HC001]		22.95	
Cover Illustration Poster (24 X 37 inches): *"From the Wisdom of the Past to Prosperity of the Future"* [PR001]		24.95	
Shipping—U.S. Priority (2–4 Days)		5.25	
Shipping—Canada Airmail (4–8 Days)		7.60	
Shipping—International Regular (4–7 Weeks)		9.80	
Subtotal:			
Sales Tax (California only): Please add 7.25% for orders delivered outside San Diego County, 7.75% for orders delivered within.			
Total:			

Toll Free Phone Order Number: 1-877-843-7788 (1-877 THE RPUT)
(U.S., Puerto Rico & Virgin Islands)

Credit Card : ☐Master Card ☐ VISA ☐AmEx ☐Discover ☐ Check

Card Number: ______________________ Expiration Date: ________

Name on Card: ______________________

On-line Orders: http://www.rput.com/store. / Fax Orders: 1-619-492-9341.
E-Mail: info@maxp.com. / Regular Mail: Enclose a copy of this order form with your credit card number or check or money order and mail to

Maximus Profectus
Order Dept. #B05
3811 Colina Dorada Drive, Unit #A-208
San Diego, CA 92124-3806